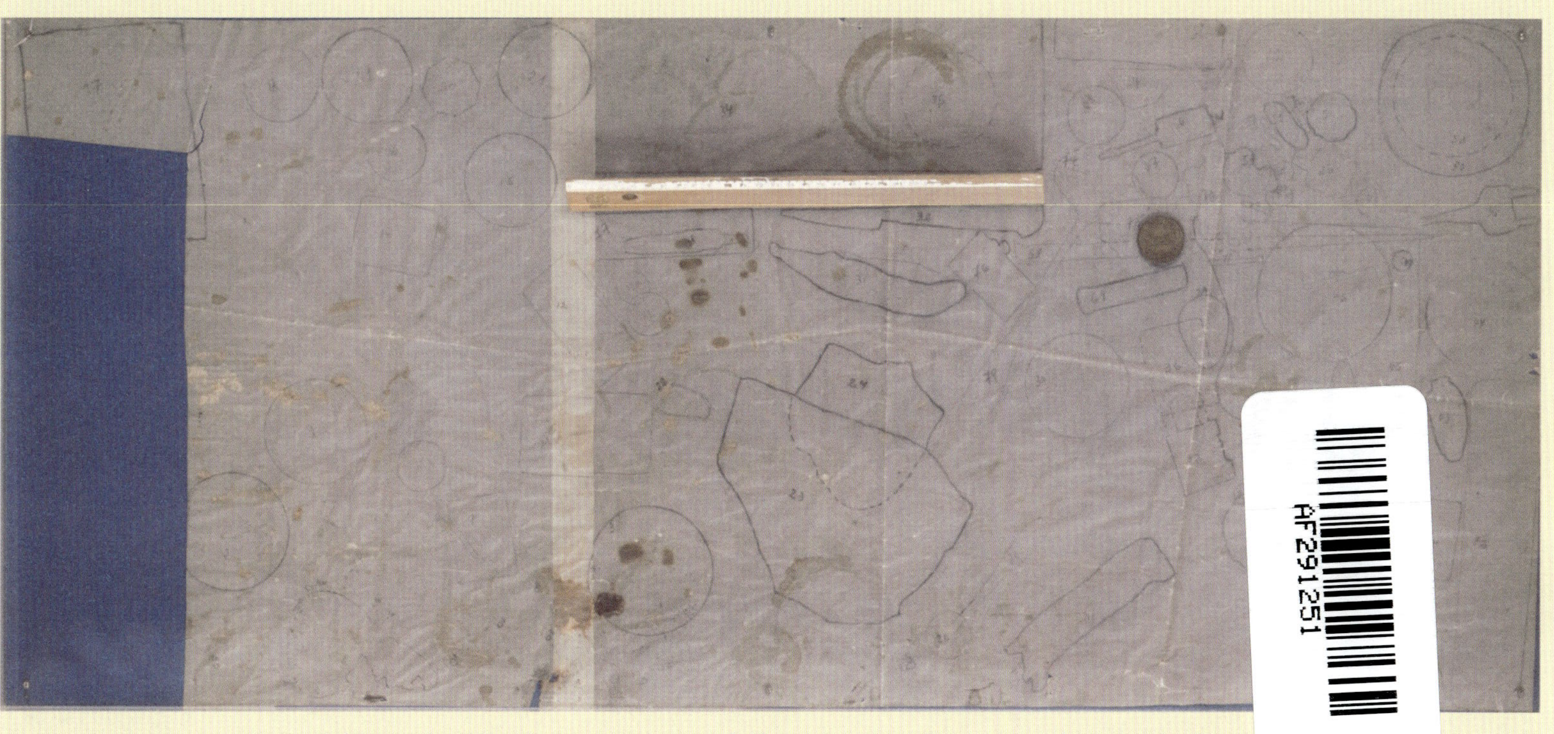

DANIEL SPOERRI, *Original drawing for "The Topographical Map of Chance"*, 1961 (objects 33 and 75 attached), Mu…, Bremen

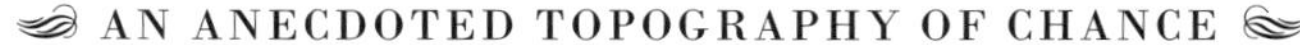

AN ANECDOTED TOPOGRAPHY OF CHANCE

An Anecdoted Topography of Chance*

*Probably definitive re-anecdoted version

by **Daniel Spoerri** *done with the help of his very dear friend*

Robert Filliou *and translated from the French and further*

anecdoted by their very dear friend **Emmett Williams***, enriched*

with still further anecdotations by their very dear friend **Dieter**

Roth *(translated from the German by Malcolm Green), with 100*

reflective illustrations by **Topor***.* Atlas Press, London 2016

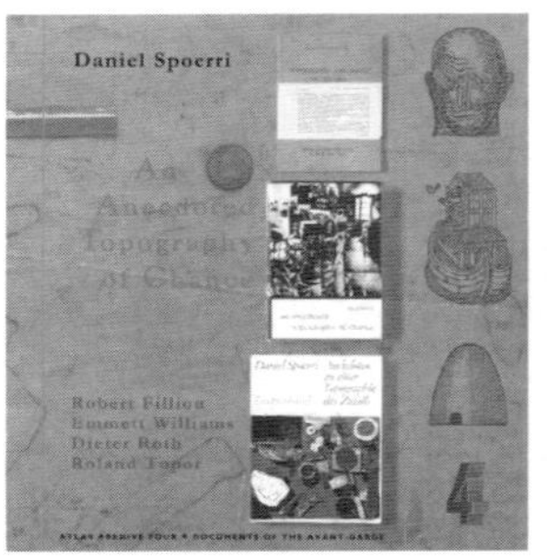 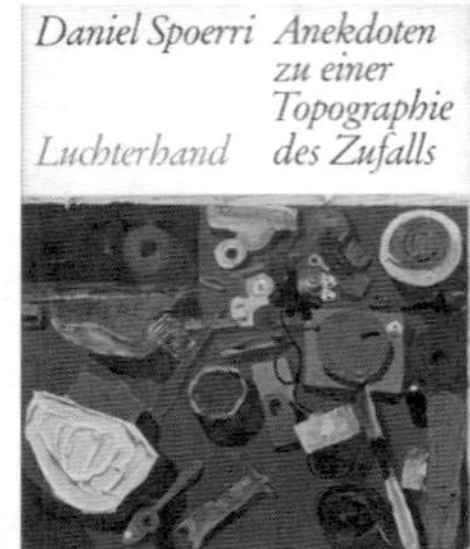 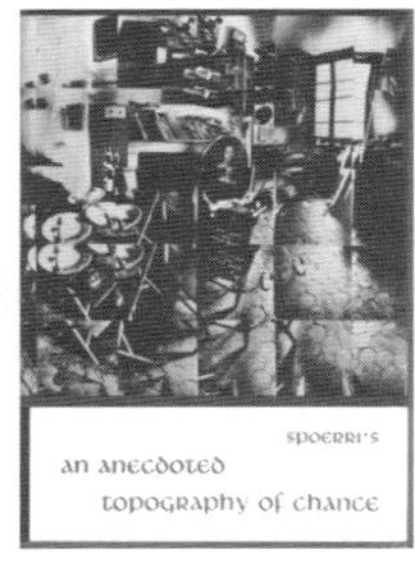 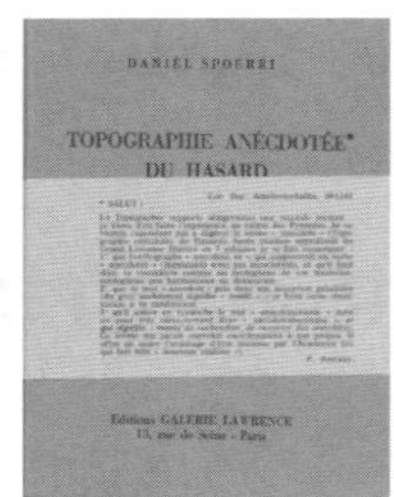

This edition first published by Atlas Press in its Arkhive series, in 1995. Atlas Press, 27 Old Gloucester st., London WC1N 3XX. ©2015, the authors and Atlas Press. Published with the permission of Daniel Spoerri and the estates of Robert Filliou, Emmett Williams, Dieter Roth and Roland Topor. All rights reserved. Thanks to Chiara Ambrosio for translating the text by Michelangelo on p.96. Printed in the UK by CPI Ltd. A CIP record for this book is available from the British Library. ISBN-13: 978-1-900565-73-8

CONTENTS

PREFACE

This is the most complete version to date of *An Anecdoted Topography of Chance* by Daniel Spoerri, co-written with Robert Filliou, Emmett Williams and Dieter Roth, and illustrated by Topor. The *Topography* describes its own origins in various places (notably in **Introduction I**, and under object **25**), but for clarity's sake it is worth summarising here.

The first version of the *Topography* appeared in lieu of an exhibition catalogue for Spoerri's exhibition at the Galerie Lawrence in Paris in February 1962.[a] Written by Spoerri, assisted by Filliou, it was a booklet of 54 pages (this edition was subsequently reprinted by the Centre Georges Pompidou in 1990, to accompany Spoerri's exhibition there, with a new introduction by Topor). At the end of 1964 Emmett Williams began translating the book into English. All of Williams's annotations were added to this translation, published by Dick Higgins's Something Else Press in New York in 1966; Spoerri wrote extra texts, and Topor's drawings were also made for this edition.

Dieter Roth's translation, together with his annotations, appeared four years later, published by Luchterhand (Neuwied). Again Spoerri added a few more annotations and extra text to the appendices (but Topor's drawings were not used).

The present version is based on the Atlas Press edition of 1995, which gathered together all the various texts from previous editions for the first time and also included new material, notably a new Introduction, annotations by three of the authors, and a number of photographs (previous editions were not illustrated apart from the drawings by Topor). It was also organised in a different and, so we hoped, clearer manner than previously.

The *Topography* is structured like a tree: narratives branch off from the first description of the objects in the form of annotations, and these in their turn may be annotated, sometimes by more than one person. One can illustrate the various levels of the text diagrammatically, for example, object **32** would look like this:

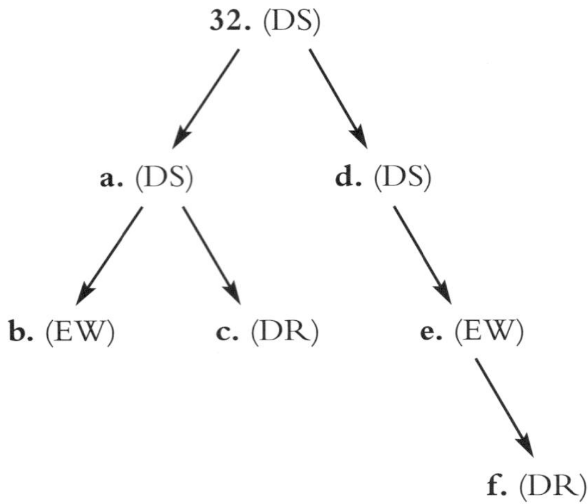

Four levels of text by three authors. The authors are indicated by their initials and the lower-case letters refer to annotations, which can often be several pages long. To make reading the *Topography* easier, the annotations are organised as follows: first-level annotations (notes to the text) are indented by 5 mm., in a slightly smaller type than the main text (the description of the object), second-level annotations (notes to notes) are in yet smaller type, and indented by 10 mm., third-level indented by 15 mm. and in yet smaller type, and so on. Annotations are indicated by a letter in bold type, thus: **a**. The authors of annotations are as follows: DS = Daniel Spoerri, EW = Emmett Williams, DR = Dieter Roth, AB = Alastair Brotchie, MG = Malcolm Green. The initial uncredited entries are from the first edition and were written by Daniel Spoerri, with the assistance of Robert Filliou. Initials are accompanied by the date of the edition in which the particular annotation first appeared. Cross-references to other parts of the book are given in square brackets, object numbers are in bold (as are the annotation letters), page numbers are in normal type. Thus [**36, a**] refers the reader to object **36**, note **a**. Object numbers refer to the map printed on both endpapers of the book. The various appendices are numbered in Roman numerals. Names included in the index are given in small capitals, and the index refers to page numbers. (AB 1995 & 2015)

    a. The principal editions of the *Topography* are depicted on p.4.

INTRODUCTIONS

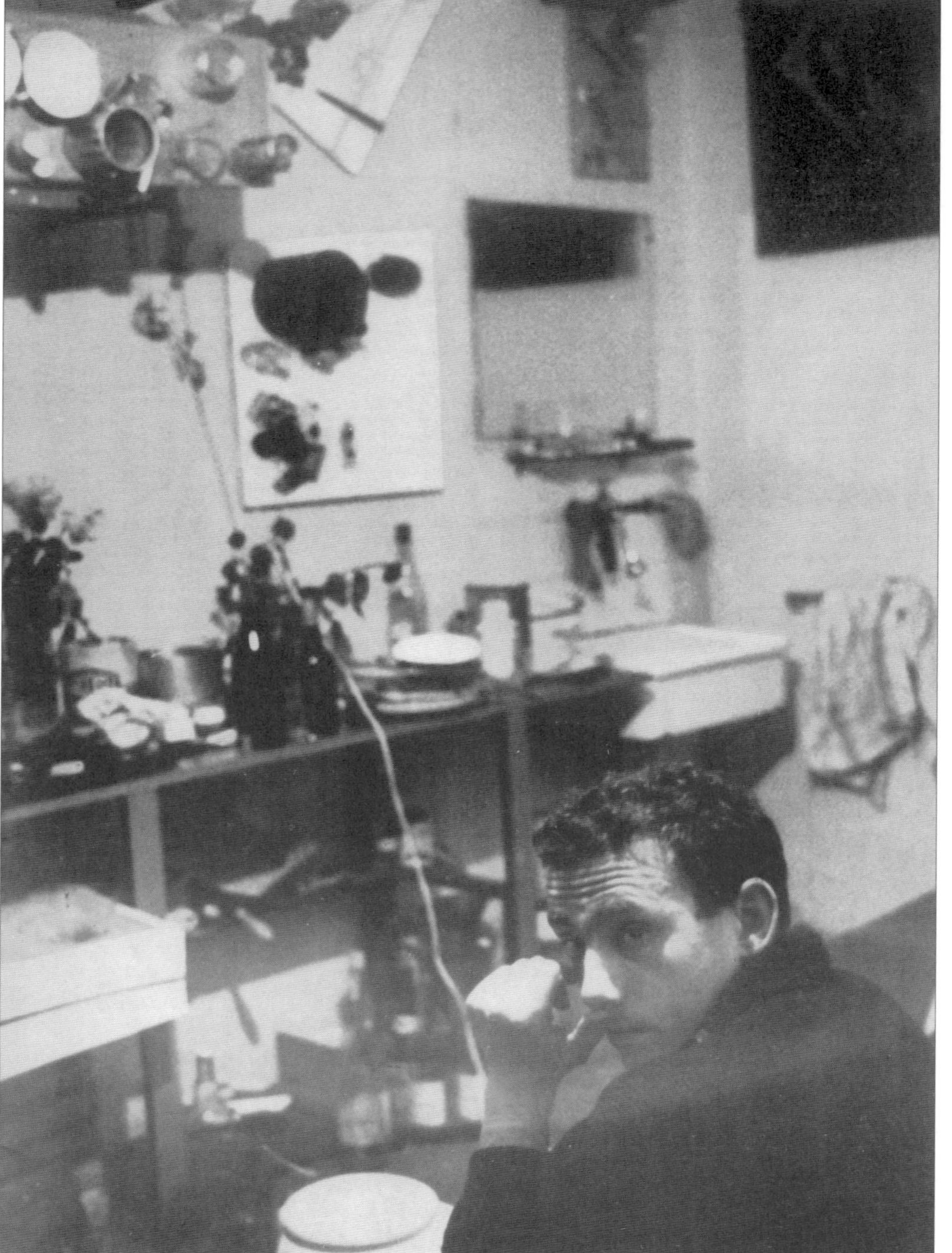

INTRODUCTION I: TO THE EDITIONS OF 1962, 1966 & 1968

In my room,[a] No. 13 on the fifth floor of the Hotel Carcassonne at 24 Rue Mouffetard, to the right of the entrance door, between the stove and the sink, stands a table that VERA painted blue one day to surprise me. I have set out here to see what the objects on a section of this table (which I could have made into a snare-picture[c] [see **Appendix II**]) might suggest to me, what they might spontaneously awaken in me in describing them: the way SHERLOCK HOLMES, starting out with a single object, could solve a crime [see **Appendix III**]; or historians, after centuries, were able to reconstitute a whole epoch from the most famous fixation in history, Pompeii.

In case it might be helpful in understanding this experiment, I should state that it was after constructing a pair of eyeglasses[d] equipped with needles to poke the eyes out that I felt the urge to recreate objects through the memory[e] instead of actually displaying them.[f]

On the inside of the dust jacket is a map[g] (the irregular shape is the same as that of the table: wishing to replace a single-burner alcohol stove with a two-burner one, I had to saw off a piece) of a topography based on chance and the disorder that I snared Oct. 17, 1961, at 3:47 p.m. Each outlined object is numbered, and the game I suggest is to choose a shape on the map and look up the corresponding numbered paragraph in the text. Notes have been added whenever there were texts or other data relating to an object.

At the end of the text is a biographical index of all persons cited in the descriptions of objects, notes and appendices. (DS 1962)

Postscriptum: The appearance of the first edition of the *Topographie Anecdotée du Hasard* was made possible by funds placed at the author's disposal by Galerie

Left: DANIEL SPOERRI in his room *c.*1961, with the blue table in the background, from the catalogue of SPOERRI'S first exhibition, at Galleria SCHWARZ, Milan, 16–30 March 1961.

LAWRENCE in Paris to publish the *Topography* in place of a more traditional catalogue and coincided with the opening of his exhibition there in February 1962.[h]

An enlarged French edition was begun four months after the commencement of the first. To show that his room was not always in disorder, and for contrast, SPOERRI added to the *Topography of Chance* a topography of order based on the blue table as it appeared Feb. 21, 1962, at 8:07 p.m. A second map (on p.248), numbered in Roman numerals, shows graphically the difference between the two situations.

This English translation, begun almost three years after the preparation of the enlarged French edition, is larger still, increased in bulk by new notes of the author, translator and others.[i]

The heights of all objects in the *Topography* are given in **Appendix I**, and printed on the jacket of the book[k] is a panoramic photograph of the author's room composed by VERA SPOERRI from fifty-five detailed photos. (EW 1966)

a. My room, too,[b] during the author's absence from Paris to prepare an exhibition in New York. Thus I begin this translation (I must here and now place myself in the position of SIGMUND FREUD who, when undertaking the translation of CHARCOT'S *Lessons* in a hotel only a few blocks away from the Hotel Carcassonne, confessed to the master that he had "motor aphasia in French but not sensory aphasia") at 9 p.m. on the first day of December 1964, only an arm's length away from the principal terrain feature of the *Topography*, the blue table. [See **Appendix V**]

(As I finished typing the words "blue table" this seventh day of July 1965 in Pfungstadt, West Germany, where I am preparing the final version of the first English edition of the *Topography*, a telegram arrived from Paris informing me of the author's forthcoming visit to oversee the last draft of the manuscript. The message in full: SATURDAYBABA LIBUBUNIGHT DANIELENKO.) (EW 1966)

b. Not my room (I worked on the *Topography* in Reykjavik in: 1965, in the rear building of Vestürgata 45; 1968, in the cellar of Grundarstíg 11 — at RAGNAR'S — and at Skolavördüstig 3a — in MAGNUS PAULSSON'S room and PAUL MAGNUSSON'S office), although in 1965 I was supposed to work through the translation of the *French edition* together with DANIEL in his room in the Rue Mouffetard (we never got round to it, first because DANIEL was already living in the Rue Rollin, and second because I stayed in bed during the days in the Rue Mouffetard sleeping it off). My relationship to the *Topography* differs moreover from that of its author in that I have difficulties in identifying with SHERLOCK HOLMES — not only do I not like objects, I am afraid of them. Nor do I like thinking about others the way FREUD did: for that I lack both the patience and the powers of observation. So, when I saw before me (just in my mind and inside my head, of course) the blue table covered with DANIEL'S playthings, I felt like (as I suppose one could put it) a small, rather naughty boy — like one of the naughty little boys who, out of enormous envy, playfully destroy other boys' (and girls') playthings as soon as they have been lent them. I feel I have constantly had to fight back the urge to destroy DANIEL'S plaything (one reader or another will doubtless say: "Yes, he has destroyed something!"). I was also handed something to play with by EMMETT (the *Topography* will show just how far I have spoilt something for EMMETT — with my nattering, battering teeth) — but it is difficult to spoil anything for EMMETT because he never leaves anything really tangible behind him.

It is also possible though that someone will come and say: "He hasn't destroyed a thing, it's impossible to convey anything in this soft, German, woolly, worn-out language, you cannot grasp anything with it — let alone destroy it. And all you can do with translation is excavate things — from the other language — and transpose them into this language here!" To which I say: "Yes, I've been playing like a little boy in a sand-pit, where I found DANIEL'S playthings and EMMETT'S footprints, and all I did was dig a bit and pile up a couple of small heaps, here and there. And obviously the occasional plaything or footprint got buried in the process."

So today, the last day of October 1968, while typing this last, hopefully very last annotation to the *Topography* here in Drakestrasse 7, in Oberkassel, Düsseldorf (not far from Drakeplatz where the peculiar BEUYS lives), I step out of the sand-pit, look back and I see DANIEL'S playthings, my heaps here and there, and in between and around them EMMETT'S footprints. And if someone were to ask where EMMETT has got to I can answer: He's gone to America and today he's in hospital because they want to remove something nasty from his head, a tumour (if it hasn't already been done), and I say, almost audibly, to myself: "May everything always turn out fine!" (DR 1968)

c. In German, *Fallenbilder*; in French, *Tableaux-Piège* [**Appendix II**], as I called my first object collages. The German name refers to the noun *Falle* (snare) and not the verb *fallen* (to fall). (DS 1968)

d. These spectacles are illustrated in *L'Optique moderne, Collection de lunettes présenté par*

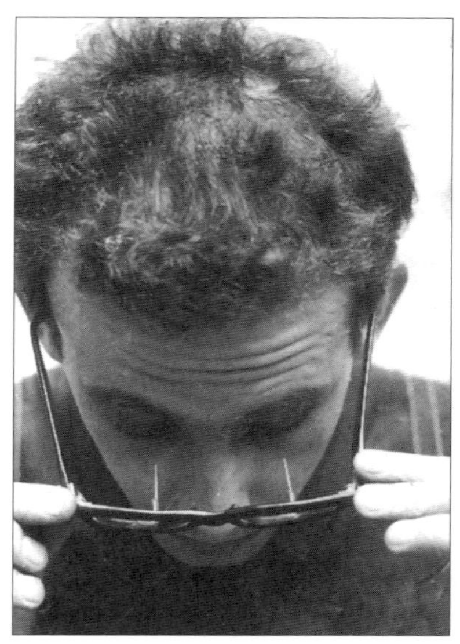

DANIEL SPOERRI avec, en regard, d'inutiles notules par FRANÇOIS DUFRÊNE, published by Fluxus. A reviewer in the London *Times Literary Supplement* of Sept. 3, 1964, described this volume as a "stout booklet of photographs showing this thin-faced author-editor-dancer-impresario wearing numerous novel types of spectacles, with characteristic small punning, assonant verses by FRANÇOIS DUFRÊNE on the even (orange-and-black) pages."

Said spectacles were first exhibited as a work of art at Galerie KOEPCKE in Copenhagen in September 1961. They were later exhibited as part of a mounted collection of spectacles in New York in 1964, and soon afterwards destroyed at a junkie party in the same city. SPOERRI was not present at the party; he managed to salvage only a few fragments of the collection.

In the Introduction [**I**] and in his notes on the development of the snare-picture [**Appendix II**] the author attributes the genesis of the present work to the threat of these dangerous spectacles. Elsewhere [**36, m**], however, he traces the idea of writing his "human garbage can" to the first time he saw one of ARMAN'S "garbage cans": "Shortly afterwards I emptied mine on the floor, and thought about how I could retrace the history of each scrap." (There is yet another, and more involved account of the origin of the *Topography* in **25, c**.) (EW 1966)

e. And so we are very concerned, sometimes about all the stuff (all the junk in front of our noses), sometimes about all the junk (all the stuff in our memory). Sometimes about people with all their stuff, sometimes about all the junk that people have produced, sometimes about stuffy people, sometimes about people's stuff, sometimes about people who make a fuss about produced stuff, sometimes about junk-dealers who mix people up with junk. And we are concerned about people (junk-dealers), and about junk-dealers (people), and about ourselves (people as junk-dealers), and once more about ourselves (junk-dealers as people). And all that stuff (all that junk) sits: sometimes in front of your nose (on your back), sometimes in your memory (inside your head), sometimes in a heap (under your backside), sometimes in your heart (on top of your stomach), sometimes on the wall (in a frame), sometimes in a book (on paper), and you start to ask: "Is my hand stuff, the way it keeps holding a heap of junk — and itself — here in front of my nose?" and sometimes: "Is my heart junk, the way it keeps wobbling and trembling under the crush of the stuff I load on myself — or keep hanging on to?" You ask, and you ask, and you ask for instance whether everything you touch turns into stuff, even if just with your tongue? And whether your tongue is for you a junk-dealer's hand? (Whatever it touches becomes a weight, as heavy at least as printer's ink. That turns to stone, even if it has once been flesh and blood.) (DR 1968)

f. "DANIEL SPOERRI, one of the masters of *nouveau réalisme* — a branch of modern art — has amassed an impressive collection of spectacles, which was first exhibited in Copenhagen in October 1961, then in Paris, October 1962, and finally in Milan, March 1963. The individual items in what is a unique collection world-wide are depicted in: *L'Optique moderne, Collection de lunettes présenté par DANIEL SPOERRI, avec, en regard, d'inutiles notules par FRANÇOIS DUFRÊNE*, Édition Fluxus, 1963."
    — *Encyclopédie des Farces, Attrapes et Mystifications*, JEAN-JACQUES PAUVERT, Paris 1966 (DS 1968)

g. It is printed on both endpapers of this edition. (AB 2015)

h. Of this edition, a London *Times Literary Supplement* reviewer wrote (Sept. 3, 1964): "Éditions Galerie LAWRENCE (13, Rue de Seine, Paris 6ᵉ) have published another of M. SPOERRI'S *jeux d'esprit*: his *Topographie Anecdotée du Hasard*. This soberly presented booklet is a catalogue of the articles that happened to be on the compiler's highly confused working, eating and drinking table at a particular instant of 1961. It is written in a scholarly style that any bibliographer, museum director or art historian might be proud of: exact particulars of the inscription on the label of the bottle of Vin des Rochers (*le velours de l'estomac*) bought that morning and drunk during the catalogue's compilation, and similar erudite details of a moderately untypical random collection of mid-twentieth-century objects." (EW 1966)

i. (*Postpostscriptum*) The German translation was begun at almost the same time, but for three years it fell, in the form of a rough draft, by the wayside, somewhere in Germany.

Only in summer 1968 was this rough version at last finished and further enlarged.**j** The German version contains:

1. The extended version of the *Topography* from 1962.

2. EMMETT WILLIAMS'S annotations — as well as those of his friends — from the English edition of 1966.

3. New annotations from DANIEL SPOERRI and his (German) translator, DIETER ROTH.

The book cover shows SPOERRI'S schematic drawing, coloured in by DIETER ROTH. (DR 1968)

j. The German version of the *Topo* came to another standstill in late summer, 1968, this time in Iceland. It had been announced for the Frankfurt Book Fair, and the waiting period was speeded up, or at least spiced up, by polite letters from father and godfathers alike:

14 June 1968

dear luchterhands, the TOPO manuscript has arrived and i got down to it straight away + i noted just how *bad* the german in it is — how could that have happened??

the translation requires *so* much work that it is quite out of the question to hand it over as it is. Consequently i am busy rewriting it.

i am writing this just so that you luchterhands don't get too impatient waiting for it. i am hurrying as best i can. i spend (on average) eight hours a day on it! is that okay?

i am not happy with the 20 pages that i have been allocated for the translations of Emmett's annotations because that is probably not enough. A THING DONE WELL CANNOT BE DONE COMPACTLY!

i wish you joy, peace + beauty! all the best till further beautiful + important things need to be letterwritten

yours zealously,

Diter Rot

Gerlafingen, Switzerland
28 June 1968

Dear Daniel,

I have gone off and will finish the *Topography* in PEACE; I could no longer work on it properly (the telephone's nearby, which keeps making you think: when will it ring again and the editor shovel his anxiety and worry in your ears and in your stomach

— plus in your heart). Yes, fair enough, a thing done well cannot be done quickly. The publisher won't be ruined if the book doesn't appear at once — and I don't want to produce something that I haven't worked through wonderfully and fantastically and that will perhaps be held up to my nose for years on end. You can't simply deliver a thing like this, a manuscript, the same way you deliver goods, can you? Unfortunately I realised that *a little* too late. Please pacify the people in Neuwied, if you can and wish to. I am still hard at it, and in a week there will once again be definitely far far more rather than far less, but I cannot hand over the manuscript in batches because I have to keep comparing the *later* sections of the *Topo* with the *earlier* ones — to see whether the numbers and references and PREFERENCES etc. tally, you see?

Here in Switzerland the summer is cool and beautiful and I am getting — I think, and I hope I am right — good and gentle ideas for the *Topo*. The day after tomorrow, 30.6.68, I am off to Iceland where perhaps it'll be even cooler and more beautiful, so that I will be able to think even better (assuming I am *already* thinking *well*). So, I am full of faith and hope.

Probably it will only take another two weeks or so until it's all there — so that the THING will perhaps make it for the book fair, who can tell? Better late and *bad* than early and *really bad*, right?

Yours, D.

Gerlafingen, Switzerland
28 June 1968

Dear master HINDERMANN,

today I can write to you, after SUFFERING for a long time, and say why, after being — quite HONESTLY — intensely, yes, genuinely and very intensively WORN OUT + DOWN (WORK), I have fled and put the momentous *deadlines* — the DEATHWATCH BEETLES that dig away at and devour the heart of a man's liberty + the heart of beauty (or at least: thoroughness) — out of my eyes, my ears, my heart + my mind:

I think it is fair to say that I am a pretty stalwart worker + have tackled + *carried out* the *momentous* task of correcting + enlarging the *Topography* — and yet I have NEVER in my LIFE handed in something that was important to me (as one might put it, more or less) without having (on handing it over) a fairly extensive feeling of CALM inside my STOMACH — or perhaps you will permit me here to say: inside my HEART. The problem right NOW is that I have yet to feel the aforementioned calm with respect to the TOPO. And I know — from experience — that I must go, drive, work, think, travel, lick, scratch, bend etc. etc. over the whole business once more before I will feel that calm which is now being mentioned for the 3rd time — and I felt that the DEADLINE, this evil DEATHWATCH BEETLE, was a STONE on whatever it is inside of you that can be weighed down by STONES, and so I fled + have taken the complete TOPOGRAPHICS with me because I *must hold it all together* so that I can hold it together *internally*, as one says, compare, juggle, control, chew, ruminate and digest it bit by bit. That is not to say that I am not sweating away hard at my JOB, as I already said, all that should be said is something to the effect of: ALLOW YOUR HEARTS TO SOFTEN towards me; put yourself in my shoes, accept the thought — along with all the concomitant feelings — that LIFE MUST BE OPEN TO THE FUTURE! (Or else one cannot see and strive towards the good, the beautiful and the true, but merely the swift and the tootling and the gaunt and the tinny.)

AND: What is an already meet deadeline, a fuell paelette, enoremouse success, the cusetomers' saetiesfied exepectaetiones, a great repuetatione — in compareiesone with the peaceable elegance of the quiet paetient antiecipaetione of the beauty of the deathwatchbeetleeless life in the quieetened paciefiecation of easy breathing?

Great thiengs (as well as the small ones) coeme frome nowe one onely frome peacefuel hearts full of patient will — or am I wrong? Have I deceived myself? Has the PEACE that I gained during my flight already sent me to sleep? Eh?

See you soon!

Yours, Diter Rot

Neuwied am Rhein

1 August 1968

Dear Diter Rot,

With regard to your lovely long letter, all that I can say is that by and large I am ready to accept what you write. But: has it ever occurred to you that perhaps others would also like to feel the calm that you describe in their stomachs or hearts during or for their work, but are unable to do so on account of you, dear Diter Rot? The deadline, this evil deathwatch beetle, is also gnawing away at me; the stone that weighs down on you — I feel its weight, too, and it increases with every day that you put the matter off. Time and again I have postponed the deadline in the face of the heftiest resistance in the company. And presumably there is not much else for me to do now than to continue to wait, patiently, but plagued and tormented by deathwatch beetles and pressed by any number of people.

So please, please: allow yourself to soften slightly, too.
Hoping to hear from you soon,
Yours, MARIO HINDERMANN

Reykjavik/Iceland
7 August 1968

Dear fellow sufferer! my, how appallingly difficult life is when one wants something one doesn't want!

Have a heart, sire, don't hate me! i live + i am *working* (on the TOPO, of course).

Yes, that's how it was: the publishing deadline (to allow that lovely term to come here to word) had been set before a complete AVERSION arose (in the Rotian innards) towards the pitiful first version of my translation, and I, D.R., in my fright, kept promising you: said yes, and: yes, it will be finished at such and such a time, yes. but that was out of fright — and not conviction — and as I then set to it was with the joy of surmounting in my bones, + i am still at it, + i am happy!… even though i suffer when you suffer. oh, don't suffer, so that i will also not have to suffer but can be happy, and with that you can be happy! Perhaps it would help you if you were to say what I am about to say and most sincerely think to all those who are oppressing you: it is not that life is short + art even shorter, no, but that life is long + art even longer!

Until very very shortly + with the battlecry: love + patience!
Your faithful Diter Rot

Düsseldorf
23 August 1968

Salute Mario!
I am glad that you have so much trust and patience. I'm really fond of you all.
So take care.

With Diter Rot we can only trust in God (the dear plaster Lord). I think simply that if he has been stalling for so long, he (the dear Lord with the pseudonym Diter Rot) will hand over something really beautiful (if not incredibly beautiful). He is one of my five best friends and I am very proud (the proudest) of them.

So *salute*, and stick up for me
Yours, Daniel

27 August 1968
Neuwied

Telegram:

REQUEST TELEGRAM SAYING WHEN TOPOGRAPHY MANUSCRIPT
READY STOP OTHERWISE MUST POSTPONE HOLIDAY STOP THANKS
AND GREETINGS HINDERMANN

Reykjavik/Iceland
1 September 1968

Dear Mr H.! the manus will arrive mid-September — it is impossible to say such
things with absolute precision, but, as I said (as one can put it). "LOVE + PATIENCE
+ JOY."

Yours, Diter Rot

Düsseldorf
8 November 1968

Salute Mario!

So now you have the whole business, our anecdote-encyclopaedia and all of the
numbers, orthography and what have you, round your neck. At any rate I know that it
will now be made irreproachably sacrosanct with perfect German fastidiousness. I am
really looking forward to it.

Here is another letter from DITER (from July 28th) to add to our correspondence
about the delays, which is also taking part in this omnium gatherum.

(Actually it is an old idea of DITER and EMMETT to make a book consisting solely
of their letters about a book that they were going to make, but never did.)

Apart from which I feel better and better by the day, as COUÉ would say.

Salute and hang on to your frayed nerves

Yours, Daniel

(DR 1968)

k. On the back endpaper of this edition. (AB 2015)

INTRODUCTION II: TO THE EDITION OF 1990

Around the beginning of the 1960s, in every Métro station, a small official handbill posted by the RATP alerted "*Messieurs les inventeurs d'épaves*"[a] that the latter, after being handed over to the relevant authorities, would be returned to them, provided it was not claimed in the mean time, after the passage of a year and a day.

So it was that I learnt, at the time when DANIEL SPOERRI was producing his snare-pictures and compiling his famous *Anecdoted Topography of Chance*, that to invent meant to find, and that a piece of wreckage was simply an item of lost luggage.

Contrary to appearances, *terra firma*, even in the absence of earthquakes, is as fluid as a liquid element, and as susceptible to the attraction of the heavens as the sea.

Our pockets, our tables, our houses are invaded by objects washed up by great terrestrial tides. Debris, fragments, crumbs, odds and ends and dust all have the consistency of fine sand; hair, pieces of thread, woolly bits of fluff evoke algae and kelp; buttons, whether those of shirts or trousers, have the pearly lustre of seashells. Same glass or plastic bottles, same beer bottles, same cola bottles, same jam jars, the same pollution in our snug interiors as on the seashore. These migrating objects which wash up in our homes have different histories, the consequence of the ebb and flow of daily life penetrating the imaginary.

They are the discreet heroes of a modern romance whose destiny leads to the dustbin by way of the vacuum cleaner. Documents to be thrown away without commentary, no flowers or wreaths.

When DANIEL SPOERRI, the worthy heir to RAYMOND ROUSSEL and MARCEL DUCHAMP, undertook in 1961 to recount in the most scrupulous manner imaginable the saga of the wreckage which had accumulated on his workbench, the *Nouveau Roman* was the last thing on his mind.

He continued, following his original idea, to trap reality in a snare. To pin it, stuffed, to the wall of a blank page. He continued his obsessive war against the watch.[b]

The watch as recorder of duration.

The watch as obligatory exhibitionism.

His intention was not to paint a complaisant self-portrait of the artist shattered into 80 relics. Nor did he desire to flaunt his worldly connections or expose his private life. He was concerned above all with exhausting the potential descriptions of a Parisian scene at a particular moment in time — just as PEREC sought to do for the Place Saint-Sulpice. In the end, objective reality organised by chance is the surest means of obtaining a true-to-life picture.

Almost 30 years later, DANIEL'S book still retains the charm and freshness of the inspiration which gave birth to it. The life contained within it becomes our own.

The *Anecdoted Topography of Chance* is an *aide-mémoire* more reliable than memory itself.

(ROLAND TOPOR, 1990, translated by Terry Hale)

a. *Épave* means both "unclaimed object, lost property" and "wreckage"; thus this sentence could be literally rendered as "Gentlemen who invent wreckage" rather than its intended meaning of "Finders of lost property". (Translator's note)

b. TOPOR exploits the double meaning of *montre*: "watch" and "show, display". (Translator's note)

INTRODUCTION III: TO THE EDITION OF 1995

It is now 33 years since the appearance of the first version of *An Anecdoted Topography of Chance*; the English and German translations, definitive at the time, followed soon afterwards. It seemed, to the editors of the series in which this version appears, that a new preface would be useful: to explore why a new edition of a work apparently so rooted in specific moments should be necessary, desirable… and delightful. We therefore noted down a few tentative observations, questions etc. and invited the authors of the *Topography* to comment upon them,[a] a procedure suggested by the book itself.

The Atlas Press Arkhive series seeks to explore areas of collective activity in keeping with the notion of an avant-garde in the arts and literature. The first appearance of the *Topography* predates the christening of the Fluxus movement by GEORGE MACIUNAS in 1962, and yet it seems perfectly[b] to embody aspects of its spirit. Later versions appeared within the context of Fluxus, and thus it seems legitimate to consider the book within this context.[g]

Fluxus, however, had and has many faces.[h] On the one hand there is MACIUNAS'S manifesto *Fluxus Art-Amusement* (1965), which pronounced, among other things: … *art-amusement must be simple, amusing, unpretentious, concerned with insignificances, require no skill or countless rehearsals, have no commodity or institutional value. [Its value] must be lowered by making it unlimited, mass-produced, obtainable by all and eventually produced by all…* On the other hand, BEN (Vautier) in a recent interview described it as *the name given by MACIUNAS around 1962 A.D. to a group of artists — Homo sapiens, egoists, hypocrites, show-offs and ruminants — who considered themselves more advanced than artists still part of the industrial era, that's to say the Bronze Age, whereas, according to MACIUNAS, Homo Fluxus had reached the level of the non-ego.* (Catalogue to the exhibition *Hors Limites*, Centre GEORGES POMPIDOU, 1994, p.117) An earlier MACIUNAS manifesto (February 1963) even centres on the demand to *promote a revolutionary flood and tide in art… to fuse the cadres of cultural, social and political revolutionaries into a united front and action.* Perhaps MACIUNAS'S programme, if he had one,[i] was itself in flux?[j]

It cannot be denied that Fluxus has been ignored for a long time, especially in England.[k] There are possible reasons for this omission: its congeniality (Anglo-Saxons expect artists to suffer for their art), and its apparent simplicity (some people don't want to understand art, it is disconcerting, art should be a serious matter etc.). Yet, like many avant-garde art movements, the avowed aim of Fluxus was the joining of life and art. It appears to have been no more successful than any of its predecessors, judging by its incorporation into museums.

The procedure of the *Topography*, its *modus operandi*, is beautifully simple: a selection of objects and the associations they evoke are described, and these in turn give rise to further associations in the form of anecdotes. An apparently infinite process is unleashed, like a stroll taken in every direction at once.[l] Perhaps it is this very simplicity (but the elegance of the execution by its various authors must also play a part), which raises so many questions. How does one finish a work like this? What principle guides the addition of anecdotes?[m] Why choose this particular selection of objects? Would any selection have produced such remarkable results? Are these objects relics, the detritus from a sort of archaeology of the present? It would be easy to stray into philosophical territory in the face of this *evidence*… As for the element of time: a moment was chosen, now many years past. How does the *Topography*, with its everlasting present, hold up after all these years? (Needless to say, the simple existence of the present edition means we consider this last question to be purely rhetorical.)

In fact, like many other matters, the *Topography* covers aspects of these questions itself; it is a machine that seems to have acquired independence from the circumstances that initiated it. Perhaps only a *collective* work can ever do this? One might compare the *Topography* to other collective works in this century, from the experiments of the Surrealists to those described in William Burroughs's *The Third Mind*.

There are other aspects of this book that allow comparison with previous enterprises: in art, for example, the idea of "fixing chance" (works by ARP and DUCHAMP being the most obvious examples). Although the *Topography* seems to do the opposite to this, whereas the "snare" pictures [see **Appendix II**] fix chance, the *Topography* remains dynamic, potential. Moreover, a book is a multiple (in which area SPOERRI was a pioneer) not a unique object.[n]

In the context of writing, rather than art, there is the process of annotation itself, which has given rise to a genre of literature all its own, a literature of digression and the forking narrative.[o] To cite the most immediate examples: LAURENCE STERNE'S *Tristram Shandy*, Count JAN POTOCKI'S *Manuscrit trouvé à Saragosse*,[p] RAYMOND ROUSSEL'S *Nouvelles Impressions d'Afrique*, VLADIMIR NABOKOV'S *Pale Fire*; Oulipian experiments such as RAYMOND QUENEAU'S *Un conte à votre façon* and ITALO CALVINO'S *If on a Winter's Night a Traveller…*; and more recently, NICHOLSON BAKER'S *The Mezzanine*. The works in this imaginary library share certain common features: humour certainly, a taste for precision, the bizarre and the banal in equal admixture, a magical evocation of the everyday, a prodigious execution.

Otherwise the structure of the *Topography* calls to mind the branching tree structure now common in computers. Beginning with any object, enough elaboration can connect it to any other (specified) object: BLAKE'S "universe in a grain of sand". In fact, despite its apparently gratuitous and chaotic structure, the *Topography* performs an almost classical aesthetic, even philosophical task: that of organising, or at least intimating a possible organisation of, a world whose complexity seems ungraspable…

To end on a more prosaic note, perhaps the Topographers might care to give a few biographical notes (as DS has done in item **78**, although this could be updated). How did they meet each other?[rs] How did the various collaborations on the book evolve? *Et cetera* and our thanks to them for allowing this reappearance under the Atlas Press imprint of a work with which we are extremely pleased to be associated. (AB/MG 1995)

a. DIETER ROTH has confined himself to a few corrections, and TOPOR decided not to add anything beyond the preface to the 1990 edition. EMMETT WILLIAMS and DANIEL SPOERRI both had comments to make, those of DANIEL SPOERRI being edited extracts from an interview he gave (in a mixture of English, French and German) in May 1995 with the authors of this introduction. (AB/MG 1995)

b. "Perfectly"[c] may be a bit strong here, and it just might possibly make the author see red. As the editors of this edition admit, the book preceded Fluxus, and so did the friendships of DANIEL and his collaborators. And despite all the anecdoting and re-anecdoting, it remains DANIEL'S book. It is true that by the time the first English-language version and the German translation appeared, Fluxus had already made waves internationally. You might wonder why, then, the authors and translators, with all their commentaries and additions, and their own involvement in the early days of Fluxus, ignored the matter almost completely except to acknowledge that DANIEL'S *L'Optique moderne* had been published in 1963 by something called Fluxus. [**Introduction I, d**]

Well, there's really no reason at all to worry about it. DICK HIGGINS, publisher of the American edition, and a Fluxus activist from the very beginning (and even before that!), made the interesting discovery some years back that "Fluxus existed before it had its name… Its participants never thought of themselves as a group until they were described as such in connection with the 'Festum Fluxorum' in Wiesbaden in 1962, by which time the participants had been doing 'Fluxus work' for four or five years." (Imagine that! Historians interested in the chronology of modern art in the second half of this century please take note.)

Whatever the case may be, in this latest edition, the fourth**d** and perhaps terminal version, there are a dozen or more artists on board who through the years have declared allegiance in part or in full to this thing called Fluxus, or have been hailed as its precursors, including the father of Fluxus himself, GEORGE MACIUNAS, who, unfortunately, will never know that he finally made it into one of his favourite books. (EW 1995)

c. AB: So here, for example, EMMETT writes about our using the word "perfectly", he obviously thinks you will object to it!…
DS: (Silent shrug.) (DS 1995)

d. Re-reading the typescript of **b** above I was startled to find "the fourth and perhaps terminal version". It is nothing of the kind. It's actually the tenth. I've had more than my share of problems with numbers, especially with the two books I have translated from DANIEL'S French, the *Topo* and the *Mythological Travels* — dates, how many times, street addresses, page numbers, how many kilometres or feet or inches, how many dollars pounds pennies or marks, weights, ages — and fortunately DANIEL caught me out on most of these errors — (I hope!) — when we sat down and compared translation and original sentence by sentence.

One of the classical instances of this wrong-number syndrome occurred in Poland not long ago, while I was addressing an assemblage of businessmen and their ladies at a fund-raising dinner for the International Artists' Museum in Lodz, of which I am honorary president. I told them that my love affair with Poland started almost eighty years ago, when my Polish mother brought me forth into the world blah blah blah blah blah blah. Afterwards there were many compliments, certainly more than I deserved for such a banal performance: how good you're looking, you don't look your age, you must have discovered the Fountain of Youth. I asked ANN NOËL how she'd liked the speech. "It was fine," she said, "but you're going on seventy, not eighty."

Sometimes I forget how to spell, too, like the time, also in Lodz, that I was making a presentation to Professor ZBIGNIEW BRZEZINSKI, the intellectual pillar of President CARTER'S administration who is still busy exploring the technetronic horizons of our allegedly post-industrial society. I was in the process of inscribing his name in the *de luxe* hand-made presentation book, TV cameras following my fingers, and for the life of me I couldn't remember how to spell his name. His son told me later that when CARTER was in the White House there was a joke circulating around town, that "if you want a good job in Washington you'd better learn how to spell ZBIGNIEW BRZEZINSKI." When I think of such moments, I wonder why DANIEL, on the announcement for the Festival of Misfits in London in 1962, described me as "the Pole with the elephant memory" [below].

GALLERY ONE 16 NORTH AUDLEY STREET GROSVENOR SQUARE LONDON W1   HYDe Park 5880

If you are too successful, and have nostalgia for the days when you were not,
if you are unsuccessful, and hope some day success will knock at your door,
if you are too beautiful, and find men in the street are bothersome,
if you are ugly, madame, and wish you were beautiful,
if you sleep profoundly at night, and feel that it is a waste of time,
if you suffer from insomnia, and have time on your hands,
if you have teeth, and no meat,
if you have meat, and no teeth,
if you belong to the weaker sex, and wish you were of the stronger,
if you're in love and it makes you suffer,
if you're loved and it bores you,
if you're rich, and envy the simple happiness of the poor,
if you're poor, and long for la Dolce Vita,
if you're afraid to die, or find no point in living,
if you're a drunkard or a teetotaler,
if you believe in heaven or believe in hell,
if you're satisfied with the colour of your skin, or would rather change it,
if you believe in yourself and are pleased with what you do,
or don't believe in yourself, and wonder what you are doing,
and why

**then come to see the
FESTIVAL OF MISFITS**

built by people who sometimes sleep soundly, sometimes don't; sometimes are hungry, sometimes overfed; sometimes feel young, rich and handsome, sometimes old, ugly and poor; sometimes believe in themselves, sometimes don't; sometimes are artists, sometimes not.
We make music which is not Music, poems that are not Poetry, paintings that are not Painting, but
music that may fit poetry
poetry that may fit paintings
paintings that may fit . . . something,
something which gives us the chance to enjoy a happy, non-specialized fantasy.

**Try it
THE FESTIVAL OF MISFITS**

Robert Filliou, one-eyed good-for-nothing Huguenot

Addi Kocpke, German professional revolutionist

Gustav Metzger, escaped Jew

Robin Page, Yukon lumberjack

Benjamin Patterson, captured alive Negro

Daniel Spoerri, Rumanian adventurer

Per Olof Ultvedt, the red-faced strongman from Sweden

Ben Vauthier, God's broker

Emmett Williams, the Pole with the elephant memory

You are invited to the opening between 10 a.m. and 6 p.m. on 23rd October. The Festival will continue until Thursday 8th November.   Admission 2s. 6d.

In conjunction with the Festival there will be a special evening at the Institute of Contemporary Arts in Dover Street at 8.15 on Wednesday, 24th October, which will include a 53 kilo poem by Robert Filliou, an Alphabet Symphony by Emmett Williams, a Paper Piece and The Triumph of Egg by Benjamin Patterson and a Do-it-yourself Chorale by Daniel Spoerri.

I almost forgot, I was adding up the *Topos*. There was the French original in 1962;[e] the Dutch translation *without a single re-anecdotation* in 1964; the 30 pages of excerpts from the then forthcoming American edition in the *Paris Review* in 1966; the two American editions, soft and hard, in 1966, we're already up to five; DIETER'S translation of my translation[f] in 1968; the reprint of the original French by the Archives of the Centre national d'art contemporaine in Paris in 1972; the micro-card edition of the American edition by WOLFGANG HAINKE in Shierbrok, Germany, in 1987; the facsimile of the original version published by the Centre GEORGES POMPIDOU in Paris in 1990, and, of course, this one, which may or may not be the 10th and perhaps terminal version. (Did I forget any, DANIEL?) (EW 1995)

e. AB: How many copies were there?

DS: Well, when LARRY RUBIN invited me to exhibit at his gallery, he told me that normally he spent 1500 francs on 1000 copies of a colour invitation card, so I asked him: "Can I do something else?" He agreed, do whatever you like, but I need 1000 copies. So I printed 1000 copies of the booklet with a very small printer and asked him to print an extra 500, that I paid 300 francs for, which I kept and gave to people. But the thousand were sent out as an invitation and they were lost, I mean most people threw them away, they found them in their mail: "What's this stupid thing, aach!" I would have thrown it away myself! (DS 1995)

f. Hi, EMMETT, I did translate: not your translations — but the first *Topo's French Text*; and after your translation had appeared I translated your *notes* — from the *English*, there was no translation of them yet. (DR 1995)

g. AB: So, how does the book relate to Fluxus?

DS: Yes, it *doesn't* relate!

AB: That's a snag!

DS: It doesn't relate because Fluxus came afterwards, the *Topography* doesn't relate to Fluxus, it's Fluxus that relates to the *Topography*. That's how the dates are…

AB: Certainly, but when the two other versions appeared, Fluxus was active by then…

DS: Yes DICK HIGGINS did the English edition, he was very much the great publisher of Fluxus, but it was a little like the Surrealists and their admiration for LAUTRÉAMONT, and of course LAUTRÉAMONT was never a Surrealist…

AB: Aha, so the *Topography* is the *Maldoror* of Fluxus! (DS 1995)

h. Some Fluxers whose faces used to be red have made about-faces, a few have lost face, and at least one lovely Fluxus face has been lifted several times. The famous "Face on the Bar-room Floor" belonged to ROBERT SERVICE, a precursor of Fluxus in the Yukon. (EW 1995)

i. He had one, all right. One of the objects on my recent collage-portrait of GEORGE is a piece of human excrement, painted one-half brown, one-half gold. It rests upon a golden plaque inscribed *Fluxus Alchemy*. As the alchemists of old sought to transmute base metals into gold, the discovery of the panacea, and the elixir of longevity, so GEORGE sought to transmute a band of prima donnas, egoists, opportunists and seekers after personal glory — you know, artists, poets and composers — into a United Front of revolutionaries dedicated to the gradual elimination of the Fine Arts. That's step one. In step two, GEORGE'S revolutionaries were to exercise the pedagogical function of teaching people the needlessness of Fluxus itself. Hmmm. Some programme. Doesn't it sound familiar? Anyway, the alchemists failed in their quest, and so did GEORGE. His band of revolutionaries turned out to be artists, with no intention of eliminating themselves. (EW 1995)

j. DS: Well, MACIUNAS was a deeply unhumouristic person, he had absolutely no sense of humour. He was a very serious person who always wanted to give a political meaning to Fluxus, which was absurd, because you can't give a political sense to absurdity.

AB: This seems rather strange. Fluxus was so humorous, all those artists' games…

DS: Yes, that was a part of it, and he probably liked that, but I think he was closest maybe to JACKSON MAC LOW with his very serious way of political thinking, and the others with their jokes were… I don't know how he felt… We never talked about it, I didn't have long talks with MACIUNAS… When he was in Paris he stayed at my place, but he was eating pills all the time, he had a huge case of different pills, he always thought he was sick — and he didn't drink like the rest of us…

And then Fluxus was very much in flux! I mean for years you didn't hear anything from MACIUNAS, when he was in the States. And when I visited him there in 1970, he was happy to see me, he invited me to dinner one evening, and he said "You know you are one of the 50 people in the 'inner circle' so you have the right to get all the Fluxus publications." I said "Yes but I can't take *all that* with me." He replied "I will send it to you, to France, but *you* have to pay the postage" — that was very funny! — so I gave him 50 dollars and it all arrived in France, in Montargis, a provincial town. It was like Christmas, I had to open it all up in front of a customs officer, who said "What *is* all that?" I tried to explain and suddenly, at a certain moment he said "Come along, pack it up and go away": it was too much for him... (DS 1995)

k. By almost everyone except the greatest living artist in England, a dear friend of all four perpetrators of the *Topography*, and a supporter of Fluxus from the beginning: RICHARD HAMILTON. (EW 1995)

l. Including musical excursions. On June 28, 1966 at 6:30 in the evening and the next morning at 9:30, the *musical* director of KPFA in Berkeley, California, broadcast a "most favourable" review of the *Topography*, in which he compared it to MARCEL DUCHAMP'S Green Box. "The reference to DUCHAMP'S book isn't gratuitous," Mr SHERE wrote to the publisher of the Something Else Press, a copy of which letter I found amongst my papers recently. "I'm currently working on an opera using it for a libretto (with DUCHAMP'S permission, of course); and I'd like to ask permission to make an oratorio out of WILLIAMS'S translation — possibly in combination with the French original. Please advise me as to the possibility of obtaining this permission..." I wonder if our publisher ever answered Mr SHERE'S letter? If not, and if it's not too late, I hereby grant permission. I'm also willing to negotiate operatic and film rights. (EW 1995)

m. DS: Well, I think that at this time, FILLIOU and I would be talking and suddenly he would say something extraordinary, a sentence of genius: baff! it was there! And we did a lot of it like this, sudden ideas had to go in. My logic after the spectacles [of *L'Optique moderne*] was related to what ARMAN was doing. He put objects, rubbish, behind glass, so, for instance you dared to go up close to it, it was interesting seeing how, here it gets rotten, and here and here, because it was sealed off... You were looking into another world, peeping in. I remember discussions about that, and thought I wanted a more tactile situation, without this separation. Another form of this was as if describing it to a blind person, as if someone had worn the spectacles [see **Introduction I, d**]. It was also important that I never glued this one down, it would only be a reference, narrated and not shown.

The book is the snare and you can look through the book... which is why I like so much MERET OPPENHEIM who occulted it even more with a layer of 15 cm. of snow… in a lousy student room in Paris: snow! Very MERET OPPENHEIM, and very Surrealist in the best sense! (DS 1995)

n. DS: No, for me a multiple has a special and very precise meaning, it has nothing to do with the classical idea of reproduction. Reproduction, bronze-casting, book-printing, lithography and so on, tries to copy an original as precisely as possible. In lithography, for example, after so many copies they say "now it becomes bad, so we finish the edition." The idea is to produce as many good copies of the original as possible… A multiple though has two aspects. It may move, for instance DIETER ROTH'S book of cut-outs, you could give it to a thousand people to frame and everyone would have a different picture on their wall. Or, it may be something made by a process, but having different results. For example, in the Restaurant SPOERRI, I took the table-top of a particular table at the end of the meal each evening and kept what was there as a multiple snare-picture, they were all different. (Although sometimes people would say "No, no, you can't have my lighter," so we said "OK! Then carry on eating!") (DS 1995)

o. While we're puzzling over these forking narratives let's get down to business, begin the begat and see where it takes us. Just for example, the RALPH and PEGEEN whom we meet in **7, b**, a box of matches, were man and wife. RALPH RUMNEY was the son of the Vicar of Wakefield and PEGEEN the daughter of PEGGY GUGGENHEIM and LAURENCE VAIL, whose son, PEGEEN'S brother SINDBAD, published some of my earliest writings in his review *Points*. Through the good graces and open houses of SINDBAD'S father I met TRISTAN TZARA [**78, a**], OSSIP ZADKINE, PIERRE DE MASSOT, KIKI DE MONTPARNASSE, NATALIE CLIFFORD BARNEY and other landmarks of the past. Many years later, while I was staying in LAURENCE'S atelier on a visit to Paris, my very dear friends DANIEL SPOERRI and ROBERT FILLIOU came to lunch one day and read the final proofs of the original French version of the *Topo* at LAURENCE'S dinner table, assisted by wines from his cellar served by me and SHARON SCIAMA [**30, a**], once the woman I loved, and whose boyfriend, ERIK DIETMANN [**Appendix VI**], DANIEL'S assistant, bloodied my nose and broke my eyeglasses one romantic midnight at ST.-GERMAIN-des-Prés. SHARON was the daughter of the poet ERNEST WALSH and KAY BOYLE [**30, a**], LAURENCE'S wife after his divorce from PEGGY GUGGENHEIM. She was raised by KAY and

LAURENCE together with SINDBAD. Her first husband was MICHEL SCIAMA, related through his mother to MARCEL PROUST [74, f], and for some years my closest friend in the world (he lured me to Paris in the first place). His second wife, a Yugoslav model, I believe (and if not she could have been), added a touch of class and glamour to the *vernissage* of DANIEL'S Édition MAT exhibition at the Galerie Loeb in 1949 [20, d, e]. Meanwhile, back at the ranch, when MICHEL and SHARON introduced me and my first wife to LAURENCE in 1949 (he was then living with CYRIL CONNOLLY'S first wife, JEANNIE) he took one look at POLLY [5, b; 30, a; and 36, b] and called her by her mother's maiden name. It seems he had been somewhat enamoured of POLLY'S mother during his Greenwich Village days. Now just think, if… (EW 1995)

p. DS: STERNE I never read, but JAN POTOCKI'S *Manuscript* I know, it's beautiful, but it's more like those Russian dolls, one inside the other.

AB: But the *Topography* is like that also.

DS: That was not the original intention, it came later in the notes, firstly I wanted to demonstrate a *piège raconté*, and then I thought, well, from a button you can explain the world, and it became this snowball and we thought in the end it will become as big as the *Grand LAROUSSE*!… but after the German translation I stopped adding things.

MG: So when does an anecdote stop being one? When is it no longer a part of the book?

DS: Well, myself, I'm not quite sure. On the one hand I agree it could go on and on, but at a certain moment it becomes indigestible… So: POTOCKI, once I met a descendant of his, and what I like most about POTOCKI he had this teapot, and for years, or months, anyhow a long time, he filed away at the knob on the lid until it was small enough to fit in his pistol, and then he shot himself with it. I hope it's true because it's such a beautiful story!

Then, ROUSSEL, I probably heard about from HARRY MATHEWS, his magazine was called *Locus Solus*, and also JOHN ASHBERY.[q] They probably told me, if you haven't read him, you must, and at that time there was still the Bibliothèque Lemerre and you could buy original editions for almost nothing, no one was reading him. Naturally he is somebody I admire, and when I was in Palermo, I went to the Grand Hotel et des Palmes and I asked for RAYMOND ROUSSEL'S room, of course they have one, they pretend it is room 300 and so and so… And so I slept in the room in which he committed suicide: another suicide! (DS 1995)

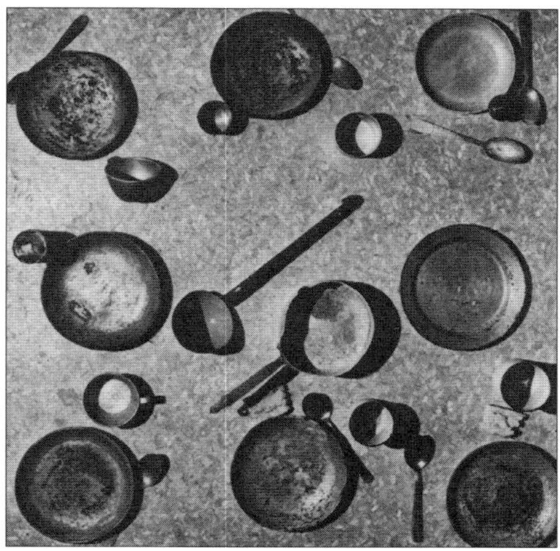

DANIEL SPOERRI, *Prisoner's Menu*, snare-picture [see **Appendix IV**, Mardi 5 Mars].

q. AB: I noticed JOHN ASHBERY was a waiter at the Galerie J., these menus are not very well explained… [See **Appendix IV**]

DS: Well that was when I turned the Galerie J. into a restaurant, each day we had a different menu and at the end of the exhibition was the *vernissage* and we exhibited all the table-tops as *"menus-pièges"* as well as the 723 cooking utensils. And this, with the *Attention* exhibition [see **6**] at KOEPCKE'S, these three things (with the *Topography*) were the most precise things I have done. And so, for example, RAYMOND HAINS, who now I've known for 35 years, makes a parallel world which is linked up only by words, puns in different languages, something he can't write down because it is so complicated… And this menu [*Vendredi 8 Mars*, **Appendix IV**] is all jokes like this, so *Coquilles St.-Jacques* as his name is JACQUES DE LA VILLEGLÉ, *Araignée de mer, sauce Heinz*, which sounds like HAINS, *Bœuf nouvelle mode* refers to Nouveau Réalisme, and so on… (DS 1995)

r. In a nutshell: DANIEL SPOERRI, born in Galati, Romania, on March 27, 1930, met DIETER ROTH, born in Hanover, Germany, on April 21, 1930, at the Café du Commerce in Bern, Switzerland, in 1953. The expatriate American EMMETT WILLIAMS, born in Greenville, South Carolina, on April 4, 1925, met DANIEL at the artists' cellar club in Darmstadt, Germany, in 1957. ROBERT FILLIOU, born in Sauve (Gard), France, on January 17, 1926, met DANIEL at La Méthode, a bistro on the Rue Descartes in Paris, France, in 1959. DANIEL introduced DIETER to EMMETT at a lively TINGUELY *vernissage* in Basle, Switzerland, in the August of 1960, and to ROBERT in a bar at the Place de la Contrescarpe in Paris in the November of the same year. This leaves the meeting of ROBERT and EMMETT unaccounted for. ROBERT'S records are of no help here: "EMMETT, I can't remember where and when we met," he wrote, way back in 1963. "I feel as if I had known you all my life." Of course there was a first time. Somewhere in Paris, and it was DANIEL who introduced us. Where and when I know not. But, as ROBERT might have said, "I am a poet, not a book-keeper." (EW 1995)

s. AB: I remember you told me how you first met ROBERT FILLIOU…

DS: Well I had just arrived in Paris and I found this room in the Rue Mouffetard, this famous *rue*, room 13 of the *vingt-quatre* and so on… and in the evening I went to a restaura… no! a bar, two minutes from there on the Rue Descartes, Bar de la Méthode, and there was a drunk sitting with just a portion of *frites*, *pommes frites*, and he was smearing the oil of the *frites* in his hair and saying "This is so good for the hair" because he was already quite bald! He was with a very beautiful maybe nineteen-year-old Danish girl. Next day — I had a little car then, a Fiat Topolino, a kind of station wagon… and I was just getting into this car and this blonde girl came running after me.

MG: The Danish girl?

DS: This Danish girl, yes, who I didn't remember, because I was drunk too, it was two o'clock in the morning or whatever, and she said "Oh, we saw each other yesterday and I have to get a mattress from somebody, can you please help me to get it?" And so I did naturally…

MG: She had to go and fetch it?

DS: She had to fetch it and because they had absolutely no money — they had been living with friends and at some point that didn't work out any more and they said to themselves okay we must leave, and they found themselves a new place but they were allowed to keep the mattress. So I collected the mattress in my Topolino, it just about fitted inside. And then we met up in the evening and that was the beginning of my friendship with FILLIOU. He was completely… I was already well informed through my other friends, through the Édition MAT which I was preparing along with DIETER ROTH, TINGUELY, BURY, SOTO and so on. I was in the picture at that time, knew all the new things that were around, and that was a completely new world for him and he was totally amazed that it existed. And so we became close friends. EMMETT was already my friend, and DIETER ROTH in Bern…

MG: You were in Bern?

DS: I was dancing there, a soloist, but as was normal in a town like that I had to dance operettas [see **78, b**] and so on… And so, shall we go and eat now? (DS 1995)

AN ANECDOTED TOPOGRAPHY OF CHANCE

Original Motto:
"This section consists of a faithful representation of the scenes from his youth, which may serve perhaps as a lesson and warning to those who have yet to outgrow this inestimable age."
— KARL PHILIPP MORITZ, *Anton Reiser*, part three, prologue (1786)

Enlarged Topo Mottoes:
"The whole world is strewn with snares, traps, gins and pitfalls…"
— GEORGE BERNARD SHAW, Epistle Dedicatory to *Man and Superman*

"Dichtungsmasse EG 750
Diese Dichtung wurde speziell entwickelt zur absoluten Dichtung von Fugen… gegen Druckverlust im Inneren bei Höhenflügen."
— HANS HADERT, *Leim und Klebstoff Fibel* (1958)

Motto for the 1968 edition:
"Ensnared! Before I could utter aught save a muffled curse, I was flung head first into an empty piano case, the heavy lid of which was instantly closed on me… I had been tricked!"
— WILLIAM LE QUEUX, "Tricked", p. 29, *The Spy's Bedside Book*, an anthology edited by GRAHAM GREENE and HUGH GREENE, RUPERT HART-DAVIS (1957)

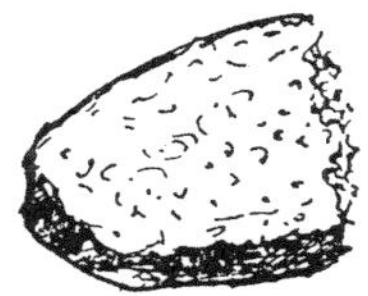

1. Piece of white bread with a bite out of it, sliced from a loaf bought yesterday (Oct. 16, 1961) but cut only this morning by the actress RENATE STEIGER, who came for breakfast with her husband, CLAUS BREMER. I don't usually eat breakfast, but since they were about to return to Switzerland, via a business detour[a] to Brussels and Hamburg, we had decided to get together once more [30]. As for the piece of bread that remained from said breakfast, KICHKA BATICHEFF took a bite out of it at noon with two soft-boiled eggs,[b] but she didn't finish it either from lack of appetite or because this snack was her second or her n^{th}.

a. The author is being imprecise by calling BREMER'S drive to Hamburg a *business detour*. It is well known that CLAUS BREMER'S mother lives in Hamburg — she has converted to Catholicism — so it would have been better to speak of a *sentimental journey*. (DS 1968)

b. The author, off and on for about three years, has been so preoccupied with the preparation of an "eggcyclopædia" that many of his friends call him "DAN THE EGG MAN". The book will explore the subject through such fields as advertising and alchemy, biology and business, cartoons and cookery, dancing and destiny, fables and feathers, garbage and games, happenings and hygiene, incubation and intrigue, journalism and juggling, the *Kabbalah* and the *Koran*, limericks and lapis lazuli, musicology and medicine, noodles and names, optics and orgasm, prophecy and poaching, quackery and quattrocento, radioactivity and ribaldry, sturgeon and sculpture, taboos and tattoos, vaginal stimulation and VIRGIL, warbling and WITTGENSTEIN, Yiddish yarns and yoga, and zombiism and Zen, to pick a few categories at random. I myself caught the egg bug from the author, and after a month of intense, and pleasurable research surrounded by my books at the Château de Ravenel was able to hand over to him more than 115 prime egg quotations in German, French, English, Spanish, Italian, Greek and Latin. (EW 1966)

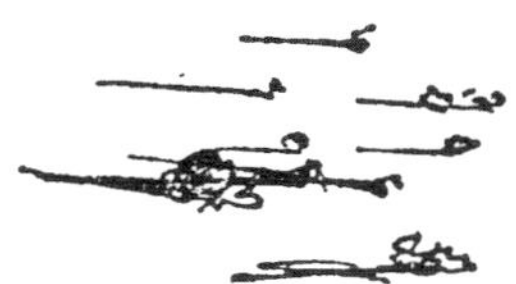

1A. Crumbs[a] from the slice of white bread with a bite out of it [1].[d]

a. "Whenever bread was sliced, a basket was placed under the knife, to catch whatever fell, to which were carefully added all the scraps from the meal, and these leftovers, fried on Sunday with a little butter, formed the festive dish for the Day of Rest."
— D.A.F.[b] DE SADE, *Justine ou les malheurs de la Vertu*, Œuvres complètes, Tome II, JEAN-JACQUES PAUVERT éditeur, Paris 1961, page 34 (JUSTINE as servant to the household of the miser MONSIEUR DU HARPIN) (DS 1962)

b. D.A.F. is a short cut through LOUIS-DONATIEN-FRANÇOIS-ALPHONSE (or ALDONZE), only son of the COMTE DE SADE, Chevalier-comte de la Coste et de Mazan, Seigneur de Saumane, Lieutenant-général pour le roi de la Haute et Basse Bresse, Bugey, Valromey et Gex.[c] Ironically, one of the Marquis's direct ancestors was the husband of PETRARCH'S LAURA. [See **25, d**] (EW 1966)

c. When it turns winter and the snow falls and you see the black word *Gex* on the white paper, it makes you think of the ravens. You can actually hear them screeching: Kex, Kex, Kex! — they are that hungry, or so you think. And at once you think of SNOW WHITE lying in her crib, wailing hideously, and it occurs to you that all the blood in the fairy tale could be left out for once. And so you press, mentally, a cake into screaming SNOW WHITE'S hand and the dear little child messes around with it amid the white bed linen until everything is beautifully mucky because the cake has become totally mushy and already you are thinking of the coming thaw. That helps — especially when you've just been thinking about DE SADE who would in fact have reintroduced blood into the story because he was very fond of children, not only nicely roasted but simply raw, and at the end of a knife. And you are on the point of thinking: He'll slash away at that little child, and then the blood will have returned once again. But then luckily the ravens interrupt your thoughts with their shrieks, these lucky ravens, which call: cakes and cookies, cakes and cookies! And now the baby in SNOW WHITE'S crib, who is also called in fact SNOW WHITE, has its mushy cake back in its hand and it gets the cookie as well and it continues to make a mess. And there's the thaw outside and such a merry, mucky messing about inside that even you, too, are glad and think: There you are, instead of continuing to put up with SADE'S tales about his knife and the blood it's perfectly all right to tell yourself and the children a bit about SNOW WHITE during warm winter weather, when it thaws, with a soft cookie and a mushy piece of cake in your hands. (DR 1968)

d. I have just received, on the day of the hanging of the five snare-pictures made by ADDI KOEPCKE under licence from me [see **Appendix II**] at the Mai Udstillingen in Copenhagen, and I hope the last day of work on this interminable[e] *Topography*, a letter from him containing a collage to which is affixed a piece of red paper, torn out of a German magazine, bearing these words: "*Stets krümelfreier Tisch durch Krümel fangleiste*" — no more crumby tablecloths thanks to Crumbscoop. (DS 1966)

e. An interminable disgusting poem.

Sundays… goes walking
and thinks of all the…
which dissolve into…
inside of all the…

Mondays… goes sweating
and smells all of the…
which divide into… and…
inside of all the…

Tuesdays… goes shitting
and hears all of the…
which plummet into the…
down through the…

Wednesdays… goes flushing
and sees all of the…
which are squeezed into the…
out through the…

Thursdays… goes fishing
and grabs all of the…
which place themselves in…
inside of all the…

Fridays… goes chopping
and grinds all of the…
which form nice piles of…
inside of all the…

Saturdays… goes feeding
and thrills about all the…
which can be dragged into the…
through the… of the…

(DR 1968)

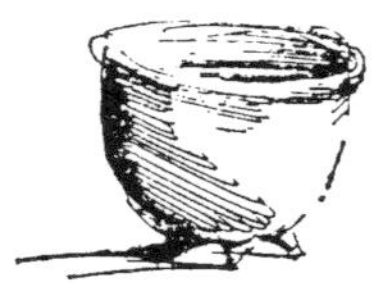

2. Pale-green egg cup of very light plastic standing on three tiny legs, bought with three others of different colour last Saturday at the Uniprix five-and-ten on Avenue GÉNÉRAL LECLERC. I was in that quarter to cash a cheque for 706 francs, payable at a bank at No. 5 on that avenue, which ARTURO SCHWARZ [see **38, f**] had sent me. Just opposite the bank is the Uniprix where I went to look for a lot of little trinkets[a] to give KICHKA'S sister, who was coming to celebrate her birthday with us in my room that afternoon. I gave her three of the egg cups, and the fourth one stayed in my room, and KICHKA used it at noon today to eat her eggs [**1, 1A**]. Still in the egg cup is the shell[b] of the egg that I bought this morning, along with three others for 35 centimes apiece, at the dairy store on the Place de la Contrescarpe, whose proprietor, at the end of the day, feeds his perishable leftovers to the neighbourhood bums, who heap coarse insults on him when they don't find the leftovers to their liking.[c] Two of these eggs were eaten by BREMER this morning and the other by RENATE [**1**].[d]

a. "Plastic vomit. This beautiful object resembles certain works of art. On a plastic base, that has been moulded at low temperature (70°), an amazingly lifelike imitation of vomited crème soup. The following ingredients can be made out:

"1. 18 pieces of badly digested ham or Caen-style tripe made of pink foam rubber (between 2 and 20 mm. long).

"2. Spinach made of rags in a nicely faded green (minced cockled plastic tissue).

"3. Finely chewed bits of EGG — both yolk and white — mixed into the whole.

"4. A pinch of parsley.

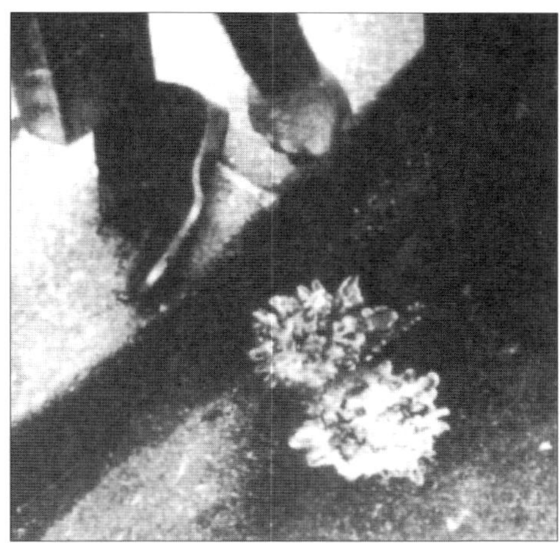

"This analysis allows one to conclude that the following meal has been consumed: egg mayonnaise, ham or tripe with spinach and yoghurt (as binder).

"This joke article is manufactured in Austria."

— *Encyclopédie des Farces, Attrapes et Mystifications*, JEAN-JACQUES PAUVERT, Paris 1966, p.439, illus. 617 (DS 1968)

b. I have consulted the file index to my EGGcyclopædia — which already contains several hundred quotations — and found an explanation: you should always completely crush EGG shells because witches and evil spirits like to make them their abode. Romanian gypsy witches sometimes even transform EGG shells into boats in which they can sail with ease to distant lands where there are riches and plenty everywhere. (DS 1968)

c. The dairy store has disappeared, giving way to yet another café, Les Arts, but the artists of the quarter have boycotted it so far. Once this week, and twice last week, I almost entered it — to get milk and cheese for breakfast. It is a hard habit to break after buying dairy products at that corner off and on since 1949. As for the bums, they are still around, sleeping and frolicking on the square except for those brief periods when the police wagons transport them to the suburbs for delousing. (EW 1966)

d. How many eggs did KICHKA eat? In **1**, the author states clearly that at noon KICHKA BATICHEFF ate a bite of white bread "with two soft-boiled eggs" (*avec deux œufs à la coque*). It was the slice of bread that she did not finish (*mais elle ne l'a pas terminée*) — singular — and not the *deux œufs* — plural.

In **2**, the author says that KICHKA used the egg cup to eat her eggs (*ses œufs*) — plural. In the egg cup, he informs us, is the shell of *one* of the eggs KICHKA ate, and this *one* of the two eggs KICHKA ate was one of four bought that morning for 35 centimes apiece. Two of these four eggs were eaten by BREMER, we are told, and one by RENATE. That leaves one egg — not two — for KICHKA to have eaten.

The eggshell debris in **4** and **4A**, as outlined on the map, is too scanty to offer any clues, and could be from any or all of the eggs, assuming in either case that most of the debris was either not placed on the blue table or later removed.

5 tells us that KICHKA salted "her egg" (*son œuf*). This could mean (a) that she ate only one egg or (b) that she ate one salted and one unsalted.

7 and **7A** would seem to rule out that she ate only one egg, and confirm that she ate one salted and one unsalted: "A match… used to light the alcohol stove… undoubtedly by KICHKA to boil her eggs" (*ses œufs*) — plural, as does **10** ("probably the very match used in place of the match in **7A**"). The burnt match in **46** is not expressly linked with the eggs and can be ignored here.

But **12** rules out what **7** and **7A** seemed to confirm, for here the author informs us that the salt from the carton of Socosel was "used by KICHKA to salt her *eggs*" (*ses œufs*) — both of them!

26, a spoon with the remains of egg yolk on it, gives no clue to how many eggs KICHKA ate, although it is most likely yolk from KICHKA'S egg or eggs, and not from BREMER'S two or STEIGER'S one. I say "most likely" because KICHKA ate her egg or eggs *after* the departure of BREMER and STEIGER; and since the author has never to my knowledge (which covers years of familiarity with his room and its contents) had more than two spoons suitable for eating eggs in the shell at any one time, the spoon or spoons that BREMER and STEIGER used was or were washed before KICHKA ate her egg or eggs.

I have pondered this problem over the months, and the only solution I have come up with is that BREMER ate but one egg. He normally enjoys a hearty breakfast, and the author might just possibly have assumed that BREMER ate more than STEIGER. After all, the situation was recreated *after* the event, and with the assistance of Vin des Rochers [see **3**].

Whatever the facts were, I feel there is more truth than coquetry in the observation of MADAME RODIER, wife of the proprietor of Les Cinq Billards café, who, seeing the author reading the page proofs of the first edition of the *Topography* in the café, remarked: "Why are you reading it if you wrote it yourself? Do you have such a short memory?"

(Since the above was written, a communication in the author's own hand from New York almost confirms my theory. Reporting on the breakfast habits of KICHKA in

America, he writes: "KICHKA still eating eggs — not just now, she is sleeping, it is 1:17 a.m. But I would say an average of two or three eggs is normal — large size B because large size A has too much white. She feels there is just as much yolk in large size B, but less white. And she prefers that.")

(A still later communication from the author would seem to end the controversy once and for all: "Sorry, EMMETT, I think the final solution is that there was already an egg on the blue table before I bought the others." Although I cannot in honesty accept the consequences of this new "fact" as any kind of "final solution" I will close the matter here and now, and leave future speculation on the matter up to other readers and editors.[e] We are, after all, dealing with a small quantity of eggs; how the problem pales when one remembers the panic of BLAISE CENDRARS, who one morning in 1920 bought nine million eggs — the cargo of three ships — and sold the whole perishable lot by phone before the end of the day.) (EW 1966)

e. They began to speculate. They speculated, and they began to hunt. They hunted and hunted and then all at once they were there in the Great Hunt. The Great EGG Hunt had descended on them, and they were unable to see anything but Easter bunnies (and no more FATHER CHRISTMASES) for all the EGGS. On top of which COLUMBUS had already died long ago, so no one could think of another solution to the EGG question apart from the Great Hunt, along the lines of: He who hunteth findeth. And they really found a lot because they hunted so intensely, they kept on hunting and hunting and consequently kept on finding and finding, so that it must be said: everlasting Easters poured down upon them until sometimes they were quite literally EGG-blind, because people can put up with anything except a stomach that is constantly stuffed full with Easter EGGS! But then whenever they had recovered slightly from the Great Hunt and their Great Finds — which together go to make up the Great Easter — they quickly resumed their EGG-sensitivity. And thus they were lured back out to the woods and meadows, where soon they got involved in EGG cultivation, and so intently that eventually they all belonged to the family of the Danes and were called either Danus or Dana or Danum, and if they had not totally degenerated in this manner and stopped completely of their own accord they would have cultivated happily ever after. (DR 1968)

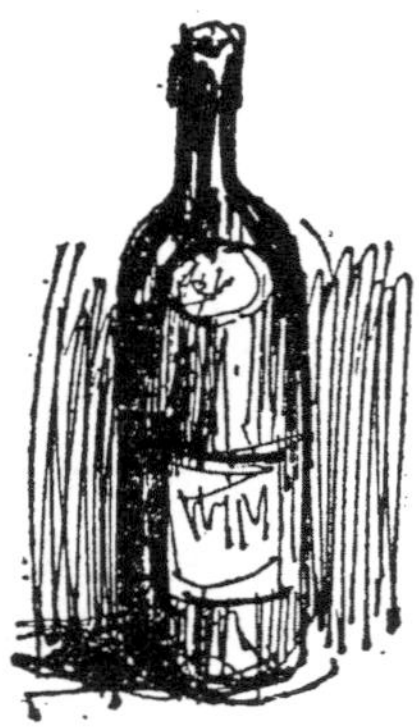

3. Litre of Vin des Rochers[a] bought on the Rue Mouffetard this morning from my regular wine dealer, who calls me the "gentleman with the deep voice" and says from time to time: "With what I have seen in this place, I could write a novel stretching from here to Place MAUBERT".[b] The litre cost 1 franc 65 centimes plus 30 centimes deposit, and with it I received a free chance on, among other things, an automobile.[d] The bottle is still half full, and I am in the process of finishing it now. [**25, 28, 28A**][e]

    a. On the label is the following data: "11% / Vin des Rochers / Lines your stomach with velvet / I guarantee this wine is made from wholesome and dependably pure juice / (illegible signature) / registered trademark / JULES LEONELLI & Co." (DS 1962)

    b. I erred. It wasn't the wine dealer who said "With what I've seen in this place I could write a novel stretching from here to Place MAUBERT,"[c] but GEORGES RODIER, proprietor of Les Cinq Billards café at Place de la Contrescarpe [see **70**]. An American, JOE CHAPEAU, set me straight on this point. He is called JOE CHAPEAU because of the filthy Spanish cowboy hat he always wears, which probably serves him as a source of inspiration for the delicate romantic portraits he paints. Just this morning MONSIEUR GEORGES expanded the philosophical observation of one of his customers, CAMILLE, that "Life is a shit sandwich" with: "Yes, and we take a bite every day." (DS 1966)

    c. From Place de la Contrescarpe, the ever more fashionable haunt of bohemians at the top of the Rue Mouffetard, that dingy but animated crooked street of markets and stalls, more picturesque than hygienic, to Place MAUBERT, called a "cesspool" by ERASMUS but today only a drab and banal annexe to the more exotic quarters of which it forms the axis, is .44 miles: a pleasant downhill walk along the Rue DESCARTES past the Esperanto bookshop, the house where VERLAINE died, a Chinese grocery store, the rear enclosing walls of the Lycée HENRI IV, the backside of ST. ÉTIENNE-du-Mont (where RACINE is buried), across the Rue CLOVIS (with remains of the medieval city walls), then down the Rue de la Montagne-STE.-GENEVIÈVE past the Polytechnic Institute, several lesbian bars and VERA'S apartment. (EW 1966)

d. "Vin des Rochers / free lottery / Series L, No. 712017 / Drawing Nov. 30, 1961." (DS 1962)

e. RAYMOND HAINS, after reading the manuscript, astonished by this reference to Vin des Rochers, one entire evening developed for my benefit a whole train of ideas that I jotted down on a dozen cards which I have since lost. All I can remember is that he started out with an analysis of an essay by ÉTIEMBLE, "PAUL CLAUDEL et le Vin des Rochers", to which**f** he wanted to reply in an article to be entitled "ÉTIEMBLE et la Purée Soma", and that he passed in review SARTRE, GIDE and all literature. (For anyone interested, his address is 26 Rue DELAMBRE, Paris 14.)**g** (DS 1962)

f. HAINS — pronounced in English the same as HANES (the renowned underpants) — did comment at a later date, if indirectly, on ÉTIEMBLE'S essay, namely in his menu for the Restaurant de la Galerie J. [see **Appendix IV**, Vendredi 8 Mars]. In March 1963 I transformed the gallery into a restaurant in which I cooked, and several Paris critics acted as waiters. The menu *Hommage à RAYMOND HAINS* consisted of, among other things, Gala cheese (GALA as in DALÍ'S wife, of whom he said: "I eat GALA"), Petit Briennois (in honour of CAMILLE BRYEN) and naturally camembert CLAUDEL. For dessert there was Far BRETON éclairs (from a baker whose name was ANDRÉ BRETON). (DS 1968)

g. To unfathom this note, I sought out HAINS at a party and attempted to communicate to him the following data: (a) that the *rocher* is the petrosal bone, and (b) that in the volume *La Réalité dépasse la fiction, ou l'humour en liberté*, by ALBERT AYCARD and JACQUELINE FRANCK (GALLIMARD, 1955), there is a photograph of a wall covered with a large poster advertising Claudel dairy products, "Normandy's best" (HAINS is from Normandy, and the author and I several years ago spent a night[h] in ST. BRIEUC[i] in a vain attempt to locate him), next to which is pasted an advertisement for the film version of PAUL CLAUDEL'S *Le Père Humilié* starring MARIA CASARÈS. After the party HAINS and I walked about the Left Bank until 8 a.m. discussing the subject, but I must confess that, like SPOERRI in the foregoing note [i.e. **e**], I wasn't able to recall a single point when I attempted to write about it the next day. (EW 1966)

h. At night, when it's dark — not in northern latitudes during the summer, nor in southern latitudes during the winter — it is so difficult to search because so little can be seen, and since what is sought is thus sometimes not seen it is very easy at night to find what is sought because so little can be seen of that which is not sought, and it is so difficult at night to find what is sought because so little can be seen of what is being sought even though little can be seen of what is not sought, but if one searches for something and finds something by day it is often not what was sought that is found because it was so bright, so bright that both eyes were so occupied with what was absolutely not sought that one might say: they were both blocked, so blocked that not even what was almost not sought found space enough in their eyes to block them, whether one likes it or not, right? (DR 1968)

i. In a letter from SPOERRI after the appearance of the American edition of the *Topography* I was told quite bluntly: "I just found out that for you ST. BRIEUC is in Normandy… and it is in Brittany." "Just found out" indeed! In the first place, SPOERRI and I went over every syllable of the English translation, sometimes, I will have to admit, using Rhine wine bottles as paperweights, so that he had the opportunity to object to my notions of French provinces while I was still on European soil. In the second place, I cannot count the number of times, during our trip to the land of the menhirs via ST. BRIEUC and the top of France, we almost came to a parting of the ways over geography. Twice I removed myself from his 2CV, slammed the door, and started walking in the opposite direction. In *his* guidebook, for example, Mont St. Michel was, of all places, in Brittany; in mine and everybody else's, of course the greatest Norman monument in France was — and remains — in Normandy. One thing we agreed on during our tour of the haunts of the Druids was that menhirs weighing 10 or 15 tons don't simply walk away when no one is looking. That, in effect, is what we were told by the director of the museum in Carnac when we reported to him that the famous fertility menhir of Plouharmel was missing. We had driven to the tiny village especially to see this much discussed monument against which infertile Bretonnes used to rub their bottoms. The peasants there claimed that they had never heard of any such thing, and that if there was anything so large and famous in the neighbourhood they would certainly have seen it because they had lived there all their lives. The closest we got to the pagan mysteries on that visit was a magic well behind a small stone church next to a swamp that didn't exactly invite penetration. Disappointed, we drove to Carnac and discussed the matter with the director of the museum. He produced a map, and the famous menhir was clearly marked on the map, though he admitted it had been drawn by his predecessor about 1907. He suggested that we go back and search again. We did, more determined than ever to solve the riddle of the missing menhir after his theory that someone might have carried it away as a monumental souvenir. While tramping around the village, we broached the question to an old Breton farmer whose French left much to be desired. He invited us to his house for cider (he had already had enough of it to be quite useless as a Baedeker), but expressed little interest in the "big rocks" which most Breton farmers find a nuisance anyway. Fertility menhir? Never heard of any such thing. Why didn't we go to this village or that to see such and such a dolmen or calvary or church? We insisted on the fertility menhir. Were we officials from Paris? Police? Our presence — and the free-flowing cider — drew other old farmers to the house, and the subject of the menhir evoked many wild tales. The men distrusted us; the women we won over by giving them a book of Breton legends we had picked up at the museum in Carnac. The women were titillated at seeing the name of their very own village in a real book, and they read aloud some of the tales they had heard when they were children (and which business-minded youngsters recite by rote to visitors to many Breton monuments — if interrupted in the middle of their sing-song history, they have to start at the beginning again). At length the old farmer "confessed". We walked with him to a hillside farm. As we reached a rocky path, he told that once upon a time, when he was a boy, they broke up the famous menhir to pave the path and roads in the vicinity, and that we were now standing on the remains of what we had come so far to find. Well, that was that, we thought, and started to walk away. Suddenly, however, our attention was drawn to a peculiar elevation near the top of the hill. When we asked what it was he dismissed it as just a pile of rocks. We walked up to it and — lo and behold! it was the missing menhir, lying on its side broken into three or four massive segments, and grown over with vines. We were victorious — but the old farmer stuck to his story. He obviously knew less about the matter than we did, and not much more than the director of the museum at Carnac, so that the SPOERRI-WILLIAMS version — that it fell over many years ago and could neither be set upright again nor carted off, considering its great weight and the inadequacy of local machinery — is as good as any future archaeologists or myth-makers might invent *ex post facto.* When we reported our discovery to the women, they confessed to having seen mysterious lights and hearing eerie sounds emanating from the spot we described. As the evening drew on, we drank more and more cider at the home of our host, and accepted an invitation from another farmer to try his brand. We left the village happier and wiser, and remained that way for several days, until, on the way back to Paris via the top of France, we crossed into the troubled borderland region of France that SPOERRI calls Brittany and I call Normandy.**j** (EW 1995, written 1968)

j. I must ask — nay, I must beg — DANIEL'S forgiveness for this outburst. He was right, ST. BRIEUC, the birthplace of RAYMOND HAINS, is in Brittany, and I was wrong, the greatest Norman monument in France is not in Normandy. This admission of ignorance probably disqualifies me from ever re-anecdoting an anecdoted Topography of France. (EW 1995)

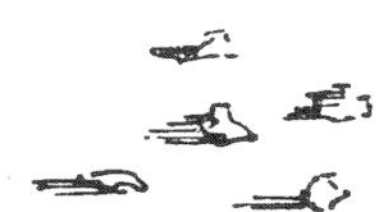

4 & 4A. Shell debris [1, 2].[a]

a. From my childhood in Romania I remember a story that impressed me very much. Robbers attack a house, and the grandmother just has time to throw some eggshells into the oven. I don't remember why the robbers open the oven, or what kind of shells they are, but they explode and blind the robbers. Without doubt I have recalled this story because I am visiting my mother in the Bernese Alps after receiving a negative criticism of the *Topography* from her in a letter that reproached me as follows (Jan. 19, 1962):

"… Other passages saddened me a little, to see that my first-born writes such stupid things; with your talent you might have created better things, certainly more refined. I still have manuscripts from the days of your youth that show promise of greater ability; but it is true that *notre monde est pourri,*[b] and your public wants to see and read such questionable things. Ah, my dear boy, don't be cross if I am a bit severe, but your mummy can't understand everything and it troubles her that her DANIEL isn't able to do something more positive with his gifts."[c] (DS 1966)

b. "Our world is rotten," French in the original. Like many a Swiss lady of her age, Mrs SPOERRI liked to season her letters with the odd sentence in French. (DS 1968)

c. SPOERRI, FILLIOU and I have often discussed the wisdom — and disillusionment — reflected in the letters of our respective mothers, who, fortunately for us, but unfortunately for them, have never met. One recent letter from my own mother counsels me that "Life is like an onion, son; you peel it off layer by layer, and sometimes you weep." With considerable pride I sent her a copy of the London *Times Literary Supplement* with ten or so pictures of my "Son of Man Trio", to which she replied that she hoped none of her friends subscribed to the London *Times*. Considering my life a failure, she often ends her letters with the painful rhetorical question: "What did Dad and I do wrong?"**d** (EW 1966)

d. Shortly after my return to the United States for the first time in 16 years, I visited my mother in Virginia and gave her a copy of the *Topography* for her birthday. She read the above section, considered it a slight invasion of privacy, but said she was pleased to see that at least I acknowledged the worries I had inflicted on her over the years. Several days later, after I was back in New York, I received a telephone call from her. She made me promise that I would not show the book to any members of her family. Why? She replied that she had been shocked to see a public declaration by her son that he was a sex fiend (she assumed that I was Mr X in **36** because the two remaining condoms were inscribed to me), a family deserter [see **5, b**] and a dope addict [see **Appendix III**], and that in my philosophy of life "life is only a shit sandwich" [see **3, b**]. Considering it all a useless battle, I didn't even bother to tell her that it was a customer at the Cinq Billards whose philosophy of life is so fatalistic, and that I have never for one minute shared that attitude. In fact, I am inclined to be an optimist, and I agree thoroughly with ROBERT FILLIOU'S saying that "There's nothing wrong with life, it's the details of living that make things so miserable." (EW 1995, written 1968)

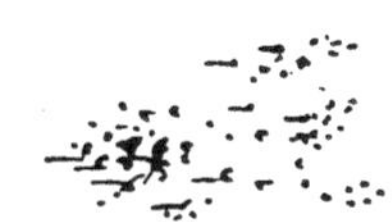

5. Grains of salt spilled[a] (as everybody does) by KICHKA while she salted her soft-boiled egg [**1, 1A, 2, 12**].

a. "The mother of a very dear friend of mine who had invited me to dinner for the first time said to me before we went to the table:'I have read all your books, very lovely, but I didn't understand a word.' I felt sorry for her because of her son, and a few minutes later, at the table, she upset the salt and I felt sorry for her again because of superstition. Everybody knows[b] that upsetting the salt brings bad luck,[c] and that writers are the salt of the earth."
— BLAISE CENDRARS, *Bourlinguer*, p.387, Éditions DENOËL, 1948 (DS 1962)

b. I less than most. In a short biographical sketch published on the occasion of the Festival der Neuen Kunst in Aachen, West Germany, July 20, 1964 (the twentieth anniversary of the plot to kill ADOLF HITLER), I pointed out:"Although I am married and have three children I live alone in a crumbling château in the heart of France's sugar-beet country. Before we were married POLLY wrote me from Washington:'We need each other like meat needs salt.' Since I don't like salt, I misunderstood, as I always do with proverbs, even those literal ones scavenged and pasted and labelled and framed into works of art by my two closest friends, DANIEL SPOERRI and ROBERT FILLIOU." [See **31, c**] (EW 1966)

c. I recall that JUDAS, in DAVINCI'S "Last Supper", has just upset the salt. (EW 1966)

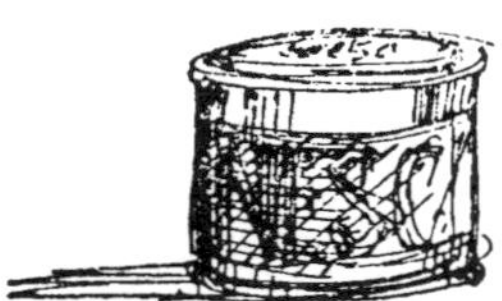

6. Jar of Nescafé with Danish label[a] that I brought back from Copenhagen Sept. 30 and which is almost empty now. I was in Denmark to help organise the "Art in Motion" (Bevægelse i Kunsten) exhibition [**34D**, **42**]. Since the museum[b] decided it could get along without my assistance I took advantage of the opportunity that ADDI KOEPCKE gave me to have a show in his gallery.[c] Fate willed that I live at ROBERT FILLIOU'S who, since he had been ordered to leave the country, gave up his apartment and let me "snare" everything I could find there: altogether ten pictures. The exhibition opened Sept. 28, 1961, at 6:30 p.m., and ran through Oct. 28. The second room of the gallery contained the pictures, the first having been turned into a grocery store [see **Appendix II**, paragraph 6] where ADDI and his wife TUT sold at regular prices groceries stamped:

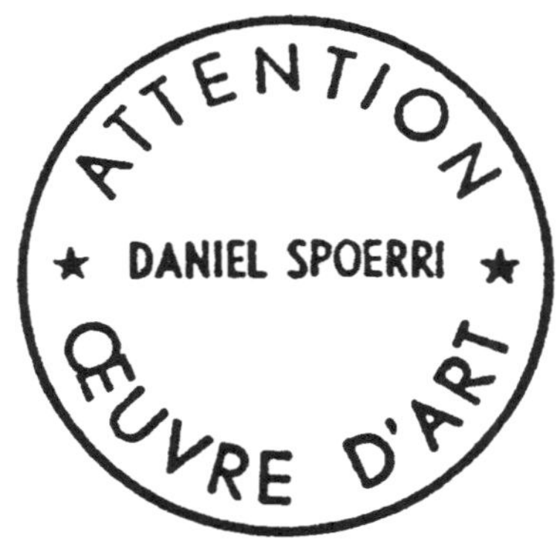

Said jar of Nescafé comes from this stock of "works of art" which, besides being just about all sold out on the opening night, included 80 bread rolls, also labelled "works of art", stuffed with rubbish kneaded into the dough, and used as catalogues. I had great trouble finding a baker who would bake the rolls, but finally the "Court Baker"[d] obliged and delivered them so punctually that I could hand them out still fresh and warm at the opening.[e] Another detail: I brought back some of the canned goods from KOEPCKE'S grocery store with the intention of keeping them, but one day when I was broke I opened them all to make supper. I can attest that this meal of "works of art" was very bad,[f] and I ask myself why.[g] [15, 19, 21]

a. "Nescafé / Fuldt opløselig pulverkaffe / 100% ren Kaffe Tryk laaget fast efter brugen." (DS 1962)

b. In the *Louisiana Museum*, which is lovely when the sun shines, you can sit in the garden and drink coffee and look at the trees and children and the sailing boats on the Skagerrak not far from Copenhagen, which is also lovely when the sun shines, or when you sit in the bars at night and watch the bearded Danes fighting with the clean-shaven Swedes, and which is lovely by day when the sun shines on the streets full of people and the shade shines into the cafés in which the fat old dears sit and gobble whipped cream from pastries. (DR 1968)

c. In Lille Kirkestræde, which is lovely even though it is only around midday that a little sun shines in. (DR 1968)

d. One of very many. (DR 1968)

e. In 1962 I exhibited 9 of these rolls in the Galerie F. The German Bread Museum sent the following written protest:

<table>
<tr><td>Mr KURT FRIED</td><td align="right">German Bread Museum, Ulm/Danube</td></tr>
<tr><td>79 Ulm/Danube</td><td align="right">Founded in 1955 by</td></tr>
<tr><td>Silvanerweg 34</td><td align="right">W. EISELEN, honorary senator</td></tr>
<tr><td></td><td align="right">Director Dr HERMANN EISELEN</td></tr>
<tr><td></td><td align="right">19.10.1962</td></tr>
</table>

Dear Mr FRIED,

I have just returned from a trip abroad to a large number of incensed telephone calls. It really is true, then, the report in your newspaper under the heading "Exciting Art Experiments". Given the underlying idea of the German Bread Museum, I also get excited when artworks consisting of "Rolls in which articles of rubbish have been baked inside" are to be produced. I assume that this state of affairs, which makes a mockery of what was once your underlying concern and your function as a founder member of our association, has slipped your attention, and I await a statement from you.

I realise of course that you will now be saying "pip-squeak" or "untalented moron". But this cannot prevent me from constantly emphasising that while pictures are being made that mock bread, over 2/3 of humanity is dying of starvation. Perhaps you consider that the two are totally unconnected. This, in my view, is far from the case. The more we destroy people's reverence for bread, the faster we will come to a sticky end when these starving masses overwhelm our world.

With my best regards,

(W. EISELEN)

Honorary senator, German Bread Museum, Ulm/Danube

The picture is now in the collection of WOLFGANG and GISELA HAHN. (DS 1968)

f. This must not be taken to imply that SPOERRI is not a good cook. Indeed, he is a first-class cook, as his performance as chef during the "Restaurant" exhibition [see **Appendix II**, paragraph 16, and **Appendix IV**] convinced the Paris art world. Nor is it to the point (if true) that, as DICK HIGGINS asserts in his charming and useful book *Postface*, "unlike EDWARD LEAR and myself, he (SPOERRI) is not at all hung up on the fantastic element in cookery." Isn't the cooking of "works of art" fantastic enough in itself? (EW 1966)

g. This question was posed in the first version of the *Topography* in January 1962. On reading the first German version on 8 July 1965, I must say that all suppers from cans taste bad.[h] (DS 1968)

h. Some suppers from cans taste good, but MARIO HINDERMANN is contradicting me yet again (6 Nov. 1968). (DR 1968)

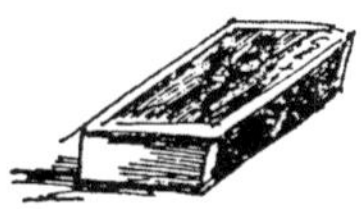

7. Box of matches bought I don't know where, on which is printed a folkloric drawing of a Marquesas islander,[a] after the custom of the S.E.I.T.A.[b]

a. This note reminded KICHKA of those children's books in which objects are personified, for example one in which matches have big eyes and slender legs. She also recalled the time at the Restaurant des Mines that the owner's wife shouted toward the kitchen: "Are those veal chops moving along?" (DS 1966)

b. S.E.I.T.A. stands for *Service d'Exploitation Industrielle des Tabacs et des Allumettes.*[c] On the table (not the blue table) in front of me as I type these notes in the author's room are four similar boxes, all empty, showing the S.E.I.T.A. artist's conception of typical Normans, Bretons and Béarnais. This morning RALPH RUMNEY woke me up at 9 a.m. (I had gone to bed at 7 a.m. after working all night at Agence France-Presse) to show me some EGG clippings [**1, b**] and to see if I would help him push his car, stalled near ST.-GERMAIN-des-Prés. I helped him, and later he drove me to the Île ST. LOUIS, where he lives, and, following a lunch prepared by PEGEEN, gave me five packs of Disque Bleu (because I was out of money and cigarettes), from one of which I copied down the key to S.E.I.T.A. Over coffee, RALPH wrote out for me the longest word in the English language: FLOCCINAUCINIHILIPILIFICATION ("jok. 1741 f. L. *flocci, nauci, nihili, pili,* w. sign. at little, at nothing [see Eton L. Grammar] + -fication. The action or habit of estimating as worthless.") As an example of its use in a sentence,

RALPH suggested that if I incorporated a note on floccinaucinihilipilification in the *Topography*, and DANIEL read it and considered it a worthless note, one could call his action a clear case of floccinaucinihilipilification. When I got back to the room I found that I had no matches (the four boxes on the table have been empty for days). I climbed upon the table and removed the matches from a similar S.E.I.T.A. matchbox (bearing the figure of an Alsatian) from an unfinished snare-picture hanging on the wall.[e] (EW 1966)

c. S.E.I.T.A., "*sei tatkräftig*"[d] as one would say in Germany, wouldn't one? You might also hear it particularly often in Düsseldorf because there, even when the sun shines, it gets so muggy that your heart slips into your pants and your brain slips into your throat, it's that muggy! And that's why the people here in Düsseldorf would then always say: Seita, be active! Especially when it's close! Because then your brain's slipped into your pants, people say: "Be an active Satan! Eh?" (DR 1968)

d. Approximately "Be active!" in English. (MG 1995)

e. According to DMITRI A. BORGMANN, of Oak Park, Illinois (quoted in Martin Gardner's notes to C.C. Bombaugh's *Oddities and Curiosities of Words and Literature*, Dover Publications, Inc., New York 1961), the longest word in the English language is pneumonoultramicroscopicsilicovolcanokoniosis — a lung disease caused by inhaling quartz dust. Sitting here in a New York heat-wave, I have no deep urge to challenge Mr BORGMANN by thumbing through *Webster's Unabridged Dictionary*, and am content to admit that whether or not it is the longest word in English, pneumonoultramicroscopicsilicovolcanokoniosis is sixteen letters longer than floccinaucinihilipilification. It is also much easier to use in a sentence. (EW 1995, written 1968)

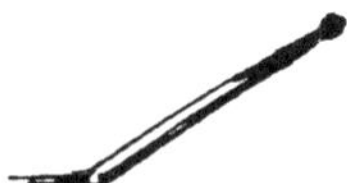

7A. A match on box in **7**, used to light the alcohol stove, located left of the table on which this *Topography* is based, undoubtedly by KICHKA to boil her eggs.[a] [**1, 1A, 2, 4 & 4A**]

a. "The spa AMÉLIE-Les–Bains belongs to Arles abbey and is famous on account of its hot baths which are said to have great healing powers. The spring is of an impressive size, the steps which lead down to the salutary water are carved from a stone that has withstood the ravages of the hot water for many centuries. The whole complex is covered by an ancient vault with a central orifice that allows daylight to enter. The construction must be the work of the Romans or the first Moorish conquerors. The source itself is located on the slope of a hill not more than 20 paces removed. The water there is so hot that once a pig fell in and was skinned instantly. And yet it would be impossible even to boil an EGG in these waters, even if it was left in them for 24 hours."
— Piganiol de la Force, 1718 (DS 1968)

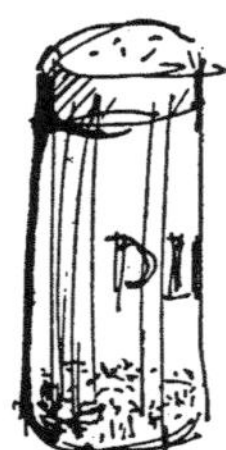

8. Pepper shaker of transparent plastic, which contained 20 grammes of white pepper, almost empty, Dipac brand, price 1 franc 20 centimes. This pepper shaker has changed position many times since the evening meal and probably isn't in its original place. The meal in question was a stew made with goat's neck, which I looked forward to very much but after three hours of cooking the meat was still uneatable, and I had to throw it out.

The sauce[a] was excellent.

a. Gravy.[b] (DR 1968)

b. Groovy. (EW 1995)

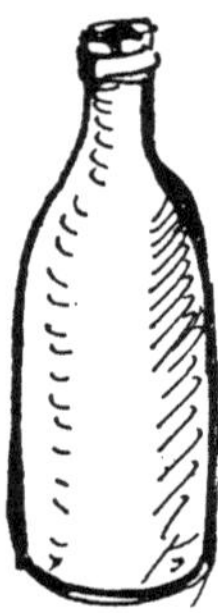

9. Half-litre bottle of milk, sealed, labelled "conditioned pasteurised[a] milk". (Subsequent note: as usual, I forgot to drink the milk, and had to throw it out later because it was completely curdled.)

    a. Excerpt from brochure accompanying the milk:"Milk — your ally / PASTEUR and our daily milk / It was a Frenchman who made possible the rational exploitation of this national wealth. A Frenchman, a scientist, PASTEUR, the father of modern hygiene and inventor of pasteurisation. This process consists of heating the milk at exactly 145 degrees FAHRENHEIT for thirty minutes in order to eliminate all the microbes and bacteria,[b] without removing any of the vitamins, then cooling it rapidly to below 50 degrees before putting it into bottles sterilised at 230 degrees in which it keeps perfectly. PASTEUR carried out this operation for the first time in a garret of the École Normale which served as a laboratory for this outstanding researcher." (DS 1962)

    b. Whatever becomes of the corpses of these little creatures? (DR 1968)

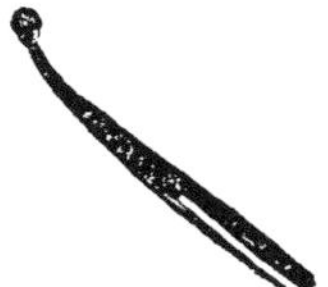

10. Burnt match undoubtedly from the box of matches described in **7**. It is probably the very match used in place of the match in **7A**.[a] In any case, both could have been used for it because the stove doesn't work well.[b]

a. Or the match described in **7A** could be the match described in **10**. (DR 1968)

b. Subsequently replaced by a two-burner butane stove. (EW 1966)

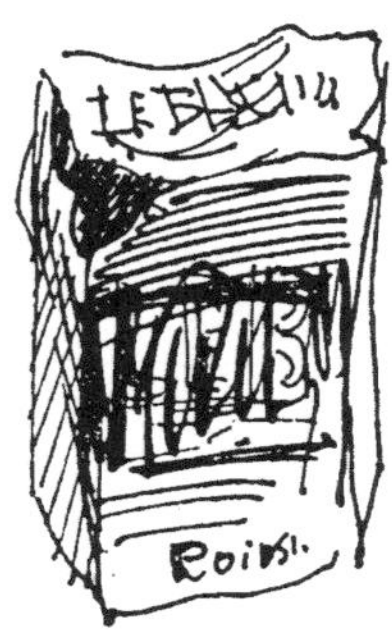

11. Box of granulated sugar, LEBAUDY-SOMMIER[a] brand, used to sugar the coffee the morning of the breakfast with BREMER and STEIGER [**1, 30**].

a. I found out recently that the birthplace of French baroque, the château of Vaux-le-Vicomte, built by NICOLAS FOUQUET, superintendent of finance of LOUIS XIV, who banished FOUQUET out of jealousy after a magnificent fête the Sun King attended at the château, is now owned by the SOMMIER sugar family, and to visit it you have to apply in writing to MADAME SOMMIER. (DS 1966)

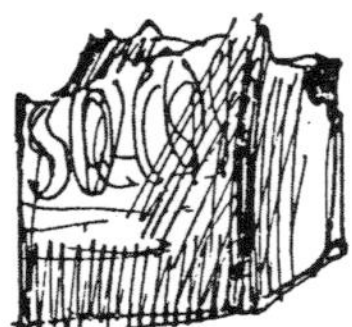

12. Carton of Socosel[a] containing 250 grammes of fine salt[c] dried by evaporation, torn at the top, half full, used by KICHKA to salt her eggs [1, 2, 5].

a. So we are very concerned. Sometimes about the salt, sometimes about the socle,[b] sometimes about the salt on its socle, sometimes about the socle under its salt. Sometimes about the socle made of books under the salt made of letters, sometimes about the salty letters on the soclish books. Sometimes about the flat printed name of the salt in the flattened printed salt packet, sometimes about the flat print of the salt packet with the flat printed name of the salt on its face. And from the flat salt on the upper face of the socle made of books ascends a salted cloud full of salty meanings, first into the eyes, then into the brain, and from the brain there ascends another one on which is written: And so we are very concerned, sometimes about the salt, sometimes about its meaning. Sometimes about the salt in our eyes, sometimes about the salt in its packet. Sometimes about the salt on its socle, sometimes about our eyes in their sockets. From them ascends a cloud on which is written, *Das Wandern ist des Müllers Lust*: "rambling is the miller's great delight". (DR 1968)

b. The *raison d'être* for this entry derives from a pun on "Socosel" based upon the German word *Sockel* for a base or plinth. The English equivalent is rather less common, its definition in the *OED* being: "Socle — a low plain block or plinth serving as a pedestal to a statue, column, vase etc." (MG 1995)

c. As the son of an evangelist, salt naturally reminds me of Biblical verses I used to hear. I took advantage of a visit to my younger brother, a future minister, to get specific quotations from the Bible bearing on salt. Naturally he cited "Ye are the salt of the earth" — in German, the salt turns "stupid" instead of "losing his savour" — because he follows my activities from afar with mistrust; but he lent me his concordance, from which I extracted all the verses containing a reference to salt:

And every oblation of thy meat shalt thou season with salt; neither shalt thou suffer the salt of the covenant of thy GOD to be lacking from thy meat offering: with all thine offerings thou shalt offer salt. — Leviticus 2:13

And that the whole land thereof is brimstone, and salt, and burning… — Deuteronomy 29:23

And ABIMELECH fought against the city all that day; and he took the city, and slew the people that was therein, and beat down the city, and sowed it with salt. — Judges 9:45

And he said, Bring me a new cruse, and put salt therein. And they brought it to him. And he went forth unto the spring of the waters, and cast the salt in there, and said, Thus saith the LORD, I have healed these waters; there shall not be from thence any more death or barren land. — II Kings 2:20–21

Now because we eat the salt of the palace and it is not fitting for us to witness the king's dishonour, therefore we send and inform the King… — EZRA 4:14

… young bullocks, and rams, and lambs, for the burnt offerings of the GOD of heaven, wheat, salt, wine, and oil, according to the appointment of the priests… — EZRA 6:9

And thou shalt offer them before the LORD, and the priests shall cast salt upon them… — EZEKIEL 43:24

Ye are the salt of the earth: but if the salt have lost his savour, wherewith shall it be salted? It is thenceforth good for nothing, but to be cast out, and to be trodden under foot of men. — MATTHEW 5:13

Salt is good: but if the salt have lost his savour, wherewith shall it be seasoned? It is neither fit for the land, nor yet for the dunghill; but men cast it out. He that hath ears to hear, let him hear. — LUKE 14:34–35

For everyone shall be salted with fire, and every sacrifice shall be salted with salt. Salt is good: but if the salt have lost his saltness, wherewith will ye season it? Have salt in yourselves, and have peace with one another. — MARK 9:49–50

Let your speech be always with grace, seasoned with salt, that ye may know how ye ought to answer every man. — COLOSSIANS 4:6

My father worked for six years preparing a concordance in Romanian; he had reached only the letter F at the time of his death, but had often expressed his hope that I would finish his work, in accordance with the Jewish tradition of spiritual succession from father to eldest son. One of his sons, at least, although the youngest, so fortunately called THEOPHIL, is following in his footsteps.[d] (DS 1966)

d. After re-reading this section in the American edition, I realised that either SPOERRI, or his brother's concordance, overlooked the most famous quotation in the Bible bearing on salt — the episode about LOT'S wife being turned into a pillar of the stuff. (EW 1995, written 1968)

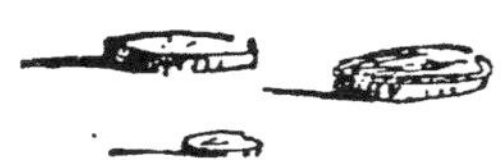

13 & 13A. Fifty- and ten–centime coins, the change left from a 1-franc piece given KICHKA to buy the white bread[a] [1, 1A, 24].

    a. I am going shopping
you should have gone shopping
he had wished he had gone shopping
she went shopping
it will have gone shopping
we should have had been shopping
you will have wished you had had to go shopping
you will have wanted to have been able to have gone shopping (DR 1968)

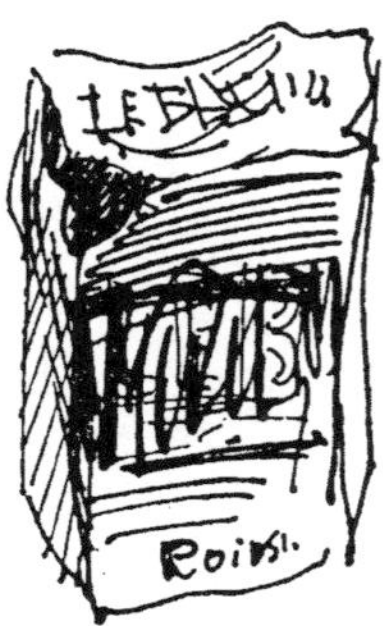

14. Package of Twining's[a] Chinese tea which I bought for a change of aroma, although I still have some Orange Pekoe left. I wanted smoked tea and they sold me this package pretending it was, which it wasn't.

    a. Recently in the Café de la Chope, Place de la Contrescarpe, I found a Twining's teabag in my cup, and printed on the cardboard tag was what must be the most idiotic couplet ever from ST. JOHN PERSE.[b] (DS 1968)

    b. The proverb must have gone roughly like this:
All you old tosspots, listen to me,
you'd do better wetting your whistles with tea
    — *TWINING'S!* [c] (DR 1968)

    c. Odd. I thought DIETER preferred TWA tea. (EW 1995)

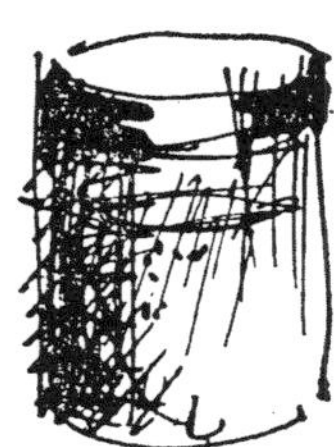

15. Jar of celery salt,[a] three-fourths full, bought in one of the IRMA chain stores in Copenhagen, price 79 øre, about 56 centimes. IRMA stocks a wide range of spices in these practical containers, all at the same astonishingly low price. I made this purchase with ROBERT FILLIOU, and I recall that the pretty blonde cashier blushed violently at our pleasantries in French. On the label is stamped "Caution, work of art".[b] [See **6** for the stamp, **19** and **21** for the container.][d]

a. "IRMA / krydderi 2 / sellerisalt / er bordsalt tørrede sellerifrø Anvendes til æggeretter, til urte- / suppe og sauce, til spaghetti-retter / og til smørrebrød." (DS 1962)

b. I almost translated "*Attention, œuvre d'art*" as "Attention, work of art". Several days ago I dug up a copy of the catalogue of the author's first one-man show at Galleria SCHWARZ in Milan (March 16-30, 1961) at the request of a bibliographer of the avant-garde in London. The catalogue contains an English version by my wife of ALAIN JOUFFROY'S early essay on SPOERRI'S snare-pictures. Re-reading this essay in my wife's words, I was startled to find "*Attention*" rendered "Caution". But of course "Caution" is the right word in this context.[c] The snare-picture that bears this title, and gave SPOERRI the idea for the stamp, was a crate with the warning in French. For the reader's information, other translators have rendered it "*Attenzione, opera d'arte*", "*Opgepast, kunstwerk*", and "*Achtung, Kunstwerk*" in Italian, Dutch and German, respectively. (EW 1966)

c. Before you look cautiously at the thing, you must first look attentively at the thing that is to be handled with caution when you are told: *Caution, work of art.* A person is only cautious of something after he has observed it, so that caution, initially at least, also contains attention — attention is the mother of caution — so now I would like to say — because I dare to: *Caution, attention, work of art.* But if you knew SPOERRI even slightly, this would make you think something along the lines of: with his stamp, SPOERRI wants to say, to draw attention to the fact, that here is a work of art in the form of an article of daily use or even consumption which can and should be used and consumed. Hence caution is not advisable because if one employed caution one would not merely rip or crack it open so as to eat or devour it, but quite simply collect it as a work of art — even if this act of collecting only absorbs a very brief moment of one's interest. In this case it would be better to say: Pay attention, here is a work of art, but dispense with any caution because it is intended to be consumed — or as was said: *Attention, work of art.* (DR 1968)

d. "Bring some fennel seeds and pepper to boil in vinegar, diluted according to taste. Pour this sauce over peeled cooked celery root. It is worth showing sufficient strength of character not to eat it right away — it will taste better tomorrow."
— Erika Sangerberg, *Alle Unsere Gewürze*, Wancura Verlag , Vienna/Cologne 1958
(DS 1966)

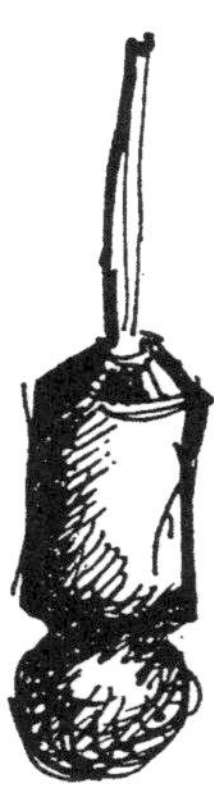

16. Container of Vanilic glue, white plastic material, consisting of a squeezable receptacle ending in a flexible tube, its flexibility allowing it to penetrate between objects you want to glue[a] without moving them. Bought in the basement of the Bazar de l'Hôtel de Ville department store two or three months ago for the sum of — if my memory is good — 26 francs. [**18, 52**][b]

   a. Surgery and glue: doctors at the University of Texas, according to an article in *Der Spiegel* in April 1962, have used glue to reconnect severed arteries. After 170 successful experiments on dogs, the doctors tried the procedure on a man. The reconnected arteries healed perfectly in seven days, faster than by suturing. (DS 1966)

   b. In some primitive cultures, houses are glued together with faecal matter.[c] (EW 1966)

     c. In some cultivated cultures, the toilets are glued together with faecal matter. (DR 1968)

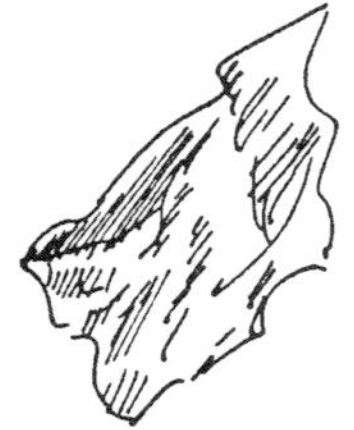

17. One of two square pockets of electric–blue Japanese silk, from a dress that VERA SPOERRI made but which she finally found prettier without pockets. I use this pocket as a pot–holder. The other one I used to pack one of the little surprises (plastic toys for "*Bout-chou*"[a]) given to KICHKA'S sister for her birthday.

    a. *Bout-chou* (cabbage stump), pet name for babies. In contrast to Germany, where babies are fished out of ponds by the stork, in France they are found inside cabbages.[b] (DS 1968)

    b. Perhaps it was this superstition which around 1840 induced people to buy seeds of the New Zealand giant cabbage at one gold franc a piece. The seeds were supposed to grow into cabbages the height of trees that would not only provide shade in summer, but also sufficient food for man and beast. The sale of these magic seeds was finally prohibited by the law courts. (DS 1968)

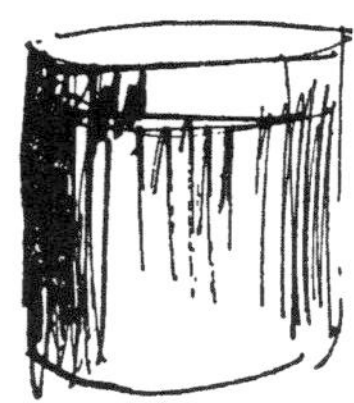

18. Transparent plastic container[a] **of VR 200 glue** bought the beginning of September at ADAM'S on the Boulevard EDGAR QUINET, accompanied by chance by JANE, English and a painter, who had heard that it was the best artists' supply shop in Paris. I used it later in Copenhagen [see **6** for Copenhagen, **16** and **52** for the glue].[b]

a. A new model, probably, since FRANÇOIS DUFRÊNE, who corrected the French text of the *Topography*, uses the same glue and was astonished by the existence of a transparent container, his — which he uses to glue his poster "bottoms" or "insides" — having always come in a can. (DS 1962)

b. I was *cocon* enough to ask ALAIN JOUFFROY to comment on the *Topography*. Here is his note to **18** [see also his notes to **32** and **34Q**]:

"The painters FERRO and PHILLIP MARTIN first mentioned this glue to me. PHILLIP MARTIN regards it as slightly superior in quality to the Vinavil that artists are currently using in Italy. It can be found at one of the basement counters at the Bazar de l'Hôtel de Ville, where it is sold sometimes in plastic containers, sometimes in cans. I have used it for my own photo-collages, and I confess that I am not insensible to the pleasure of feeling it coat my fingers with a thin transparent film (which makes me think of the cocoons caterpillars secrete around themselves before moulting) after an hour or two of work. VR 200 and Vinavil are certainly among the most fascinating mediums an artist can use today, and constitute the material origin of a very large number of works of art that, without them, would have been inconceivable." (DS 1966)

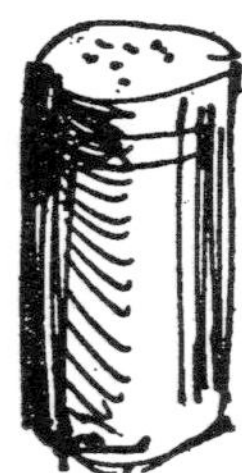

19. Jar of curry powder[a] bought at IRMA'S [**15**, **21**], stamped "Caution, work of art" [**6**]. As everybody knows, or doesn't, curry is not simply a particular spice, but rather a mixture of ginger, coriander, pepper, garam masala and a powder resembling saffron[b] (whose name I have forgotten, although it is in my collection of 150 herbs and spices), which gives the curry[d] its colour.

a. "Karry / er et blandingskrydderi, der bestaar / af ca. 10 forskellige krydderier. An- / vendes i saucer, salater og sammenkogte retter, til ris og makaroniretter / m.m." (DS 1962)

b. Curcuma. "The strong aroma, hot flavour and bright yellow colour of curcuma powder explains its frequent use as a colourative, especially in the making of curries. Curry powder (*poudre de cari*) is a mixture of curcuma, powdered cloves, cumin, coriander and other aromatic products.[c] It is widespread in countries with hot climates, such as India, Indo-China and Malaya, as well as the Antilles. It is well known in England, but less so in France."
— *Les Épices, l'Ancienne Mode*, 1963 (DS 1968)

c. So if they don't fade away, they will smell happily ever after. (DR 1968)

d. I have asked DICK HIGGINS, a specialist in Indian cuisine, for one of his curry recipes:

Three Day Curry

— a style more than a recipe —

Friday, 9:15 — Start about one quart of water. When it is boiling, put the bones from six pounds of lamb legs (boned) in a pot. Separately, start a cup of oil heating. And elsewhere, mix eight ounces of turmeric, eight ounces of ground cumin seed (cumino), twelve ounces of coriander, four ounces of garam masala (available from any good spice store that carries oriental seasonings), one ounce of grated galangal root (available through herbalists), one ounce of star anise (also available through herbalists: IMPORTANT, it is not sweet like anise seeds) and six ounces of ground cardamom. Cut a lemon in half, squeeze both halves into the oil and throw in the rinds. Lower the temperature down to a slow boil.

10:00 — Cut up three tomatoes, and add them to the boiling lemon brew. Add in about six ounces of the mixed seasoning, hereafter referred to as "curry powder", which it only in a way is, since it is incomplete. As soon as the powders are dissolved, add the lemon and curry brew to the lamb stock pot. Let it cook fairly slowly.

11:00 — Cut up four medium onions. Add them in.

11:35 — Remove all oil that you can, and put it in a frying pan. The quantity is not critical. Heat it almost to burning. Throw in the six pounds of lamb legs, already mentioned. Sauté them.

11:45 — As soon as the lamb is sealed on the outside (and juicy inside), add it and about four ounces of curry powder to the growing curry. Start a few cups of water boiling over the bones in a separate pot.

Saturday, 12:10 a.m. — Turn down both the fire under the curry and the fire under the bones as low as possible. Here one is interested in evaporation, not cooking. Go to bed.

7:30 — Turn off the fire. Add the bone water to the curry. Place in a cool place.

8:30 — Place the curry in a refrigerator.

6:00 p.m. — Skim all lamb fat that has risen completely off. But save it. Mix up two ounces star anise, two ounces ginger, two ounces pepper, six ounces ground cumin, one ounce cloves, three ounces fenugreek (available at most spice stores) and one ounce grated galangal root. This is hereafter referred to as "Sanbar powder" which it is not, but which it resembles.

6:20 — Cut up five tomatoes and two onions. Add them into the curry. Turn the heat up until there is a very slow boil. Slowly mix in four ounces each of Sanbar and curry. When the whole mix seems smooth, lower the temperature, and leave it be, slowly steaming. In the mean time, put about a pound of dhal or any lentils into a pot, and let them soak overnight. Squeeze a couple of lemons over them if possible. Also, take a pound of whole wheat flour, called "hunters' meal" in its commonest commercial form in the United States, and slowly add half a pound of butter to it. Dissolve the butter and dough with a cup of boiling water. Add a little salt and a very little baking powder. The more flour one sprinkles on one's hands and on the mixing board, the easier it will be to do this. Wrap the flour in a flour-sprinkled clean dishrag, and keep it in the refrigerator. Add a couple of cups of water to the curry.

11:30 — Turn off the curry completely. Let it steep until —

Sunday, 11:05 a.m. — Turn up slow heat under the curry and the now-soaked dhal or lentils. Add eight ounces of curry powder and eight of Sanbar to the curry, and add four ounces of Sanbar powder and two of garam masala to the dhal. Add sufficient water to the dhal to make it like a very thick split pea soup in texture. Let everything cook very slowly.

1:00 p.m. — Turn off the curry, and let it steep some more. This is your last chance to add any additional curry powder or vegetables, if these seem called for. Continue to allow the dhal to cook, very, very slowly.

6:30 — Heat an oven fairly high. Heat a frying pan, or, better, a skillet, as hot as possible. Take the dough, and divide it into parts. Place each part on to a floured board and, with the thumbs, press it till it is about a quarter inch (or less) thick and six inches in diameter. Put some of the lamb fat saved from Friday on to the skillet. When it is browned and about to burn, put a few dough patties in it. You can call the resultant bread "paratha". Douse it with plenty of extra lamb fat (or, if necessary, butter). It is best when it is brown or has reddish freckles on a paler background. The dhal will probably require a cup or so of water, six dried chilli peppers, and a few ounces of curry powder: add all, till you have a fairly spicy mix about the consistency of thick split pea soup, as before. Heat up. As soon as all three curry dishes are quite hot, throw a few dashes of hot sauce into the curry, and mix it in. Place a paratha off-centre on each plate. Serve the curry on to the far side of it. Put some dhal on the curry. A side dish of yoghurt should be available: if the dish is too hot for some, yoghurt has a magical and delightful cooling effect. Another traditional side dish, supplementary to yoghurt, is made by cutting up a cool, large onion, and sprinkling lemon juice and hot sauce over it. The mixture is then stirred well, kept cool till serving, and served uncooked. This also has a cooling effect in conjunction with the curry. A final traditional note: in South Arabia, from where this dish hails, rice is normally used, in addition to the paratha, as a substance on to which the curry is served. For Western tastes, the rice often seems a bit too much, though others will dispense with the paratha rather than the rice. Serves eight.[e] (DS 1966)

    e. So if they don't die, they will mix happily ever after. (DR 1968)

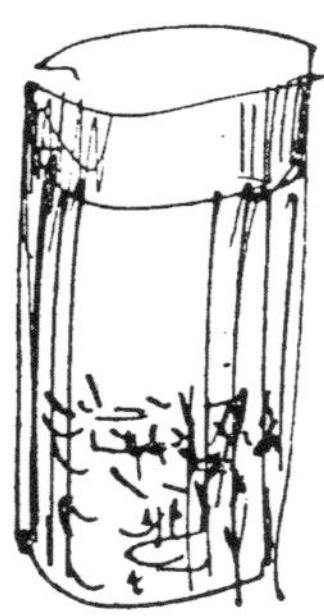

20. Pretty glass jar of sweet basil[abc] bought at Konsum Bolaget in Stockholm two days after the opening of the MAT[d] (multiplication of transformable art) exhibition there [**34E** and **42**], in the Vallingatan 42 gallery which, by chance, belongs to the Konsum Bolaget chain. It was through the intermediation of PER OLOF ULTVEDT, who was at that time artistic adviser to the gallery, that I organised this exhibition comprising multiplied works of AGAM, ALBERS, BURY, DUCHAMP, MALINA, MARI, MUNARI, MAN RAY, ROTH, SOTO, TINGUELY and VASARELY.[h] At the same time I bought two other jars in the same format, the first of celery salt [**15**] which belongs to the snare-picture called "Flat-Iron" (the iron keeps falling off, I don't know for what reason; on the subject of glue see **16**, **18** and **52**), the second of Old Hickory Smoked Salt, to be found on the snare-picture "KICHKA'S Breakfast" bearing, pasted underneath, the notice: "Do not touch, reserved for KICHKA" because she is very fond of it.[i]

a. "Kockens Basilikum används till; Tomaträtter, gula ärter, grönsaksoppor och fiskrätter, sallader, Kockens AB Stockholm." (DS 1962)

b. Many persons read and re-read the proofs of the first edition of the *Topography*, yet one error slipped through: basil was mis-spelled *"basilique"* in French, instead of *"basilic"*. The father of FRANÇOIS DUFRÊNE called my attention to the error, and to the triple signification of the sound in French: the herb, the mythological monster and the building. (DS 1966)

c. "The Greeks called their king *basileus*, and basil is still called 'king's herb' in Germany. Perhaps it played a mystical role in royal ceremonies because of its imposing aroma, or was used to ward off the fatal glance of the basilisk. This little herb is luxuriantly overgrown with superstition. The most ludicrous concerns the scorpion. Basil was formerly believed to be an antidote for scorpion bites; yet, if one rubbed basil leaves between two rocks, and covered them with a vase, a scorpion was supposed to come forth."

— Erika Sangerberg, *Alle Unsere Gewürze*, Wancura Verlag, Vienna/Cologne 1958

(DS 1966)

d. Introduction to the catalogue:

"Édition MAT is the first attempt to multiply art[e] outside the classical processes of reproduction (lithography, bronze casting, tapestry etc.).

"For each work we have sought the means of multiplication it deserves. To this end, the idea inherent in the work must express itself without 'personal handwriting', which would permit only reproduction and not multiplication.

"Objective, static art permits only quantitative multiplication of an idea fixed in the model, and even if it assures a wide diffusion of the object, the multiplication adds nothing to it. For animated objects, moving or changing optically, electrically or through the physical intervention of the spectator-collaborator, multiplication renders justice to the infinite possibilities of transformation.

"Each work is signed by the artist, and each will be offered in a limited edition of 100 numbered works for sale at the same price, $40, taking no account of the imponderables that influence the market value of a work of art." — DANIEL SPOERRI, November 1959 (DS 1962)

e. At the present time, around 1968, an astonishing number of people who sail and fish under the same colours fail to quote or in any way acknowledge DANIEL SPOERRI'S definition of multiples, which is the first ever. Probably these people simply don't understand it. But nowadays there are so many multiples that one *could* talk of a multiplication of the multiplication idea if, in keeping with SPOERRI'S standpoint, they really were multiplied works which move or can be changed. But the things that are multiplying away at every corner of the globe can be as little changed as the weedy[f] beards the new multiplicators allow to grow down into their old etching, litho and letter presses, thus letting these faithful veterans of the industrial revolution be degraded into moustache-curling machines. (DR 1968)

f. (Translator's query): "*Dünnbärte*? Are these really thing/scrawny/weedy beards in the literal sense? Grown by artists?" (MG 1995)

g. thin, the meaning in this case (beards grown by the "Multiplikanten", the multipliers. In german, if something "has grown a beard" it is meant to be old, better: outmoded; the machines for winding these beards was, a long time ago, called "Bartwickelmaschinen")

(DR 1995)

h. After eight exhibitions in Europe, SPOERRI stopped production of the MAT collection. Then in 1964, at the suggestion of KARL GERSTNER, it was revived, with the help of Galerie der Spiegel in Cologne. The 1964 collection of twelve new objects is almost sold out (July 12, 1965), and the 1965 and 1966 collections are in preparation, as well as the new Édition MAT-MOT, which will publish visual poetry. (EW 1966)

i. The author says here that the iron keeps falling off his snare-picture "Flat-Iron". Is it possible that the Old Hickory Smoked Salt has fallen off "KICHKA'S Breakfast"? At any rate, it does not appear in the illustration of this snare-picture in the Museum of Modern Art's "The Art of Assemblage" (page 132). And in the museum's illustrated list of painting and sculpture acquired from January through December 1961, the work is described as follows: "KICHKA'S Breakfast, 1960. Wooden chair, with board across seat, with coffee pot, tumbler, china, egg cups, egg shells, cigarette butts, spoons, tin cans etc. 14⅜″ high, 27½″ deep (36.6 x 69.3 x 65.4 cm.). PHILIP C. JOHNSON Fund. 391.61." In the museum's checklist of new acquisitions exhibited from Nov. 20, 1962, to Jan. 13, 1963, the same description is reprinted. The checklist includes the following data in connection with the picture: "SPOERRI calls himself a 'paster of found situations'.[j] 'I was waiting for the visit of three people who wished to come to see my tricks. Two hours before they came I pasted together the morning's breakfast which was still there by chance. (This chance was very lucky besides, because this breakfast I had had with KICHKA…)' Significance? 'A breakfast hung on the wall, which defies the laws of gravity and the angle of view to which we are accustomed.' " If the Old Hickory Smoked Salt was originally part of this snare-picture, apparently it was not able to defy the laws of gravity as long as the coffee pot, tumbler, china, egg cups, egg shells, cigarette butts, spoons, tin cans etc.[k] (EW 1966)

j. Mostly handed to him on a plate. (DR 1968)

k. "You are wrong about the Old Hickory Smoked Salt. It belongs to 'KICHKA'S Breakfast No. 2' and naturally you can't find it on 'KICHKA'S Breakfast No. 1'. ARTURO SCHWARZ has 'KICHKA'S Breakfast No. 2' in Milan. But please keep the note. DANIEL." (DS 1966)

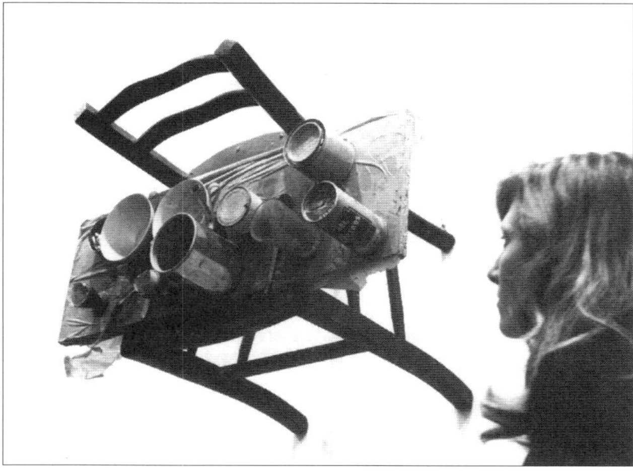

DANIEL SPOERRI, *Kichka's Breakfast I,*[1] 1960, Collection of the Museum of Modern Art, New York.

1. Since the publication of the photograph, many people assume the figure in it is KICHKA; in fact it is HÉLÈNE DE LA TOUR, now married to M. DE CANCHY, first secretary to the French Minister for Culture. (DS 1995)

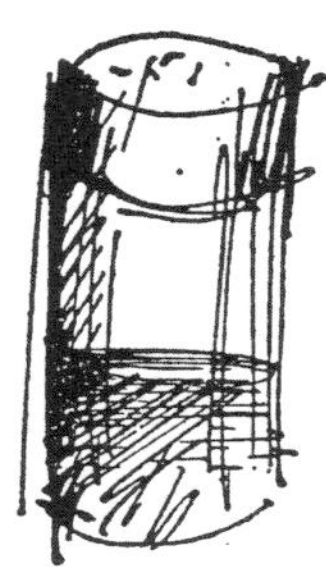

21. Jar of mild paprika[a] bought at IRMA'S [**15, 19**], to be used before July 1962.[b]

a. "Paprika / er Modne, tørrede, pulveriserede / baer af spansk peber. Anvendes til / ategte kødretter, fiskretter og sam-ø menkogte retter." (DS 1962)

b. Romanian peasants eat a breakfast consisting of *paprikas szalonna* (fat bacon rolled in hot paprika and smoked), a slice of *mamaliga* (cold corn-meal mush), a green pepper and a raw onion. Scientific research has shown this combination to be nutritionally ideal, containing everything the body needs and in the right proportion. (DS 1966)

22. Small, light-blue rubber "bracelet" bought Oct. 10, 1961, at my newsagent's. ROBERT FILLIOU used rubber bands to *momify* his signature on a card placed inside a half-litre milk container, in turn "measured" with five and a half small bricks of water colour fastened to the container with six bands, which he gave me in Copenhagen, where he exhibited it at Galerie KOEPCKE.[a]

The original signature having disappeared, he promised to make me a new one as soon as he returned to Paris. Since he makes a habit of letting things drag (me too), he certainly would not have kept his word if I hadn't needed a photo of this "measurement and *momification*" for eventual publication in a book called *Projects of Young Architects* (a project of STEFAN WEWERKA).[d] I used the rubber bands that FILLIOU didn't need in a little surprise package given to KICHKA'S sister for her birthday, with the dedication: "More bracelets than a queen."

[a] Excerpt from the catalogue of ROBERT FILLIOU'S exhibition at Galerie KOEPCKE in Copenhagen, June 1961 (original in English):

"Note on *Momified* and Measured Objects:

"Perhaps talking, certainly recording one's words on tape, creating, making durable, making one's own, employing the possessive — all these things imply *momifying*[b] an object, a thing, an emotion, intuition, idea…

"(Here is a chair. VAN GOGH paints it. In a sense, he *momifies* it. SPOERRI uses it in a snare-picture. In a sense, he *momifies* it.)

"*De-momifying* what others — or yourself — have done also is creating… Others, time, death are great *de-momificators*. I have wanted to see what the result would be if I *momified* directly some objects, with strings, elastic, thread, rope… whatever happened to be within easy reach at the time.

"POIPOI.

"Some of the objects are due to mere measurements. I thought of measuring things according to the criterion of the moment. For instance, my height is 60-odd tomatoes, and I am 111,225 Copenhagen–Paris train trips old. The metric system itself, of course, can contribute to this identification. POIPOI." **[35]** (DS 1962)

b. "Three mummies, three mummies
were lying in my grave,
when up came young ROBERT
and dragged the three away.

"'Oh ROBBERTY, oh ROBBERTA,
leave us mummies be,
or else we'll all de-mummify
and chop you up for tea!'

"'You mummies resting in your grave,
Please don't be such dummies
for if you start to chop me up
you'll get lots of tiny *demummified mummies!*'"**c** (DR 1968)

c. Dear Mummy,

Something's been tickling my conscience ever since the *Topo* first appeared — yes, even in the original French version — and it's this: I knew all along that when ROBERT was doing all that *momifying* and *de-momifying* and *momificating* and *de-momificating* he had mummies in mind, which he pronounced *momies*. Perhaps I should have changed it. But I decided to leave it the way ROBERT wrote it and said it, and, now that ROBERT is no more, I'm happy I did. It adds a little nostalgic touch to the book. Well, it does for me

DIETER put it into good Deutsch for the German edition. I suppose he had to, or else he couldn't have appended his *Drei Mumien* verses. (I'm anxious to see the English translation of *that*. Glad *I* don't have to do it.)

More on the subject of translations. In a recent letter, ALASTAIR BROTCHIE mentions that MALCOLM GREEN, his fellow editor of this edition of the *Topo*, "has taken the German text to Nepal to translate it." *Quelle coincidence!* Or perhaps I should say, *Welch ein Zufall!* Because UWE CLAUS has taken the English text of my forthcoming book about GEORGE MACIUNAS to Nepal to translate it into German. What is it about Nepal that attracts these translators? Why, do you know how ANN NOËL'S UNCLE HERBERT, who led a Gurkha regiment in the good old days of Empire, amused himself in his spare time? Translating Nepalese poetry. (EW 1995)

d. My own contribution to this volume, which never appeared, was "A Poetic Memorial to the WIDOW OF THE UNKNOWN SOLDIER", to be constructed by swift birds. (EW 1966)

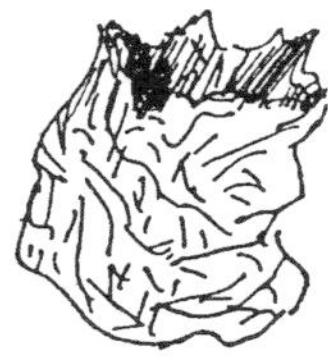

23. White paper bag which contained the eggs[a] [**1, 1A, 2, 4** & **4A, 5, 12**].

a. Really? (DR 1968)

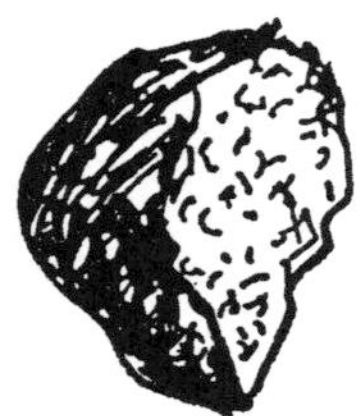

24. Chunk from the same loaf of white bread as the piece with a bite out of it, and from which RENATE STEIGER cut a slice [**1, 1A, 13 & 13A**].

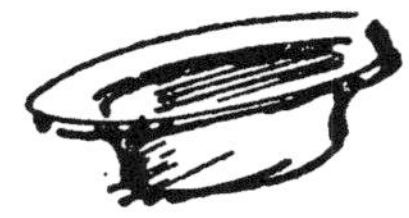

25. Stopper of tricoloured plastic, black-green-red, from the bottle of wine described in **3**. Only Vin des Rochers uses these tricoloured stoppers, and only since a short time, because they realised (a) that the colourless stopper previously used was almost invisible and that you were always pouring with the stopper still in and (b) that people collect them to make front-door curtains, like the one the owner of a movie on the Rue CHAMPOLLION made last year, but with plain ones, and pointed out to me: "It takes a lot of drinking to make a curtain like this."[a] [**34L, 49, 57, 67**]

a. During the final reading of the manuscript, while I am trying in vain to write how intrigued I was to learn that other brands of wine are now using marble-coloured stoppers or caps stamped with numbers and letters of the alphabet, MARIANNE and MICHÈLE RICARD are talking about pink mattresses, square ones, blue-grey, flowered — proof enough that I absolutely must end this *Topography*, something I have been saying for weeks[b] without result.[c] (DS 1962)

b. For years. (DS 1966)

c. The idea for this *Topography* in its present form was captured almost by chance on magnetic tape during the course of a conversation between ROBERT FILLIOU and myself in October 1961. It turned out to be decisive to the realisation of my project. Here are excerpts:

DS: More wine?

RF: Yes.

DS: No, but what interests me… have I told you about my new idea? Sure, I've already told you before, but now it… it… it preoccupies me. I've already bought the tracing paper to make…

RF: Oh yes.

DS: … what I already told you about, and now seriously I really want to do it. To make… I don't know, I told you before, just like that, in the clouds, but now it… it… it preoccupies me more and more. I mean I really want to do it, no more pictures, that's too spectacular, you look at it, you say ah that's nice, but to have only the design, only the… what do you call it?

RF: Yes, yes, the… the… the form, the…

DS: Not quite, the…

RF: … the outline.

DS: That's it, the outline. You know, numbered, and it will be the same size on paper, outlined like a detail, like a topographic map of chance for a given moment, and the design would be numbered, with a book underneath — a fold-out, number such and such, you know, what's this?, and I would like to explain very fully. For example, everything here. I'd have to explain that this is a tape recorder, because no one would know what it was, it would just be a square… a rectangle.

RF: Yeah.

DS: A tape recorder bought in Amsterdam, and why? Well, because I had a lot of money from my… from… you know, make a little… what do you call it when the police… when you have an accident the police make out a… a report.

RF: Yes yes.

DS: It's also a map, with only the outline of the cars, the wheels.

RF: Yes.

DS: Who put on the brakes, things of that kind, and that's what I'd like to do, to make it completely… It's a bit too external, I think, to make it… to… to… to… I want to put it back into the spectator's imagination.

RF: Yes.

DS: And besides, it's a kind of game, a kind of game like dice. You ask what's this? No. 15? You never or only rarely will you know what it is, because for example when you think… well here, there are twenty or so bottles, and…

RF: And you wouldn't be able to tell what they were.

DS: Right, because it's… it's…

RF: Only the things that have a very definite shape, like knives, something like that.

DS: Yes yes, knives, that's very good.

RF: Everything that… everything that…

DS: Knives, forks, and I don't know what all.

RF: Yes yes.

DS: There are very few things… but for example, there are thirty or so things here that would make only circles, and what are they? One is celery salt from Copenhagen, and so on, stamped "Caution, work of art," and then… well, I explain why and all that.

RF: Yes yes.

DS: I'll have to find a style. You know, not to relate a lot of twattle… and I think it would be a very amusing game.

RF: Yes yes, very.

DS: Here on the wall, the snare-pictures… everything is spectacular and visible to the maximum, you see bread, you see things that stand out, volumes, all kinds of things that extend beyond the shape, and all that, but in the other, in the outline, it would be completely different… well, like the subconscious and the conscious, you know, you'll see only numbers, nothing at all, and you will read… a novel… before a topolo… a topographic map of chance. But it'll be difficult. I think that for the moment I will… I'm going to cover the table with tracing paper to begin with, and I'm going to pretend that I've forgotten all about it, until the day I say all right, here goes, and after I make exactly… after I make… from that tracing paper another tracing paper, precise, exact, I'm going to almost paint it, you know, so that it'll be almost like a picture, but a technical picture, without any trace of individuality.

RF: Yes yes.

DS: With the text nearby, so that people will be able to say: "Ah, No. 13, the circle, that's Jaffa Gold cucumber pickles…"

RF: Ha-ha.

DS: "… found at…" I think it will be pretty interesting to give both.

RF: Yes yes.

DS: Because at the moment it seems to me… it's the most challenging thing I'm able to do at the moment… The things on the wall are too easy for me now.

…

DS: Without the outline the topography wouldn't make any sense, and without the text the outline wouldn't make sense. That would be to withdraw completely and give only a geographic map, like when you travel through France using a map. For example, during my vacation I visited the Fontaine-de-Vaucluse. I didn't know what it was, but it was marked with three stars, I didn't know whether it was a Roman thing, a monument, or what have you, and you know this pool, in summer it's nothing at all, just a hole with a little water in it,[d] and I was really deceived,[e] and still it was marked with three stars, and there you are, that's the topographic map for me, and the experience will be exactly the same. Someone will take No. 5. What is it? A piece of wood, a cigarette butt. You can say a lot about a cigarette butt, a mere cigarette butt, you could have a whole novel under it, you could say that it's a… I don't know what all.

RF: Where it comes from.

DS: Where it comes from, that's very important.

RF: That there's lipstick on it.

DS: Yes. For example, look at that black…

RF: There will be lipstick on it.

DS: … look at that black mark there. It could be from your pen, the pen you sign your work with, and how you sign in such and such a fashion in making a… a… *momification* of your signature.

RF: Yes.

DS: And that *momification* of the signature signifies for you the *momification* of a work, and it follows that… and so on and so on, and it could be carried pretty far…

RF: Yes yes.

DS: … for a little black mark. And nearby would be something that… that's identified as just a knife. And related stories. On my way to the Fontaine-de-Vaucluse I saw many things much more interesting that weren't marked by three stars, not even by one star, and that's what I'd like to see.

RF: Like when you go to church to get married and on the way you meet a lot of girls who are prettier than your wife.

…

RF: Most people understand life only when they go to the movies.

DS: Yes, it's… they go to make their…

RF: … their own… they understand very well, for example, a woman who cuckolds her husband on the screen, and they leave the movie saying "What a fine film."

DS: Yes.

RF: But when somebody tells them, "You see that woman, she is cheating on her husband," they call her a slut. But what I mean is something more violent, but similar. The element of taking something and isolating it.

DS: Yes.

RF: There is always the… the…

DS: I… I believe… I… I think what you said, to add something being the same as isolating… to add something isn't the same as isolating… I don't know…

RF: I have seen a lot of things in reproductions of paintings, in REMBRANDT, for example, details… you see more, a hand, how he does the hands, they specialised in things like that.

DS: Yes yes yes.

RF: Right now you're holding a bottle and pouring something to drink, I don't really notice the hand, but they… it's…

DS: It's… it's…

RF: It's there that they started… they started all that… that… the plastic perception that exists… it's… it's they who started it, who elaborated it, and from the most obvious things, that which man himself is, and it's… it was in accordance with their conception of life.

DS: It's there that you also see… If you look through a book on Romanesque art with marvellous photos of details you see things you never saw before.

RF: Yes, it's a way to understand things better. I've been saying all along that you should send a letter to people, signed with your name, and say: "Look at what you have on your table at this moment…"

DS: I wanted to do that, I even wanted to ask them to glue it up themselves, but I can't ask people to submit themselves to such boring exactitude. If I do it myself that's something else, because I identify myself with such things. Just to look, that's a good idea, but they do it automatically after seeing my pictures, and that's one of the reasons I make them. That's better, to look, just to look.

RF: Or a telephone call. You call them and say: "Look around you." That's the whole conversation.

DS: Oh.

RF: It makes a kind of poem, saying what there is.

DS: It's because of that I'd like to make… that I'm going to make topographies. Because it turns history completely upside down, and everybody can begin to imagine the object, and I hope they start looking around their own homes.

RF: Yes.

DS: And that they will be able to imagine more than I could myself… (DS 1962)

d. This is, of course, the haunt of PETRARCH, one of the three "fountains" of Italian literature, whose favourite spot was the grotto where the Sorgue starts its course. SPOERRI was there at the wrong time of the year; at flood-time, the pool that disappointed him so much overflows in roaring cascades, and might very well have taken his breath away (although he is seldom victimised by the masterworks of nature). Only a few miles away is the family castle of the MARQUIS DE SADE, one of whose ancestors, HUGUES DE SADE, married PETRARCH'S immortal LAURA. [See **1A, b**]

Another Italian, MICHELANGELO, was also drawn to a watering-place — but for reasons far different from PETRARCH'S. In what must be one of the oldest testimonial letters on record, MICHELANGELO wrote to his nephew: "Day and night for two months I drank from the waters of a fountain lying forty miles from Rome; its waters break stones, and did indeed break mine, so that I was able to expel most of them in my urine." The letter, signed and dated 1549, is reproduced on the label of Fiuggi table water. (EW 1966)

e. "There is a tradition that the turning point in his thinking took place during the sacrifice of the Second Russian–Polish Army, almost wiped out in East Prussia. COUNT ALFRED KORZYBSKI, then a staff officer, had prepared an attack. He carefully studied the maps. But the maps didn't show a deep ditch in which the Prussian machine-gunners were positioned. This could be the origin of the famous motto of general semantics: 'The map is not the territory.' "

— GABRIEL VERALDI, "Le Père de la sémantique générale", *Planète*, 6, Sept.-Oct. 1962

This passage, which I read about a year after having expressed my own deception by maps, intrigued me a great deal. (DS 1966)

26. Small aluminium spoon, a real bargain, bought at the drugstore on Rue LACÉPÈDE opposite the Hotel Beau Séjour, where MADAME MARABELLE[a] claims that someone is tapping her gas and threatens to write the city gas company about it. She has also sent countless complaints to the transport authorities because the buses stand at the bus stop in front of her house with their engines running, and pollute the air. On the spoon, remains of EGG yolk [**1**, **2**, **4** & **4A**].

a. It is also futile to search for MADAME MARABELLE at the Place de la Contrescarpe. Her hotel still stands there, but she has now turned eighty and her son has sent her away — perhaps in fact to the Ticino, where she was born. (DS 1968)

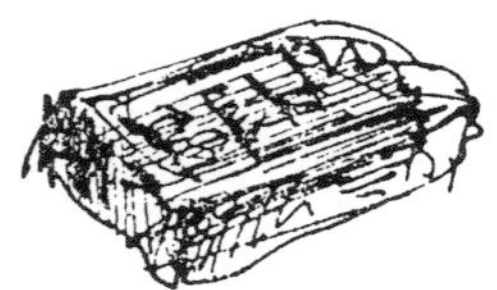

27. Quarter of a pound of butter wrapped in gold–coloured silver foil, now half finished, Premier brand [1, 24].[a]

a. "In Belgium, during the First World War, LÉOPOLD MAGRITTE (the father of the Surrealist) sold common or garden salt water in pharmacy bottles to the farmers to conserve their black market butter. But all accusations would have been in vain because salt has, according to the encyclopaedias, the property of conservation."

— *Encyclopédie des Farces, Attrapes et Mystifications*, JEAN-JACQUES PAUVERT, Paris 1966 (DS 1968)

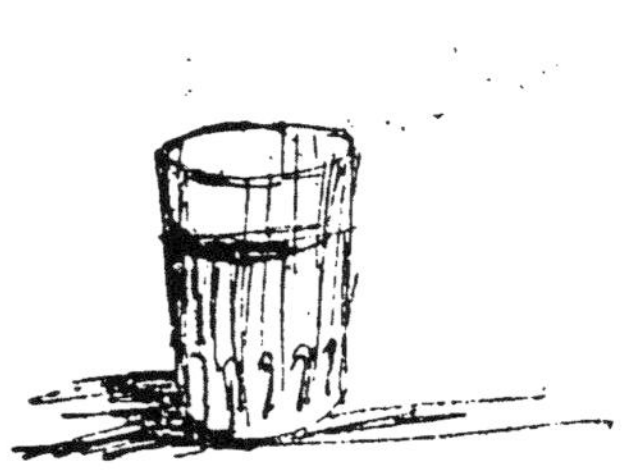

28. Glass of wine that I am in the process of drinking, but which I always put back in its original position [3].

28A. Wine stain[a] from the wine glass in **28**. In reality an ink blot that is trying to look like a wine stain.

   a. An unintentional orthographic variant of the author's name.[b] [See ALAIN JOUFFROY'S note to **34Q**] (EW 1966)

   b. In the German version the German word for *wine glass* has been used for the word *wine glass*. (DR 1968)

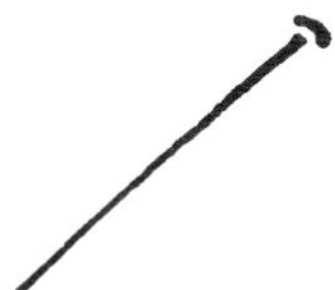

29. Pin from a spectacularly folded new grey sports shirt, bought at the Uniprix on the Avenue GÉNÉRAL LECLERC [see **2**] for 20 francs, after being insulted by the salesgirl because I didn't know my size, which turned out to be 39.[a] The salesgirl didn't have that size on the shelf, so she went to the stockroom to look for it, and during that time I met a nurse, whose name I no longer remember but who hangs out around my quarter; but I recall very well that she stank that day, and that she insisted on accompanying me in the store while I shopped around for all the ridiculous trinkets I bought for KICHKA'S sister's birthday.

a. I didn't reckon with the fact that the laundry I take my shirts to uses all sorts of chemical junk that shrinks them. Now I buy size 41.[b] (DS 1966)

b. Now that I know that chemical junk is used not only to launder shirts, but also to make them, I buy size 43. (DR 1968)

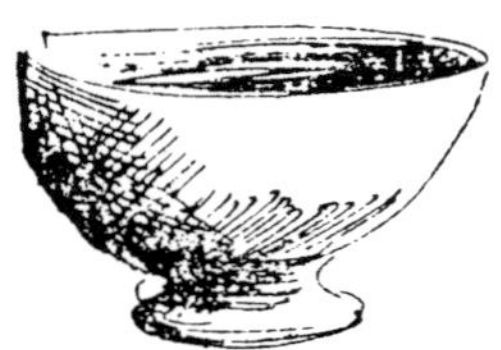

30. Glazed earthenware bowl, yellow outside, white inside, half full of Nescafé [6] served to the American negro composer BENJAMIN PATTERSON[a] (author of a score for bass violin in which the instrument emits sounds by the removal of objects inserted between the strings and elsewhere), who paid me a visit during breakfast [1] and who, learning that BREMER was returning to Switzerland by car, decided then and there to take advantage of the opportunity and accompany him as far as Brussels, thinking it would be easier to hitch-hike from there to Cologne to pick up his bass and bring it to Paris. (BREMER asked him to do a performance at the Municipal Theatre in Bern next February as part of a programme he was preparing in which the public would participate, details of which they were to discuss in BREMER'S CITROËN 2CV.)[d]

a. To my knowledge, my only namesake is the son of BENJAMIN PATTERSON, EVERETT EMMETT PATTERSON.[b] I have not yet met him. I was baptised OSCAR EMMETT WILLIAMS, and for many years was known as OSCAR, but so many people mistook me for OSCAR WILLIAMS the anthologist that I decided to use EMMETT instead of OSCAR. The mother of my dear and long-time friend SHARON SCIAMA, KAY BOYLE, almost refused to come downstairs to dinner before our first meeting, thinking that SHARON'S friend "OSCAR" must be the anthologist. And once my old KENYON College colleague ANTHONY HECHT, who had just seen POLLY and me off on the QUEEN ELIZABETH, received a telephone call, the dialogue of which ran something like this:

"Yes, this is ANTHONY HECHT."

"This is OSCAR WILLIAMS."

"Come on now, I just put OSCAR and POLLY on the QUEEN ELIZABETH."

"Is there more than one OSCAR WILLIAMS?"

"Why yes, I know several… Wait a minute. Is this…"

Yes, it was the anthologist. And through the years people introduced to me by those old friends who still call me OSCAR have often handed me manuscripts to be included in my next anthology. One of the more outspoken of them once took my hand and said: "I've always wanted to meet the poor man's DYLAN THOMAS."[c] (EW 1966)

b. Since the above was written, I have met EVERETT EMMETT PATTERSON, whose name, it turns out, is really *ENNIS* EMMETT PATTERSON. When I first returned to New York in 1966, my bedroom was separated by only a thin wall from the room of ENNIS EMMETT and his younger sister BARBRO. Their early morning romping would wake me up by six or seven o'clock, and gave me an undeserved — and welcome — reputation as an early riser. ENNIS EMMETT — called ENNIS by his father and mother, but not by me — so far is too young to have read the *Topography*, but holds no grudge against me for getting his name wrong. (EW 1995, written 1968)

c. EMMETT has also joined the ranks of the anthologists (*An Anthology of Concrete Poetry*, Something Else Press, New York 1967), so it is easy to imagine a telephone conversation — or maybe it has already occurred — running something like this:

"Yes, this is WILLIAMS the anthologist."

"But this is WILLIAMS the anthologist."

"Come on now, I just edited the new anthology."

"Is there more than one anthologist called WILLIAMS?"

"Why yes, I know several… Wait a minute. Is this…"

Right, it was the anthologist. (DR 1968)

d. The programme never took place, but I myself have since bought a CITROËN 2CV. (DS 1966)

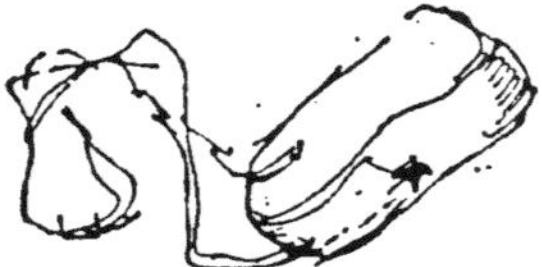

31. Outline of a plastic bag for my new PHILIPS electric razor, leaning against a wooden box [**34**]. Bought the same day I decided to glue up a board on which my old razor was lying among a pile of other things. By coincidence, there was a publicity campaign in progress that day, and I got a 5-franc reduction; if I had come a day earlier, according to the dealer, I would have got a 10-franc discount — the custom, for PHILIPS at least, around Easter.[a] The snare-picture in question was exhibited afterwards at the Festival of Nouveaux Réalistes at Nice (July 13, 1961), where the wire was plugged in so everyone could see that the immobilised razor still worked [**43**]. The picture was almost stolen when I drove to Nice with RAYMOND HAINS in the 4CV of JEANINE DE GOLDSCHMIDT. At Lyon, where we spent the night in a hotel close to the railway station, someone forced open a car door, made off with only a shirt that HAINS had bought at the House of 100,000 Shirts in Paris, the thief apparently having panicked when he found he couldn't lift the razor and other objects solidly glued to the board.[c]

a. "Who would believe that the art of shaving goes back hardly a century and a half? 'The glory of teaching civilised man to shave himself,' writes GRIMM, 'is reserved for all eternity for MONSIEUR PERREL: Would God he had appeared forty years earlier!' PERRET — and not PERREL — 'master cutler and tradesman', in publishing his *Pogonotomy, or the Art of Learning to Shave Oneself*, had little doubt of the service he would render his contemporaries. Its publication had one advantage, however — it accustomed gentlemen of fashion to wash their faces."

— DR CABANÈS,^b *Mœurs intimes du Passé*, ALBIN MICHEL, Paris 1908, p.151 (DS 1966)

b. DR CABANÈS and GRIMM obviously overrate PERRET'S contribution to the art of pogonotomy. Long before the birth of CHRIST (who himself did so much to popularise the beard), ALEXANDER THE GREAT ordered his soldiers to shave off their beards to prevent the enemy from using them as handles. PLINY, in his *Natural History* (Book VII, Ch. LIX), writes: "The first barbers that entered Italy came out of Sicily 454 years after the foundation of Rome. They were brought in by P. TICINIUS MENA… The first to shave daily was SCIPIO AFRICANUS, and after him the EMPEROR AUGUSTUS." LUCIUS TARQUINIUS PRISCUS, to whom we owe the sewers of Rome, introduced another hygienic reform to the Eternal City: shaving. CAESAR tells us that the Britons and Celts were clean shaven. WILLIAM THE CONQUEROR ordered the English princes to cut off their beards, and SHAKESPEARE'S plays are full of jokes about barbers. PETER THE GREAT, who considered beards "a useless embarrassment", levied a tax on them. This measure was repealed by a beardless monarch who apparently was very fond of them: CATHERINE THE GREAT. (EW 1966)

c. I was once surprised, and somewhat put out, to find my own BRAUN electric razor attached to the SPOERRI-FILLIOU proverb "A Close Shave", on exhibit at the Galerie J. in Paris. I had left the razor in SPOERRI'S room, where it lay for several months before incorporation into a work of art. Of course, I should have known better, as author of the first published review of the first edition of the *Topography*, in which I wrote: "You've heard about the man who came to dinner and stayed for months. But did you ever hear about the artist who came to dinner and took the table with him when he left? Not only took it away, but hung it up and exhibited it as a work of art." (EW 1966)

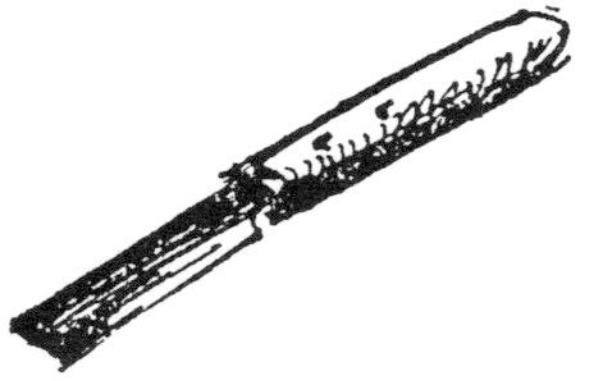

32. Paring knife with a black wooden handle and a very rusty blade, point broken off, bought for 3 francs and 40 centimes only a week ago along with two snail tongs at the cutlery shop at the foot of the Rue Mouffetard. I made this purchase because I liked the contrast between the long handle and the short blade, but without noticing that it wasn't stainless steel. The point was broken off the same day in trying to open clams, the most hermetically sealed of all shellfish. The only way KICHKA found to open them was to wait until they opened up slightly to breathe, then insert the blade rapidly, which took her the whole day. (If anyone knows a more efficient method, please write me.)[a][d]

a. DE LA VILLEGLÉ has since informed me that all one needs is an ordinary oyster knife, which costs about 1 franc. But the real revelation came with the introduction of a truly monstrous machine at the annual LÉPINE competition,[b] in 1962. It sells for about 35 francs, and here are excerpts from the prospectus:

"EASY OYSTERS:[c] for opening oysters of all sizes and varieties. Hurrah for EASY OYSTERS! Gone are your oyster-opening woes. No more cut hands, because the semi-automatic EASY OYSTERS machine opens the oysters for you. EASY OYSTERS consists of a base with a slot to insert the oyster, with adjustable clamps to hold the oyster in place. EASY OYSTERS comes with an adjustable hand-grip blade movable in all directions, and can be fastened to your table. Simply…" (DS 1966)

b. The "Concours LÉPINE" is an annual exposition in Paris where inventors and small manufacturers have shown off their wares since 1901. It derives its name from a former prefect of police, LOUIS LÉPINE (1846-1933). MARCEL DUCHAMP introduced his Rotoreliefs at the 1935 gathering — and wasn't able to sell a single set. (EW 1966)

c. Milady has an "Oyster opener"
A strapping lad who loves to grope her —
And bears his name with a certain pride,
For many an old maid has been surprised,
That not only her eyes were opened wide. (DR 1968)

d. Note by ALAIN JOUFFROY: "For opening shellfish, and clams in particular, I can think of no one who would know how to do it better than PHILIPPE HIQUILY, whose work often puts one in mind of giant clams."[e] (DS 1966)

e. To "open clams" is one of the more colourful euphemisms for sexual intercourse. In this connection, as well as the author's search for the best instrument to open these hermetically sealed creatures, it is interesting to contemplate the giant West Indian clam[f] which reaches a length of three feet and weighs up to twenty pounds. (EW 1966)

f. In Switzerland one would call something like that *en ufgschtellte Waidlig* (an upturned barge). (DR 1968)

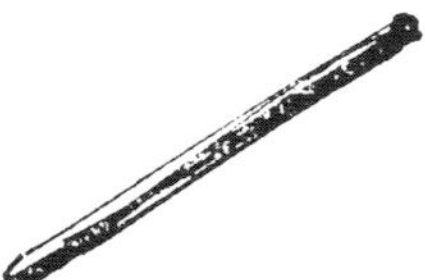

33. Wooden ruler 30 centimetres long, leaning against a wooden box [**34**], used by VERA for enlarging photos before I brought her a special device on returning from my first trip to Copenhagen, which must have been around the end of January 1961, because MARCELLE, the daughter of MARIANNE STAFFELDT, the wife of ROBERT FILLIOU, whose brother's name is MARCEL, had just been born, and I'm told she was born Jan. 14. I have tried to recall how the ruler got where it is,[a] but since the box and all the objects around it have been where they are for a long time, I suppose I used it one day and just left it there.[b]

a. Rulers get to where they are when the people who have allowed them to end up there have not seen a horizon for a long while. Then they make themselves a horizon and go off to it. And although at that moment they had not thought: it's time to think about the horizon (they had actually thought: it's time to think about enlarging photos!), it's often the case that, sooner or later, one goes off to the horizon — as in this moment now, when I am going off to the horizon which the ruler on the blue table forms before my nose when I read about it.

Even when a man and woman are screaming outside of your window at night because they're screaming at each other you think that the screaming won't go off to the horizon because it penetrates the room in which you are lying and sleeping but then wake up in and hear it, or does it go off to the horizon after all? For when you wander out of your room after you are awake — even if it's the middle of the darkest night — with these thoughts, as they are called, and the inner images of screaming men and women, aren't you going off?

When something cannot jump over lines because it doesn't want to, not even rulers, but simply looks at it all, then it goes off to the horizon, and this line, this ruler, and the horizon will become, because it is something that can be jumped over, something to be jumped over as you go off to it. And if you do so, do what is called going-off-to-something, you are already on what you think you are off to, because you are already trampling about on it with your inner feet, are walking along it while you picture it to yourself. So what you think you are moving towards, you are already on that, but you are not on what one walks about on when you are going-along-something. You don't go anywhere, but simply go along something.

For when you go off to something the going-off-to-something acts as if there were something apart from myself, far away, which I go towards going-towards-somethingly. But the joy of having found it outside of myself in the form of something that goes along outside, this joy holds it firmly inside of me. This joy says: I, this joy, is the joy in something which you believe not to be, but which is in fact inside of you because I, the joy in something apart from yourself, am inside of you. So I am a part of you, aren't I?

And so once again there's an opportunity to say something, namely: once again one can speak of something outside as something inside. Yes, and that's fun. (DR 1968)

b. VERA came from Frankfurt-am-Main the end of February 1962 to photograph my exhibition at Galerie LAWRENCE. During her brief stay she received the following telegram, which I opened thinking it was for me:

    =42 W PARIB F =4071 TA FRANKF D

       COL 24 5+

    44 FRANKFURTMAIN 10 7 0952 =

    HAARSCHWANZ BESORGEN = MUTTI +

    (get pony-tail — mummy) (DS 1966)

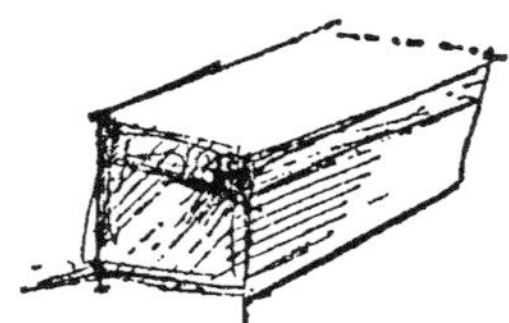

34. Worm-eaten joined wooden box with broken hinges, size 30 x 30 x 10 centimetres, on one end two overlapping old labels with illegible inscriptions, and on the other end the penned notice: "edelweiss 10", which came from a stock of about 35 boxes of various formats probably found in the run-down store-room of an ironmonger, to judge from their labels and inscriptions.

Bought at the Flea Market along with the table they were on, to make a snare-picture. I was assisted during this purchase by STANISLAUS SALM,[a] who used to be a bookbinder, but after his training at the dance school I used to direct in Bern[c] he became a dancer and danced in the operetta "MARCO POLO" at the Théâtre du Châtelet, and who presently weighs beef at Les Halles. While I was snaring the picture "The Boxes", I suddenly decided to make a snare-picture of a snare-picture, that is to say, to glue all the tools I was using, without finishing gluing the boxes. Those that remained form part of another picture, "MONSIEUR BITOS", named after a little man in wood who figures in the picture, whose prick sticks out when you press his head.[d]

a. Salm[b] is a Maltese unit of measurement equal to 8.2 bushels. I remarked this to SALM the one and only time I met him (in the author's room) and he seemed surprised. Since this meeting, SALM was killed in an automobile accident in Switzerland. (EW 1966)

b. A SALM is also a *Salm*, "salmon" in German. They are caught by people wherever and whenever it is allowed or possible or done. They do this by casting lines at the ends

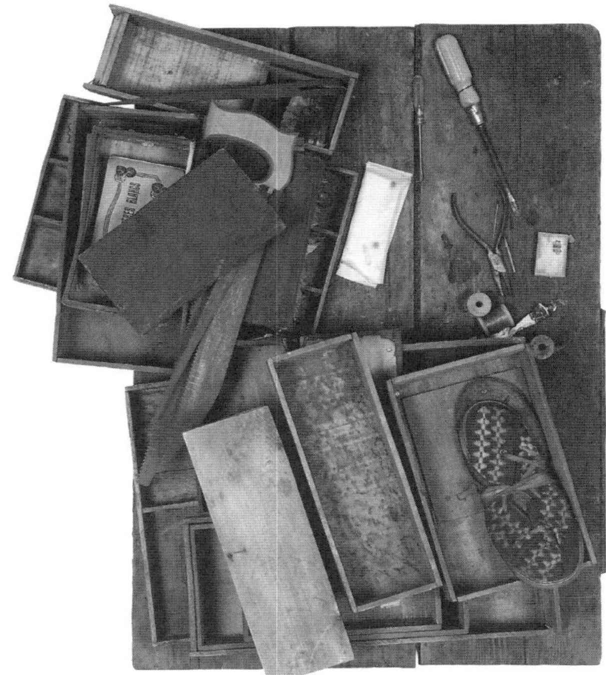

Left: DANIEL SPOERRI, *The Boxes*, 1961, Musée Nationale d'Art Moderne, Paris (Centre POMPIDOU).

Below: DANIEL SPOERRI, *Monsieur Bitos*, 1961, Kunstmuseum Winterthur.

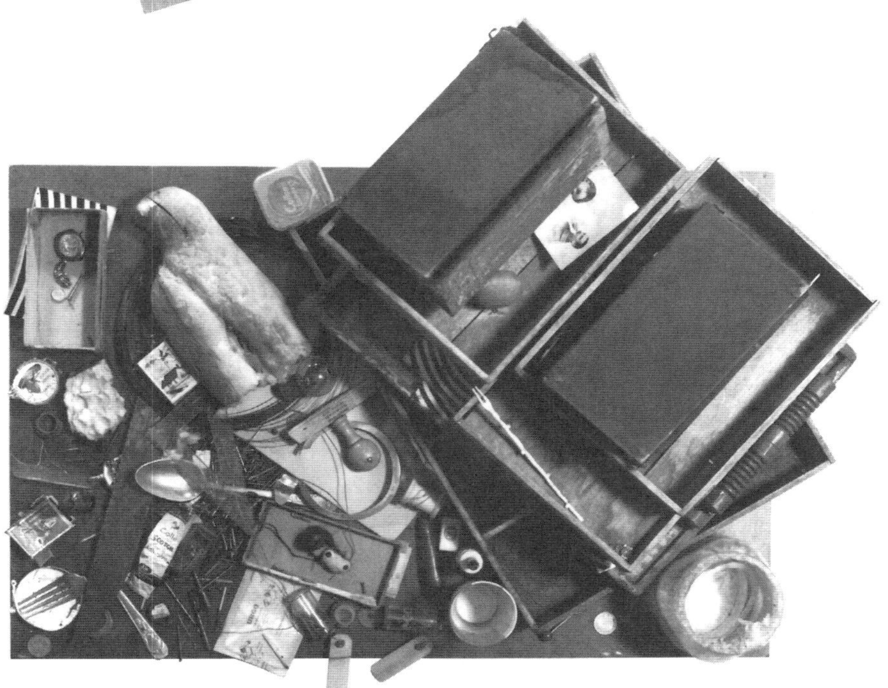

of poles above barbed hooks, on which something that entices the salmon is stuck, to there where the salmon, this enormous fish, travels past: into the fresh water. They let the trusty fish bite on the enticement with the hook inside — deep into the enticement down on to the hook which hooks deep into the front part of the salmon where its mouth is. And the salmon is fixed firmly with its mouth on the hook. At that the wicked people who are not well-disposed towards the salmon but only towards themselves, these people tear and lug the trusty salmon out of its lovely-laughing liquid element and hit it stone-dead. And they tear and tug the soft, fresh innards of the salmon right out from the salmon's inside and throw it away and place the remainder, the outside, in a concave implement used for frying or boiling animals and plants and cook the salmon's outside inside. And then once the outer salmon is done, they then take it out and eat it, and even that little bit of inside which had been cooked with the salmon's outside, that which people refer to as the bones, even that is removed from the outside, cast aside and stamped on frequently to the words: "Leave it alone, children (*sic*), it'll tread in, it's good for the carpet!" (DR 1968)

c. It is lovely in Bern, even when the sun doesn't shine because then perhaps it's raining, but even when it isn't raining it's lovely, especially then when the sun shines, but also when you walk in the rain, if on occasion the sun is not shining, down along the river which is there called the Aare and which also flows through the small town of Solothurn, which is also very lovely, especially lovely, without a doubt, when you walk down along the river there and the sun shines, but it is especially lovely in Basle, very special, when the sun shines there on the river which is called the Rhine, and you can walk along it and see how lovely it is there. (DR 1968)

d. MONSIEUR BITOS was sold to me by an ambulant bonbon salesman at the Flea Market. I paid him 3 francs. The contraption seems to be a degenerate form of the old PRIAPIC figures, on which subject I read by chance recently:

"A traveller, MONSIEUR DE GRANDPRÉ, witnessed, in 1787, a pantomime performed by masked men who carried with 'affectation', that was his expression, a huge phallus which they moved by means of a cord. HERODOTUS, who assisted at a similar ceremony more than 2,000 years earlier, wrote an almost identical description: 'The Egyptians celebrate the feast of BACCHUS almost in the same manner as the Greeks; but, in place of the phallus, they use figures about a cubit in height, which they move by means of a cord. The women carry these figures, on which the *membrum virile* is almost as large as the body, through the market-towns and villages. A flute player marches at the head of the procession; the others follow, chanting praises to BACCHUS.'"

— DR CABANÈS, *Mœurs intimes du Passé*, ALBIN MICHEL, Paris 1908, pp.245–46 (DS 1966)

34 (continued). The box described above for whatever reason it got into its present position,[a] I have since filled up with the following incongruous objects:

a. Out of the brown, warm but hard and angular hollowed hand comes the long, thin, cold poke and the soft but coy sow and the confused, wicked but tied tie and the bright, smooth but inwardly dark dwarfess and the double-deckered flathead and the aspiring but depressed twins and the outwardly soft but inwardly hard villain and another bright, smooth but inwardly coarse dwarfess and the plump and peaceful but stupid, shallow rolypolyess and the two-cornered, cunning but tepid minisod and the glum but biting hard yob and the dark and despondent but absent-minded little hand and the venomous green nipper and the sluggish but biting stuff and the innocent but wicked, crushed cripple, to name but a few — BUCKET FULL foresees, as can be seen, it all; he opens the one eye and with its help looks inside himself. We are sitting here and thinking: He sees it inside of his head, it is standing in front of the one eye which he has turned inwards and opened, and because he sees it it sits inside of his eye. Now perhaps you will say: He doesn't see it inside of his eye but inside his head! But another person has joined us who says to us all: BUCKET FULL sees it in his eye inside his head! And at that everyone calms down. (DR 1968)

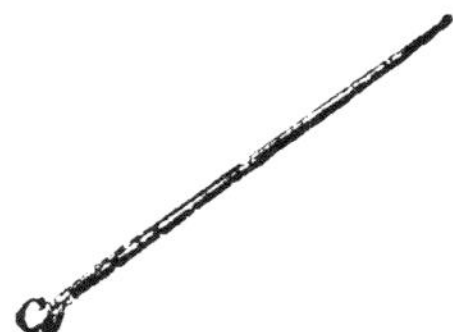

34A. Knitting needle 24.5 cm. long, grey with a light–blue plastic tip,[a] "ARIEL 4,5", which most likely belonged to VERA.[b]

a. Is that the *uppermost* tip or the *bottom-most* tip? Does the knitting needle — if it is made of grey metal — have a plastic knob at its bottom-most end, or does it — if it is made of grey plastic — simply have a blue tip? (DR 1968)

b. Is it "ARIEL 4,5" or "ARIEL 4.5"? The original object is no longer in SPOERRI'S possession, and he cannot recall whether a comma or period joined (or separated) the 4 and 5. For the sake of accuracy I call attention to both possibilities. (EW 1966)

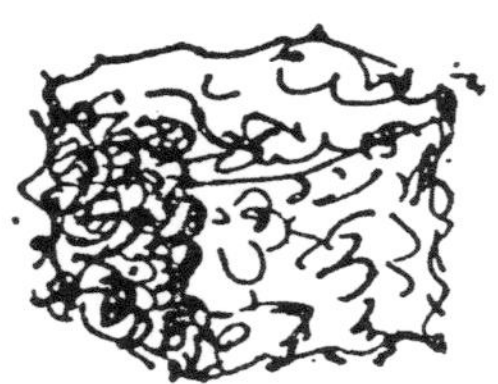

34B. Small cube-shaped sponge from the plastic box of a game by MUNARI which contained other materials to be used in making transparencies [61, 77].

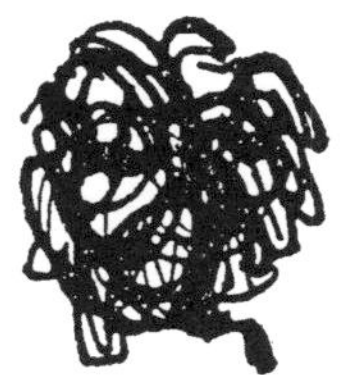

34C. Ball of scrap wire cut from the backs of snare-pictures (I use wire to fasten some objects), picked up and saved through false economy.[a]

a. Aha! Horizontality! (The fact that it can be rolled up and even more, and that the entire world is just a tangled ball because people have all rolled up their horizon with themselves included — all one big ball. The fact is though, that the ball here, the world, is actually just the great wide horizon.) That's been done quite according to the book! (DR 1968)

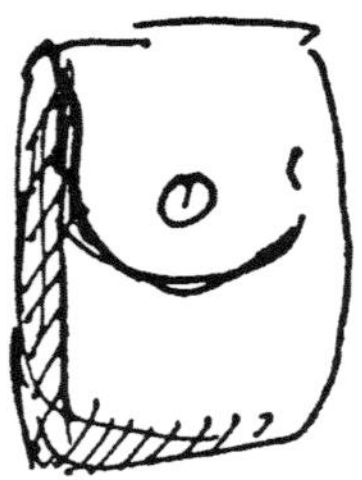

34D. White plastic case for a tape recorder battery. I bought the tape recorder while I was in Amsterdam [see **25, c**] during the "Art in Motion" exhibition; the batteries were used up and replaced shortly afterwards in Stockholm, where PONTUS HULTEN, director of the Moderna Museet, arranged the same exhibition. I fell asleep with the tape recorder running, and used up the batteries overnight.[a]

a. On the subject of museums and exhibitions: spending a day with ROBERT FILLIOU on the Rue des Rosiers, where he lived after his expulsion from Denmark, and which is the main street of the Jewish quarter in Paris, we saw inside a store about twenty hens in a wall of cages. (In this quarter poultry is kept alive until killed according to kosher ritual.) As we ventured in, without wishing to we provoked a dispute between an old man seated on a chair and a bad-tempered little old woman plucking a hen. He wanted us to come in, but she let us know that her shop wasn't a museum. He assured her that we weren't going to eat up her chickens, but she repeated over and over again: "No museum here, this isn't a museum." Finally driven out, but amused, FILLIOU remarked that the incident rated a note in the *Topography*, for it was certainly in "NADIA'S Live Poultry, Strictly Kosher" shop that the BRANCUSI egg in the Moderna Museet in Stockholm was hatched.[b] (DS 1966)

b. More on the subject of museums: ALLAN KAPROW wrote (2/19/65) in his introduction to "DANIEL SPOERRI'S Room No. 631 at the Chelsea Hotel", an exhibition sponsored by the Green Gallery in New York in March 1965:

"… artists have paid only partial attention to how deeply their works reflect and utilise the environment in which they were created. They speak about the light at the seashore appearing in their colours; the profound effect upon their dreams of the filth and reek of urine-soaked studio-loft buildings, the pounding of the subway under their feet… Yet, when their works are shown in the neo-classical gallery-box, it is supposed that these qualities of the environment are brought out *a fortiori* and that the gallery will have no other effect than to focus upon the essentials of the work.

"This is patently absurd, utter blindness. Today nine out of ten artists' work is absolutely desiccated by the powerful purity of the gallery and museum atmosphere. Everything whispers 'sh, sh, don't touch.' If art once was thought to be made from life in order to leave life, now the great bulk of modern creativity is deliberately mixed with life in order to affirm it.

"SPOERRI'S philosophical works were made in a hotel room, where he slept, made love, cooked marvellous meals, and defecated. His constructions crowded the space,[c] mingling with the bed, the clothes, the odour of lasagne. One must pick one's way through this intriguing mess. Where does the work of art end, and life begin? Look into peep holes, turn a mirror and see the reflected curtain, lift the test-tube phallus of a flowered hermaphrodite, contemplate an embalmed meal once eaten, the shoes of lovers facing one another. Here there is no hallucination, only wholeness.

"I suggested that SPOERRI invite the public to see his room, as it is being lived in, not as a memento or shrine. It was in line with his own intentions. I was convinced that his work would never appear as meaningfully again. By agreeing, he has contributed to the eventual death of the art gallery and museums. This death will take time, but meanwhile, the world has become endlessly available." (EW 1966)

c. And the room felt filled! (DR 1968)

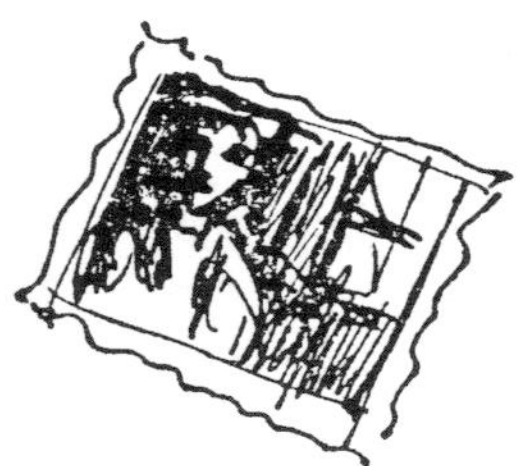

34E. Stereotype of a photo-portrait of DIETER ROTH[a] from two angles, size 4.7 x 4.7 cm., intended originally for the 1959 Édition MAT catalogue [20], but which I didn't use, WILLI ADAM, a lithographer, having been able to persuade his employer to make all the stereotypes for the catalogue in exchange for the objects in the MAT collection. ADAM didn't like this photo, and he wrote DIETER ROTH, whom he knows very well, to have another one taken, which finally served the purpose.[h]

a. Biographical note from the 1959 Édition MAT catalogue:

"DIETER ROTH, born 1930 in Hanover, Germany. 1943 — Zurich. 1947 — Bern: commercial art, furniture, painting, etc. 1956 — Copenhagen: textiles, writing, films, painting. Since 1957 — Reykjavik:[b] writing, films, books, printing."[d] (DS 1962)

b. From a letter by DR to DS:

… the tym iz ryp and the beliz ov hyumaniti ar swelling evriwun iz pregnant for thair iz no spirichyul burth kontrol it is neseseri to invent mental kontraseptivz and nominayt a saynt hoo wil unrol them ova the hedz of the projusirz this saynt must nachurali be the larst exarmpul ov the purfikt purson hoo iz and noz and meenz and can do absolootli evrithing and thus duz nuthing and has nuthing exsept that he kastraits the Devil and az waz sed handz owt kontraseptivz so then wen the extant standz there sivd and konsentraytid it is loded onto nyu wurldz and then a tayp with the ror ov gunz from the sekund wurld wor and the nifgrinding ov the ston aj iz set going the blesed on the nyu wurlds wayv thair thinking capz and the wurldz speed off into spays the saynt remaynz behind on irth and pix up a fyu anteex wich ar lying arownd abandond: sex insens holmeel bred winking brazierz grilz novulz baybeez hobi horsiz taybulz frenzeez publik bathz rubba coshiz seryusnes in al itz dir lord beli-ayk…[c] (DS 1968)

> **c.** Reading this excerpt brings to mind a critic for the *Frankfurter Allgemeine* and his Lichtenberg-cudgel — and the way he lashed out with lovely quotations — a method which can equally be used for letters: *From now on letters will not only be written by people who do not understand them and read by people who do not understand them and cited by people who do not understand them and printed by people who do not understand them and then read by people who do not understand them, but also criticised by people who do not understand them.* (DS 1968)

d. Since 1959 — writing, films, books, printing, New York, Yale, translating the *Topography* into German.[e] [And see **Introduction I, i**] (EW 1966)

> **e.** Subsequently in Philadelphia, Providence R.I., Reykjavik, Cologne, Basle, London,[f] Düsseldorf, Reykjavik, Düsseldorf:[g] books, paintings, translating the German translation of the *Topography* into German. (DR 1968)

> > **f.** In Her Majesty the QUEEN'S service. The letter of dismissal from Her Majesty the QUEEN'S servants: "When his term here has finished, he will receive a P45 form. He should take this to his nearest local tax office, and they will request that he fill out a form." (DR 1968)

> > **g.** And then he rode off and raced round, and said: that's so that he can see something so that he can have something to think about and something to look at, can see all the junk, all the stuff outside through the window, and the faster he races past the fuller the window becomes. But so that he can even see what's outside the window he himself must be able to see something besides, and that's the other which he always takes with him so that he can see it besides, besides that which he sees outside of the train window if he has not just zoomed off in a plane because if he has not brought something to see besides he will also be unable to see the other, which always shits the porthole full from outside, assuming he has not actually gone by car. (DR 1968)

h. ADAM wrote that you cannot see the man behind all the cigarette smoke. (DR 1968)

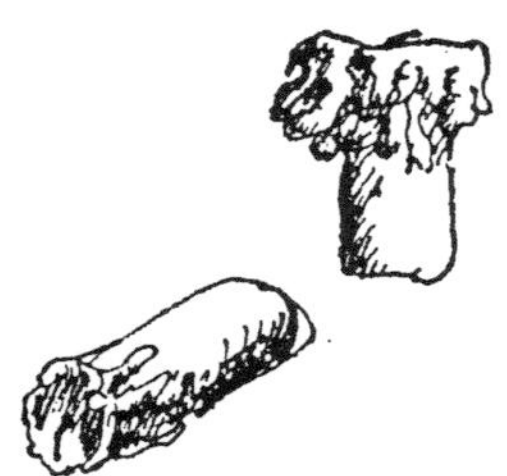

34F. Two candle butts one of which was squeezed near the wick when the wax was still warm. I remember neither their use nor their origin, but since I often blow out fuses by plugging in all kinds of apparatuses and art objects, there is nothing astonishing about their presence in my room. In the crypt at Vézelay, the candles the pilgrims light in honour of the VIRGIN plop down on to a sheet of iron where the wax makes a very lovely picture, as HAINS pointed out to me on our trip to Nice [31].

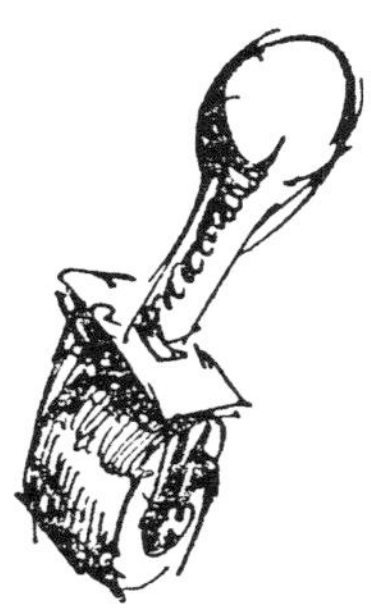

34G. Metal stencils of prime numbers[a] up to 13, of which the 1 is missing, used to number the review *material.*[b] (There were four numbers: 1, 2, 3 and 5.) These title-numbers were used for the following reason: just as a prime number can be divided only by 1 or by itself, so the contents of my review could be understood only through the contents itself, and not through comparisons or interpretations.

a. Jan. 30, 1962, ROBERT FILLIOU heard on the radio that the prime American prime number had been discovered with the aid of an electronic brain at the University of California:

$$(2^{2442} - 1)$$

(DS 1966)

b. The review *material*, as its name implies, was intended to propagate concrete poetry, in which I myself was interested at the time (1957-59). Its aim was to eliminate the subjective point of view of the author, and present poetic material that the reader could do with as he saw fit. Some of the texts, "ideograms", appealed to the optical sense by their typographical arrangement. Here is an example by DIETER ROTH, who composed the second number of the review:

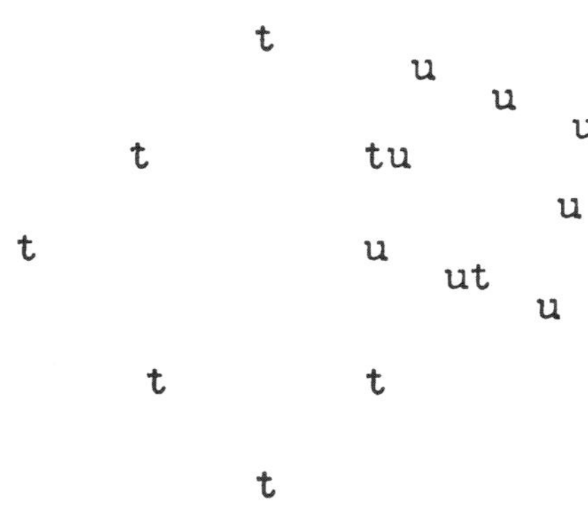

Two squares, interlocking, form at their intersection the two little words "ut" and "tu". A possible interpretation would be that there is no meeting without reciprocal influences.

Other texts were "constellations" (a word imposed by EUGEN GOMRINGER), intended for the ear as well as the eye, in which words or letters were arranged according to a rhythmical system. Here is an example (translated from the original French) by EMMETT WILLIAMS, who composed the third number of the review:

<pre>
              abcdefghijklmnopqrstuvwxyz
      abcdefghijklmnopqrstuvwxyz
          abcdefghijklmnopqrstuvwxyz
          abcdefghijklmnopqrstuvwxyz
       abcdefghijklmnopqrstuvwxyz
            abcdefghijklmnopqrstuvwxyz
           abcdefghijklmnopqrstuvwxyz
      abcdefghijklmnopqrstuvwxyz
</pre>

And in German (1968):

<pre>
a b c d e f g h i j k l m n o p q r s t u v w x y z
                  a b c d e f g h i j k l m n o p q r s t u v w x y z
           a b c d e f g h i j k l m n o p q r s t u v w x y z
             a b c d e f g h i j k l m n o p q r s t u v w x y z
           a b c d e f g h i j k l m n o p q r s t u v w x y z
a b c d e f g h i j k l m n o p q r s t u v w x y z
a b c d e f g h i j k l m n o p q r s t u v w x y z
             a b c d e f g h i j k l m n o p q r s t u v w x y z
</pre>

Eight horizontal alphabetical rows are linked together by a familiar interjection, whose eight letters determine the typographical arrangement. (DS 1966)

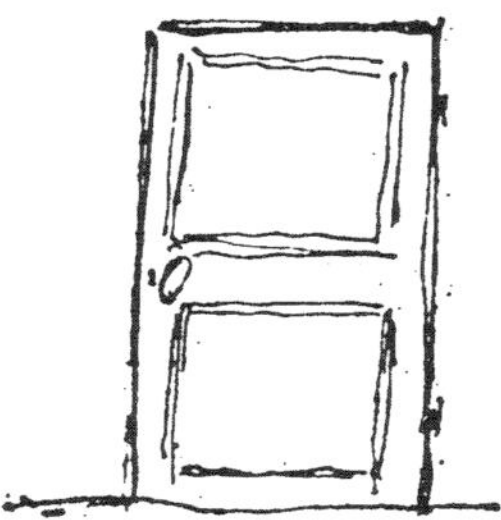

34H. Yellow plastic case for drills. I use the drills to make holes in the surfaces to which I fasten objects in my snare-pictures with wire. On the back of the case, the inscription "Made in Western Germany" [**34C**].

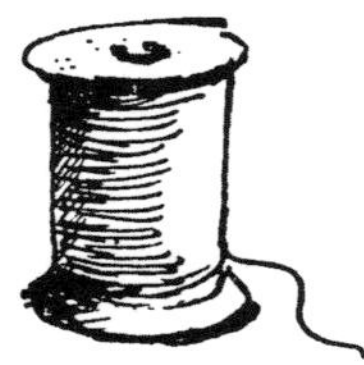

341. Spool of Tubino white thread the origin of which I don't know.

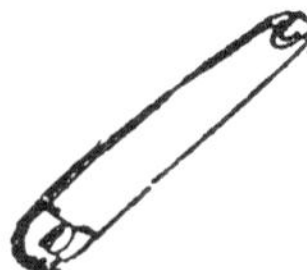

34J. Safety pin.[a]

a. From a prospectus distributed by the baby-food firm JAQUEMAIRE:

"The Second Mamma: You must change baby frequently, because contact with urine and faecal matter can easily cause his sensitive skin to break out in a rash. If the infant has only urinated, you need only wash him lightly, dry him and apply powder. But if he has made matter, you must first remove it, then wash the area with tepid water and cotton, dry carefully without rubbing, and powder thoroughly. If you change baby after feeding, handle him delicately in order not to cause vomiting. French swaddling-clothes include a linen or fine cotton shirt with sleeves, and a knitted wool vest. These should overhang the navel and cover the stomach lightly. They are put on from the front, crossed in back without tying, and fastened with *one or two safety pins*."[b] (DS 1962)

b. Safety pins[c] have been used as ear ornaments in Africa. (EW 1966)

c. One large safety pin = 2 safety pins = 2 x 2 small safety pins.
One onceuponatime = one small itis = one itllbe.
Translation exercise:
Two little safety pins are going to have a scrap with a safety pin, which will almost be the same as when four small safety pins once got mixed up with a large former safety pin or when a safety pin cuts a large safety pin in half. Question: *With whom must one half of the large halved safety pin fight and against which adversary so that we can forecast a draw?* (DR 1968)

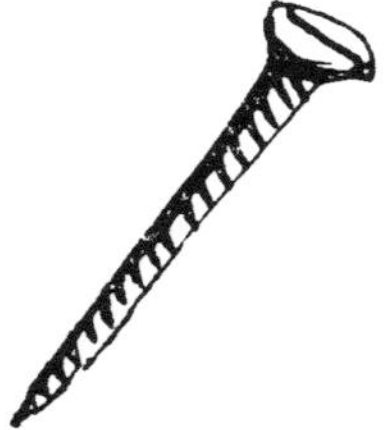

34K. Large screw that says something to me, but not enough for me to remember what.

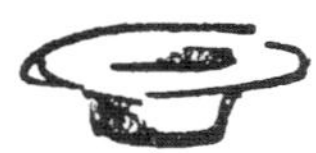

34L. Dark–blue plastic stopper from a bottle of wine [**3**, **25**, **49**, **57**, **67**].

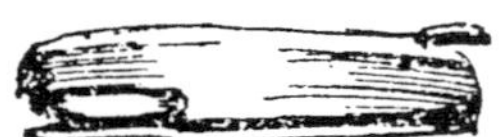

34M. Red stapler (Swingline Tot 50)[a] bought at Orléans or Chartres for about 6 francs. One Sunday I stopped off there (Orléans or Chartres) with VERA and, I believe, WILLI ADAM to visit the cathedral, and in a shop where we bought postcards this stapler caught my fancy: it was the smallest I had ever seen.

    a. Trillions of terrific tots'd tell
trillions of terrific tales
if trillions of terrific tots told
trillions of terrific tales (DR 1968)

34N. Iron rod in the shape of a Z that FELIX LEU twisted to hang on my wall an aquarium in which he wanted to exhibit as a work of art a beef heart STANISLAUS SALM got for him cheap at Les Halles. He thought he had sealed it hermetically, but after two days the odour was so strong[a] I had to throw it out. Afterwards, the aquarium sheltered my collection of five leeches, which died during my last absence.

a. The stinking heart.[b] (DR 1968)

b. Once upon a time there was a heart that had grown old and grey and gave off an odour. It lay there in its glass coffin and the people walked by. Many of them said something. One said: "There's such a strong smell." Another said: "It stinks." A third said: "It is a stone, a touchstone which tests people. It tests people to see what words they carry about inside them. Whoever has smell inside them says: 'It smells.' Whoever has stench inside them says: 'It stinks.' Whoever has stone inside them says: 'It is a stone!' " (DR 1968)

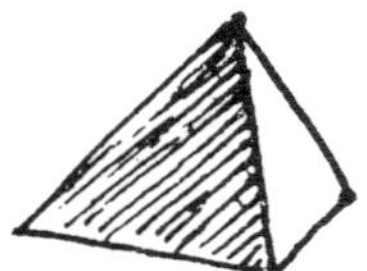

34O. Small plastic pyramids alternately transparent and grey, hinged together at the base and along the sides, part of a model made by ANDRÉ THOMKINS[a] and an architect[d] to illustrate their idea for a mobile architecture based on the same principle.[e] I had intended to dedicate one of the numbers of the review *material* [**34G**] to the work of ANDRÉ THOMKINS, whose idea of "laque-dynamorphose"[f] I used during an evening at the I.C.A. (Institute of Contemporary Arts) in London in March 1960 [**34B, 61, 77**].

   a. LEB ANDRÉ MAL AM ERDNABEL[b] (DR 1968)

     b. "André try living at the navel of the Earth"[c] (MG 1995)

      c. Yeah, but just try making a palindrome out of *that.* (EW 1995)

d. Architecture (regardless of whether they, the architects, erect this or that wherever) is judged by whether you can go into it when you want to go into it, and whether you can go round it when you want to — and even if you can't do what you want to do, it (architecture) is good because it is then good for something, namely for feeling like a child again (as a child you can't always do what you want). Architecture is also judged by whether the people inside (inside the things which they, the architects, have erected) get what they want — but the architecture is still good when they don't get it because once again you feel like a child (like in the days when you didn't get all you wanted). And the architecture is also good if it is much too large for you, because then you also feel once more like a child. And when it (the architects' architecture) is too small, it is nevertheless good for making you feel like a child because then the architecture seems like a toy. So whether it is thus or thus, architecture always makes children of everyone, and that is why it is always good. (DR 1968)

e. Although I have held these "small plastic pyramids" in my hand, I am at a loss, being neither a geometer nor an architect, to describe their functioning any better than SPOERRI'S attempt — which I find inadequate.

I asked ANDRÉ THOMKINS to assist me in clearing up the matter, and received the following letter:

Dear EMMETT,

It is the truth! Whereas you have learned French, I am still unable to explain things in English. I will visit my ancestors one of these days to learn it — we will see.

You want some notes on **34O**:

— It is the geometry of the smoke ring, or that of the inner-tube that one bunches up with both hands to find the hole — the elasticity replaced by a play of hinges.

— This wonderful principle I owe to PAUL SCHATZ, inventor of the celebrated *Stülpkubus* (turn-up cube).

— It is built with plastic pseudo-tetrahedrons, the base angles of which are 60°, those of the apex 110°. ECKHARD SCHULZE-FIELITZ, architectural chess player, made it for me.

— The angle of intersection of the base and that of the apex alternately serve as hinges. As the object revolves around its axis it is transformed several times according to the irregularity of its systole and diastole.

— In geometric syntax, one adds a mechanical verb to the substantive. Thus I call it a mecanohedron. Applied to an architectural structure, the mecanohedron consists of a whole governed by the continuity of fragments of evolution.

— It could serve to articulate habitable space, either real or of the kind that might satisfy the speculative needs of an emancipated society in a world free of drudgery. In the mean time, the smoke ring is coiled up in the inner-tube.

—You see, it's just that, you hold it in your hand, you turn it, it goes click–clack and it pinches, you think of a pile of things because it doesn't resemble anything, not even a soft-boiled egg. It was made above all to be translated into English by EMMETT WILLIAMS. (EW 1966)

f. "Laque-dynamorphose:

"This is a simple method of banalisation of the contemporary styles of painting like Tachism and Action Painting — like photography, which was a banalisation of the realistic technique of painting. Particular attention should be given to the movement of the lacquer and colours on the surface of the water instead of the static result on the paper.

"Directions: Fill up the dish with water. Put a few drops of water glass in it. With the stick take a little lacquer and let it fall on the surface in drops or streaks, let it spread, or blow with the straw. When you like the pattern you take a piece of paper, lay it on the surface and the pattern will be fixed. Variations can be made without water glass, but with different paints, with a drop of alcohol, with a small electric battery, with sugar, salt, or you can let the lacquer dry a moment, and then draw on the surface.

"Commentary: Within the limits that this material imposes you can consciously employ different means. But in spite of that, this method is governed to a high degree by chance, because of its enormous plastic variability, and that is why it is an appropriate medium for the individual to express his own psychic personality on condition that everyone interprets these instructions in his own way."

— English text distributed to the I.C.A. audience (DS 1962)

34P. Bent nail I don't know from what.

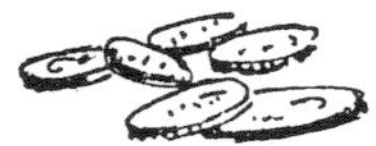

34Q. Coins three 5-øre pieces, two of them aluminium and one copper; three 25-øre pieces (some kind of alloy); four 10-øre pieces; one Danish crown; three German 10-pfennig pieces and one 5-pfennig piece; one French 50-franc piece; and a 50-something piece (the inscription is in Hebrew).[a]

a. Note by ALAIN JOUFFROY: "This box and its contents remind me of the 'Can of Involuntary Secret Noise' that SPOERRI presented to me in January 1961, with a dedication on the label signed with orthographic variants of his name: DANIEL SPÖRRI — SPOERRI — SPOERRI-FEINSTEIN — SPÖRRI-FEINSTEIN — SPÖRRI-FAINSTEIN — SPOERRI-FAINSTAIN. [See also **28A, a**] On shaking the aluminium can, which contained among other things a key, an empty spool of ACKERMANN'S black thread, one slightly yellowish die, a large safety pin, a tube of paste, an old franc and a compass glued to a pen, one could really hear an incomprehensible noise, similar to that made by those toy puzzles with which one can play for hours trying to return tiny ball bearings to their pockets. This 'Can of Involuntary Secret Noise', which I hung up on my wall between a bronze Benin mask and a MANINA picture, given to me on my last birthday and consisting of pieces of lead glued to brown wood, may have been presented to me by SPOERRI to thank me for the article I wrote about him for his first exhibition (*Mostra Personale*, Galleria SCHWARZ, Milan, March 16-30, 1961). My introductory text, entitled 'The Snare-Pictures of DANIEL SPOERRI' [see **15, b**], ends with the words: 'The idea of reality is to reinvent, as everybody knows.' But I'm not certain. Maybe he gave it to me, without knowing it, for the symbolical meanings of the objects which it contained, and in particular the key, the compass glued to the pen, the empty spool of black thread and the yellowing die. Key-compass-pen-spool-die constitute, to my eyes, an ensemble of meanings, well tied together, that summarise, like the images of a poem, the half-conscious, half-unconscious impulses that have compelled me since the age of seventeen. I would be interested in knowing if the snare-pictures and objects SPOERRI has given to others correspond as well, and as subtly, to their personalities and sensibilities. (New fact: In trying to find out what there was deep down in the can, which still contains many small objects impossible to identify — among which, no doubt, is the perpetrator of the 'involuntary noise' — I uncoupled the pen and the compass. Thus I am certain that the source of the secret noise ought not be probed.)"[b] (DS 1966)

b. What is the secret that JOUFFROY thinks he ought not probe, and why is the hidden noise involuntary? This dilemma calls to mind immediately the 1916 semi Readymade of MARCEL DUCHAMP, "With hidden noise" (*à bruit secret*), called by ULF LINDE "one of the most puzzling things DUCHAMP has ever done."[c] In the catalogue accompanying the recent DUCHAMP show at Galleria SCHWARZ, LINDE describes it as "a ball of twine mounted between two metal plates, the latter with strange texts engraved on them. There is an object hidden inside the ball of twine — an object put there by WALTER C. ARENSBERG. And the object gives out a sound when in contact with the plates (the voice of the bride?)."

The inscription on the plates — a telegraphic compound of French and English words with periods replacing missing letters — has no special significance, according to DUCHAMP:

P.G	.ECIDES	DEBARRASSE.
LE.	D.SERT.	F.URNIS.ENT
AS	HOW.V.R	COR.ESPONDS

and on the lower plate:

.IR.	CAR.E	LONGSEA
F.NE,	HEA.,	.O.SQUE
TE.U	S.ARP	BAR.AIN

No *special* significance. The system, at least, is obvious.

There is no intentional mystification in the SPOERRI object, and the inscription, too, bears the mark of the artist's straightforwardness. He confided to me recently that after he finished gluing the object he discovered that he hadn't glued it as well as he had intended; and that when he shook it and heard a noise, he called it exactly what it was: "involuntary" because it was unintentional and "secret" because he didn't know the source. As long as JOUFFROY refuses to get to the bottom of the matter — or the can — SPOERRI'S "secret" will remain hidden. (EW 1966)

c. Why is there anything "most puzzling" on (or under or by or in or around) DUCHAMP'S thing? If one looks aside (or keeps away) from the *superlative* here and then simply says (or asks): "What constitutes the puzzling?" I could at once come and say (or reply): "The puzzling is something that does something to me, and I cannot stop it because I don't know where it is located and don't know who it is that is doing it (or is it), and furthermore I know that I do not (or will never) know who it is (or who does it) because it is located at the edge of the (or my) world (the two worlds are in any case the same), and it is there at the edge of my world so that I cannot (or can never) reach it and stop it, regardless of whether at the edge of the inner or at the edge of the outer world, because it does not jut (or poke) far enough into my world, however large I keep trying to make (or extend or inflate) the latter, for me to grab it." And if one surmises what I might then be about to say, and says: "Right," I would then come a step closer and say: "That thing there from DUCHAMP, I can grasp it with my hands (which is one way of reaching it), and I can stop that thing inasmuch as it is doing something (to wit making a noise). I can stop the noise inasmuch as I can put it down. Why should one shake it? I can reach it, I can stop it, and so I cannot call it puzzling — let alone *most puzzling*, or am I wrong?" (DR 1968)

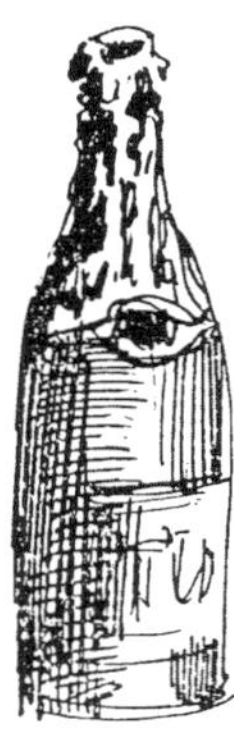

35. On box 34, a bottle of TUBORG beer, grade FF, the label of which has been replaced by a facsimile of the original doctored up to read "KOEPCKE, Poipoi, FILLIOU", because it was used at the opening of FILLIOU'S Poipoi exhibition in Copenhagen.[a]

a. "Somewhere in Africa, I was told, when two persons meet they ask each other: How is your cow?… and how is your field?… and how is your oldest son?… and how is your house?… and so on, reviewing in this way all their possessions until one of them says:

POIPOI

to which the other answers

POIPOI

Then they break off, and at times start all over again.

"What I'm presenting here is the result of some (let's say) meetings with myself: how is my chair?… how are my numbers?… how are my buttocks of BRIGITTE BARDOT?… how are my passengers of the Caravelle?… how is my thirty-second thought of PASCAL?… how am I?… how is my man in revolt?… all this to end with a POIPOI, something taking care, more or less, for the time being, of the unanswered question — while I (we) break off.

POIPOI!"

(Original in English) (DS 1962)

36. Gold-coloured package, Blausiegel[a] brand, with a tongue-flap opening, containing two of the original three condoms,[b] with the notice: "Genuine only in this package. Carefully tested several times. Known and proven trustworthy for decades." The pack was obtained by inserting a 1-mark coin in an automatic dispenser in the men's room of a nightclub[c] in Krefeld, Germany, where I went with JEAN TINGUELY[f] in August 1960 to help him prepare his second exhibition of scrap-metal objects at the Museum Haus LANGE. The missing condom was used, during one of my absences, by X, who later told me the use he had put it to in my Parisian[k] hotel room: the prickly surface of his sheathed sex, studded with raisins, aroused his companion more than usual.[1]

a. "Zur Vorlage bei Ihrem Fachhändler! / Ich bitte um diskrete Aushändigung eines Päckchens / Blausiegel B3-BR3-B6-BR6 'Export' 'Queen' 'BF2 Spezial' / Oder 'BF3 Flüssig-feucht' gewüschtes bitte unterstreichen / Rückseite bitte beachten. Kennen Sie schon Blausiegel BF2 Spezial den Gummischutz mit der gleitfähigen Beschichtung? / Fordern Sie Prospekt — ohne viel Worte nur gegen Vorlage dieses Hinweiszettels — bei Ihrem Fachhändler. Neu. BF3 Flüssig-feucht. Kontroll Coupon: IJ 387646." (DS 1962)

b. I have in my possession a full-scale map of the blue table to which is affixed the Blausiegel package containing the remaining two condoms. The map is inscribed (in French): "No. 36. Original object from the *Anecdoted Topography of Chance*. For OSCAR-

EMMETT-POLLY-WILLIAMS. Thank you, my friends. Jan. 1962. DANIEL SPOERRI."
And on the inside tongue-flap of the package itself: "For EMMETT, one of my three
friends. DANIEL." (EW 1966)

c. The sole vestige of the guitarist-singer-composer JEAN-PIERRE SUC, who
committed suicide on the Paris-Montpellier train in 1960, and with whom I used to
pass the evening from time to time at a nightclub in the quarter, is a *de luxe* condom
terminating in a hand. After SUC'S death, his studio on the Rue CARDINAL
LEMOINE (formerly Rue des Fossés SAINT-VICTOR) was rented by EVA AEPPLI. I
helped her clean up the infernal disorder and found the condom, which I threw into
the drawer of a small table, later made into a snare-picture**d** along with everything on
it and in it and now in the possession of ENRICO BAJ. During a visit to Paris ENRICO
asked me (someone had put the bug in his ear) if all the objects fastened to the table
were fixed solidly, because it hangs over his costly radio set in a *de luxe***e** apartment in
Milan. (DS 1966)

> **d.** Is a snare object an object that lies in a snare (the thing lies firmly on the table), or is
> the snare object the snare in which the object lies (the table that holds the object firmly
> glued)? Or is the snare object perhaps both together: an object that lies in a snare plus
> a snare in which an object is lying? No, isn't it rather the two simultaneously than the
> two together? That is to say: isn't it both an object that is lying in a snare as well as a
> snare in which an object is lying? Or is it perhaps simply that the object (as the thing
> which is made from an object in a snare or a snare with an object inside), the whole of
> it, is that object which lies inside of the snare — or is it the snare in which the object
> lies? But to continue: what if the snare, in the case of the snare object, was not an object?
> And if in addition the object, as demonstrated by the object of the snare object, was not
> a snare? Such that the snarishness of the snare object was only the thought about the
> snare? And the objectness of the snare object was just the thought about an object? So
> that the snare object is caught in a snare: the thought acting as a snare — or the snare
> object holds on to an object firmly: the thought acting as an object? But what else is
> the thought than a snare-layer or the stepper-into-the-snare, the person who is thinking?
> Does the person step into the snare which the snare object so obligingly sets him, and
> is he lying firmly inside the object? Or does the snare object step into the snare which
> the person has so obligingly set, and lie firmly inside the person? (DR 1968)

e. The *de luxe* condom in the *de luxe* apartment, that's the cat among the catnip. (DR 1968)

f. *Two precursors of* JEAN TINGUELY (excerpts from a conversation snared on magnetic tape):

DS: You were going to tell me about…

RF: PLATO.

DS: That's right, PLATO.

RF: PLATO, inventor of the perpetual motion machine. I knew him in 1944, or maybe 1945, or 43, 46 or 48. I was in school at Alès.

DS: You were living in Alès?

RF: I was at Nîmes before that — I come from Sauve and that's not far from Nîmes — but I was kicked out of school at Nîmes and they sent me to Alès. Anyway, everybody there knew PLATO. He exhibited his machine at the market place, right opposite the school. He had a wheelbarrow, and he would descend — he lived high up, Alès is a mining town — he lived high up… in a hut… and he would descend and cross the whole town with his wheelbarrow. And over the wheelbarrow was a big sheet of canvas so you couldn't see what was underneath. Well, he would arrive at the market place and choose a spot, and as I remember it, it was always close to the school.

DS: Yes.

RF: And then he'd remove the canvas and lift out the machine… It was huge… And then he'd put up a poster. The poster said in large letters: MACHINE FOR SALE. And lower down, in small letters, it said: man for sale. Then he'd start crying out "Step right up, see the perpetual motion machine." And that machine! It had a big wheel and a little wheel, I remember it very well. It was held together with belts, ropes and wire and it was always falling apart and breaking down. He would start turning a crank… you know, real enthusiastically… and it…

DS: And nothing happened?

RF: It was a perpetual motion machine… because when he turned the crank the little wheel would turn and…

DS: I mean it didn't really do anything.

RF: Nothing… nothing else, that is.

DS: Only the wheels.

RF: And other things… It was put together in a pretty strange way, as I said. For example, the belt went up and down and around. And he would say: "This is the perpetual motion machine." But when there were farmers around, you know, they would look at the thing and say: "That's not perpetual motion… It keeps stopping… The thing doesn't even work." Well, then PLATO would say: "That's why the man is for sale, too."

DS: Ah yes.

RF: "I'm ready and willing to turn it all the time," he'd answer.

DS: Basically very logical.

RF: "I'm selling myself with the machine," he'd remind them.

DS: And as long as he turned it, it would work.

RF: Yes, you had to buy both.

DS: That way it would be perpetual motion.

RF: Right.

DS: Because he was perfectly willing to turn it all the time.

RF: And there was no answer to that. The people made him a lot of propositions, and that gave him a lot of pleasure. For example, I remember once my uncle took me to a café and there was PLATO at the bar. He knew my uncle — FLORENT MALZAC the mechanic, BIG FLO they called him, a real drinker, a big shot… Everybody knew him because it was a small town, you know. Anyway, I bought PLATO a glass of white wine. He looked like a bum… made his living collecting cigarette butts… He was big, and well built, but… but disgusting… always filthy.

DS: How old was he?

RF: He was about 40 then. Anyway, while he was drinking the wine I had bought him, he told me — I can see every detail, he was very vivid, you know the southern type, dark and full of life. Well, he bent over and confided to me: "These people — they think I'm crazy… and I know I am. But I think *they're* crazy and don't realise it."

DS: How many times do you estimate he exhibited his machine?

RF: Well, when I arrived on the scene — I was a kid then — he was already a town phenomenon. Just when he started I don't know. But a long time before I got there, I suppose, because he was already so famous. You know, in the towns of the Midi they treat people like that very well. After all, they're nice and harmless.

DS: Medieval tradition… the sacred fool.

RF: PLATO was accepted in the town… as a type. And whenever you talk with someone from Alès the subject comes up… and the destruction of the perpetual motion machine.

DS: It was destroyed?

RF: Once in the south of Spain — in Malaga it was — I met a guy from Alès I hadn't seen in ten years. And I asked him immediately about PLATO. And he replied that PLATO was dead. How did he die? I asked. And he said: "It was fantastic. One day he decided to modernise his machine…"

DS: Ha ha.

RF: Up at his place. He bought, or he found, or someone gave him — I don't know how he could possibly have bought it, he was always flat broke — a bottle of butane gas.

DS: Ah!

RF: And then, just what he was going to do to the machine I don't know, but there were tubes and pipes, and he lit a match…

DS: Yes yes.

RF: … and everything blew up.

DS: And PLATO with it?

RF: And PLATO with it.

DS: Amazing.

RF: And that was the end of PLATO.

DS: And of the machine that destroyed not only itself but its creator as well. That's some story. Then there's ANTON MÜLLER,[g] the one I told you about once…

RF: Ah, the Swiss.

DS: A Swiss nut who really invented something. A machine to cut the… to cut the… the fungus from grape vines… so that it wasn't necessary to… to… what do you call it?

RF: To stoop.

DS: That's right, to bend down. It would cut off the fungus with a kind of… a pair of long scissors, something like that. MÜLLER really invented it, and they use it to this day. But he didn't know very much about patents and someone swiped it and got all the credit. Well, this deranged him, and he wandered around the canton of Vaud like an idiot… through the vineyards… really deranged… and since he was born in the canton of Bern they placed him in an asylum… in the canton of Bern.

RF: But he wasn't really dangerous, was he?

DS: Well, he was in a pretty bad way. Bitterly disappointed. He told everybody off. Then he started sleeping in lavatories… you know, in the urinals of the asylum. He lay down in them and didn't want to get up. He was soaked with urine… He stank… It

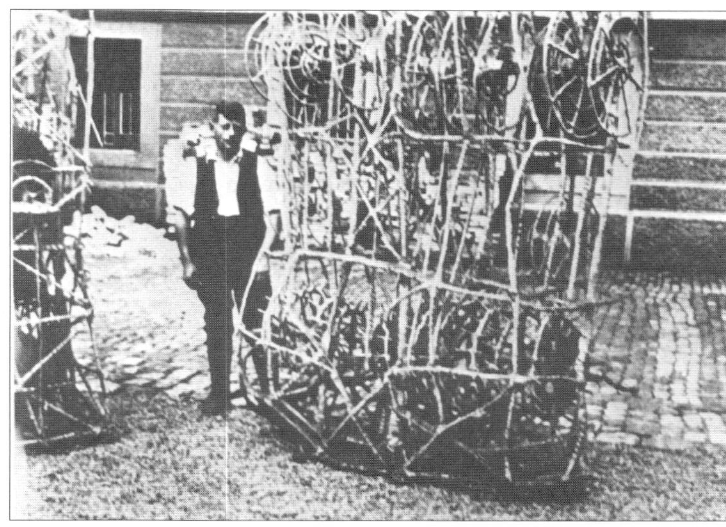

ANTON MÜLLER with his machines in the courtyard of the Müsingen Asylum.

was really terrible. But for several years — in those days they didn't do much for the insane, they didn't know what to do for them — they just let him be.

RF: How long ago was this?

DS: I think he entered the asylum about 1913 and stayed there until 1927 or 1930.

RF: Did he die there?

DS: Yes, he died in the asylum. Anyway, he started building machines… with old wire, junk, tree branches and so on. I had a photo…

RF: Someone photographed them?

DS: The doctors, because the machines were something… six feet tall and twelve feet wide… in the garden of the asylum.

RF: You know, I wonder if… if anyone took pictures of PLATO'S perpetual motion machine. The next time I'm in Alès I'm going to find out.

DS: It was published in the catalogue… as a precursor of… of the art of movement… at Stockholm. Anyway, he made the machines and the only problem was that they didn't run very smoothly. You know, he didn't have any… the gears stuck… he never ate his butter, and spread it over the gears…

RF: To oil them.

DS: And not only butter. He pissed on the gears, too, and he jerked off on them… It stank like… It was terrible… rancid butter, urine, sperm… all sorts of… well, finally they stopped him from making them… so he took up drawing… and they're marvellous, the finest drawings I've ever seen made by an insane person.

RF: Where are the machines now?

DS: They destroyed them, they stank.

RF: Destroyed them?

DS: Yes, they threw them away. Old branches… you know, junk.

RF: So there are only these photos…

DS: Only one still exists.

RF: Oh la la.

DS: And there are no photos of him at all. Well, he became more and more phlegmatic, this… this HERR MÜLLER, and finally he made a huge pile of… of garbage, if you like… branches, all sorts of… all the crap he could find… a huge pile… It was like a grotto… a kind of opening in the pile… and he contemplated it… At 8 o'clock in the morning he would go there with a little stool, and he would sit there until lunchtime looking at it… the opening… a kind of… of… what do you call it… like a cunt… a vulva…

RF: Yes.

DS: … of a woman. In the afternoon he'd go there again. And he did this for years and years, just sat in front of the hole… looking at the hole…

RF: Yes.

DS: … and he got sicker and sicker…

RF: But in general they treated him very well, didn't they?

DS: … and finally he died.

RF: I mean he was well treated because they… they let him be, they didn't prevent him…

DS: They let him go the limit of his madness.

RF: Yes.

DS: He was creative in his madness, and they let him carry out his ideas as far as he could… like an artist

RF: Yes.

DS: While today they give such people injections immediately and replace them in a social environment and all that… They stop them from going the limit.

RF: Right.

DS: And that's why there aren't any more… any more creative madmen.[i]

RF: Right.

DS: Because as soon as they get lost in a fixed idea… every artist basically…

RF: They psy…

DS: … every artist has a… **j**

RF: They psychoanalyse them, they…

DS: Yes, they immediately take away their…

RF: Yes.

DS: … the fixed idea… and then it's finished.

…

DS: This all proves that basically… you know, for all inventions there were always… the automobile, the motor and so on… there have always been… almost… it proves that basically the insane… they are the true inventors.

RF: Yes.

DS: They are really on the track of something, but they simply don't know how to realise it… They don't bring it to fruition, and it's only after someone like… like TINGUELY today… and even today there are people who think TINGUELY is crazy…

RF: Yes yes yes.

DS: … and that's absolutely not true… and it's absolutely necessary to believe that something… sensed by… almost sensed by… the insane, by people who are completely outside… people who are disencumbered of… of traditional logic.

RF: Yes.

DS: Until someone… without knowing…

RF: Yes.

DS: … that these types ever existed…

RF: Yes yes.

DS: … is able to put the finishing touches…

RF: Yes yes yes.

DS: … on such things.

RF: Yes, and in this sense PLATO and ANTON MÜLLER were precursors.

DS: And TINGUELY agrees completely. They were the true precursors of TINGUELY, and not the recognised artists.

RF: Right.

DS: I think that they are the real…

RF: They started something, and they went as far as they could, and PLATO even died at it.

DS: Yes.

RF: PLATO is really someone who died for his art… or his science.

DS: Yes, he's a… he's a…

RF: A hero of art.

DS: A hero! (DS 1966)

g. I first heard about ANTON MÜLLER in 1959. My Fish Poem, along with the first universal poems and the Poetry Clock, were conceived as part of an *Hommage pour ANTON MÜLLER* by JEAN TINGUELY, SPOERRI and myself at the Galerie 59 in Aschaffenburg. I had already settled the aquarium problem and arranged for the alphabetisation of live carp**h** with the director of the gallery, HEINER RUTHS, when about a week before the opening TINGUELY and SPOERRI requested a postponement of several months because icy roads and snow prevented them from transporting their works and material from Paris to Bavaria. Request refused. "That's really a bit too much [*ein dicker Hund*]," RUTHS wrote to TINGUELY and SPOERRI, "… I just spoke with poor EMMETT on Saturday 10/12/60 and his project is all ready." I have never tasted carp since that day without thinking of ANTON MÜLLER. (EW 1966)

h. In Basle on the Rhine I once saw a large basket full of straw in a lovely shop where you can buy yourself a drink and a bite. There was a lovely shop girl in her pinafore, as white as a goose, who was busy unpacking what had been packed in straw and packed into the basket. And I started to hum a little song to myself, so, in my head: "*Hushaby, what's rustling in the straw?*" My what a lovely song! And as this shop girl inside her lovely pinafore unpacked the creatures that were packed in the straw, I unpacked, but all very respectably — just in my mind, of course — this girl from her white pinafore. That was just like plucking a goose, and inside in my head I could see my naked shop girl's goose pimples and I was also getting goose pimples from doing the unpacking. But then I saw what the naked shop girl was unpacking: carp from France! They were still alive and gasping for water in a way that turned my lovely shop girl's goose flesh into cold grey carp skin. Oh, and with that my naked, unpacked shop girl disappeared completely from my inner eye to be replaced by the suffering carp — even though they had already completely filled my outer eye — along with a couple of grey clouds which were already waiting in front of the shop door as I left, and sprinkled my bald head with a cold rain that made it tingle. (DR 1968)

i. This is, of course, a dangerously absurd point of view. JOHN GEORGE HAIGH, the English acid bath killer, in addition to indulging his derangement to the extent of murdering nine persons and ingeniously reducing their bodies to sludge (he delighted in doing a job well, "like an artist painting a picture"), had the inventors' bug, too. Among his discoveries were a device to enable the blind to thread needles, and a silent hammer. Such inventions "call for imagination and concentrated thought," HAIGH testified; "they are something out of the ordinary. I thought I was creating something. I enjoyed the constant fight against the unknown." (EW 1966)

j. Hopefully! (DR 1968)

k. In Switzerland '*Parisians*' are condoms, because condoms there are '*Parisians*'. (DR 1968)

l. LOUIS PERGAUD relates in *De Goupil à MARGOT* how the female suffers terribly during penetration because the sex of the male is barbed.[m] (DS 1962)

m. During one of my trips to Basle, KARL GERSTNER, a purist of the mathematical and geometrical school of abstract painting, and to whom I am bound by a strange friendship based on the law of contrasts, expressed astonishment at my French writing style, and cited as an example the phrase "*truffé de raisins secs, son sexe, m'a-t-il dit, excitait davantage sa compagne par sa surface granulée*" (rendered here as "the prickly surface of his sheathed sex, studded with raisins, aroused his companion more than usual"), comparing it with the best phrases of MALLARMÉ.[n] I took this opportunity to tell him that I consider the *Topography* a garbage can ("the human garbage can") and that nothing restrains me from accepting anything that can be accumulated in it, and that in this specific case the alliterative phrase was furnished by FRANÇOIS DUFRÊNE [**18, a; 45, a; 52, a; 62, c**]. On the subject of garbage cans,[p] the idea for the *Topography*[q] came to me about two years ago, when I first saw one of ARMAN'S "garbage cans". Not long afterwards I emptied mine on the floor, examined the contents, and thought about how I could retrace the history of each scrap. (DS 1966)

n. DOROTHY PODBER of New York City, seeking an alliterative equivalent of this phrase in English, came up with "male moles have prickly pricks." But the success of the alliteration is offset by the inappropriateness of the figure to the context. TOM WASMUTH suggested a play on the words "raisin" and "raising", but this seemed to me too homely for the rather sophisticated situation. I sought to capture the spirit of the original encounter in my rendition, "the prickly surface of his sheathed sex, studded with raisins," the alliteration creeping in quite by accident.

It would be interesting to speculate on the preparation of the female organ of sex to "surprise" the male, as the male does to the female with the raisins. In this connection I cite two advertisements printed in a brochure of the Akafune Drug Company of Yokohama:

1. JUGENOL: Stimurant (*sic*) for women. Ladies, who do not feel better when uniting with men, should use this. When used, you will receive days. Aged ladies who have too roomy vagina, should use this; then you will regain the same condition as a virgin. Take one tablet and dissolve it with your spit, and then paste it around your vagina.**o** Price 400 Yen.

2. GOLD MUSIC-BALL: This ball automatically plays music, which can be enjoyed by both sexes. Trying is believing. This is to be inserted into the female organ with your fingers. With every movement of it, a very exciting sound will be heard to your excitement. Price 800 Yen. (EW 1966)

o. Sometimes when you hear or see the word VAGINA it is best to go outside (if you are not already outside) and sit beside the broadest river you can find. Then you should have a look to see whether you cannot spot a pair of birds that are just saying Good Night, or, if you have a pair of binoculars on you (which you should always have with you if you want to get keen insights into the ways of the world), you should peer into and down it to see whether or not a for-once-sociable wolf is not just saying Good Night to the solitary sheep over yonder, on the other, as-far-as-possibly removed bank of the river. Then you should wait calmly until (with your right eye screwed tightly shut) the bitter wolf sinks, in the form of a black or deep blue point, behind the hill to the left, to the very back of the left lens of the binoculars, and until (now with your left eye tightly screwed shut behind its half of the binoculars) the sweet sheep sinks in the form of a grey or pale blue point behind the hill to the right, far away at the very back of the right lens of the binoculars. And then you can remain quietly seated until (if it has not grown too cold) it has grown completely dark, and you should look and see whether all of this has calmed you down nicely. It is best in fact if you don't go home any more, but wait until morning, then take the first plane and fly away.

— KAN IN'CHEN, *Wie man starke Wörter verdaut*, Taucherverlag RIESER, Hochkirchen-Cologne 1968 (DR 1968)

p. "I have several times had occasion to speak of 'rubbish-pits', and that is the most convenient term, but it is not necessarily the true description. Often these pits, which might be fifteen or twenty feet deep, were intended simply as receptacles for refuse, as was, for instance, the case with the pits attached to the Level V temple in which we found the discarded *ex votos* from the shrine; but sometimes they were really sewage pits… The graves and the rubbish-pits with their contents of pottery, etc., were the more valuable because it was seldom that a complete vessel could be found in houses so badly denuded as were those of Level II; they supplied the intact examples while the houses yielded an immense amount of broken sherds and reliable evidence for their date."

— SIR LEONARD WOOLLEY, *A Forgotten Kingdom* (A record of the results obtained from the recent important excavation of two mounds, Atchana and al Mina, in the Turkish Hatay, with 24 plates and numerous figures), Penguin Books, p. 155 (EW 1966)

q. Anyone who has anything in DANIEL SPOERRI'S *Topography*, anyone who has, for instance, added something, might start to think: "Might this be garbage that I am writing here now? Am I not writing something, but producing garbage, throwing away, instead?" Personally, I comfort myself when visited by such thoughts by thinking: "This writing here, that's not an act of throwing away, but for the moment simply of throwing — of throwing in, into the garbage can called the *Topography* — and even when the act of throwing in has been fully completed, when I have finished writing, the stuff is not thrown away at once but printed first — for it is hard to imagine that SPOERRI will let anything put him off — and once it has been printed it won't be so easy to throw away, as everyone can see." And when — sometimes when I have stomach-ache or am in a bad mood — I then continue thinking and say: "But sadly, that is exactly what is so new and remarkable about it, about SPOERRI'S idea: that the writing, and what is described by the writing, and the relationship between the described and the description, and the writing when it comes back from the press, and the oppressive description (which the printer must first print on his press, whereupon the printed impression oppresses the reader), that this is all garbage! What then?" Yes, so then I often think a bit further and can sometimes say to myself: "Right, fine, so people are intent on making garbage! Let them be the obsessed shitters they are! And may the life in which the garbage-possessed people live be The Great Shit-in!" I just take it as it is, I take it — as SPOERRI says — as it comes. And it simply shouldn't bother me and it should not stop me from continuing to live. But then afterwards I sometimes say to myself: "Oha, how revolting, how absolutely shitty!" and then that seems to be the last word on the matter — which it often is. Yet sometimes something else does occur to me after all — to say to myself (and if you like, to you): "Keep quiet, keep still my boy (or girl)! When one says something one only says the opposite of what one says — which, thank GOD, cannot be proved." (DR 1968)

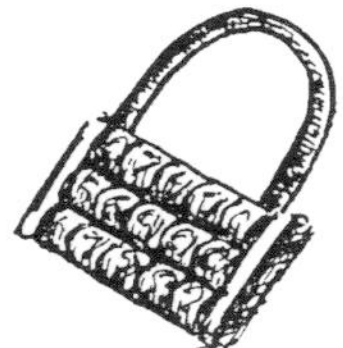

37. Lock for my room opened by the secret combination 4-1-6, bought after my return from Denmark 15 days ago because the combination to the old lock (same brand, S.O.S.,[a] secret combination 5-5-5) was known to so many people, and I ascertained that my room had been visited several times during my absence and that phonograph records had disappeared. One day, for example, returning unexpectedly from a trip, I found the room occupied by four huge Senegalese direct from Africa. Not knowing where to find free lodging for a while, they were let into my room during the night. (While on this subject, I give notice that I have just changed the lock again.)[b] [See **Appendix VI**, *Anecdoted Topography of Order*, object VII]

a. "No more thieves with an S.O.S. lock / 1,000 combinations / Precision, elegance, security / Each S.O.S. lock is sold with its own combination of three numbers, stamped on the metal disc shackled to the lock. To open the lock: place the three numbers of the combination (from top to bottom, as shown) opposite the 'O' and pull the shackle up; to close: press the shackle down and scramble the numbers. Beware of imitations. Ask for S.O.S." (DS 1966)

b. This habit seems beyond repair. I returned to SPOERRI'S room after midnight shortly before Christmas and found the following note from MARILYN HARRIS, a Bennington girl and secretary of ILEANA SONNABEND:

"Dearest EMMETT: A Christmas Poem: So this is where you live / My. / Happy

days are here again, / and when I found that you / I just had to come tell you. / Pour-
tant there was / only the padlock, / Which is well known to me now / … What is that
THING on the wall in front of the desk? / SCHLACKE let me in, who else / knows
the combination? / … Did you take an inventory of the articles in this room? / Your
Kinortine drew a comment / not from / your loving / " (signed) (EW 1966)

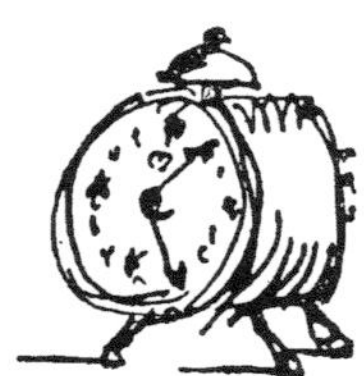

38. Alcarm clock[a] bought in January 1961 after its predecessor was glued to the snare-picture "It Isn't ARMAN'S Garbage Can".[f] This new clock, trademarked ALOUETTE Japy,[n] got its face smashed and was repaired three times by the repairman at Place de la Contrescarpe; then the face got smashed again.

a. My alarm clock takes the place of a wristwatch.[b] I have owned only one wristwatch in my life, which worked perfectly for seven years before I mislaid it. It was given to me the day of my twentieth birthday. On that day I had visited a HERR ADLER, an Austrian Jewish poet who once received the poetry prize of the city of Basle, and who retained a very peculiar way of smoking from his days of internment in a concentration camp: lipping the cigarette, sucking in the smoke, puffing it out and inhaling it back, then expelling it and sucking it back in again as though each cigarette might be his last. At that age I still thought of myself as a poet,[c] and having confidence in the judgement of HERR ADLER I had taken him some poems, which I read to him. At his place was a lady Ph.D., a professor of literature at the University of Basle. Following my reading, she asked me if I had a watch. After my negative response she declared that I must get one — to get some idea of time and cadence — and she invited me to accompany her home, where she gave me the wristwatch. It was my first present of the day. (The lady Ph.D. wasn't aware that it was my birthday, and one to which I attached much importance: because from that day on I was an adult and no longer had to present myself to the board of minors which had me under surveillance because I lived alone and without regular employment.)

The second present was given to me by a waitress[d] at the Café Tropic whom I admired very much but never dared tell of my admiration. She had learned from someone that on that day I had turned twenty, and as I entered the café and ordered my usual cup of coffee, she brought the cup and four cakes, saying that she was giving them to me for my birthday, and this touched me very much.

The third present was from HANS SCHWEIZER, nicknamed SNAKY JACK (*Schlangehansi*). He owed his nickname to a fondness for reptiles, which he raised in his apartment (he slept in the kitchen, they in the living-room; he ate bread and cheese, and the boa, for example, devoured rabbits) and about whom he wrote an article a year for the review *Herbarium*. Since he was weak in grammar and short on style, I helped him prepare his articles, which wasn't easy: he was so meticulously exact! On March 27, 1950,[e] he timidly left a shoe box on my table and then fled. Inside I found a hundred sheets of typing paper (clumsily rolled up and tied with a cord), half a pound of butter and a chocolate bar. SNAKY JACK was a petty employee of a Basle insurance firm, where he was proud never to have missed a day of work in 30 years. He hated women, and I don't think he had ever known one, all his love being concentrated on his dangerous fad. He told me once that, just as other men perpetuate themselves through their children, his name would figure for ever in science through his reptiles: for one day he had discovered a snake hitherto unknown, which now bears his name: *Vipera vipera svizzeri*. (DS 1966)

b. Wristwatches are handcuffs, they lay an alloy, steely or golden grip around the wrist and their twin sisters sit in banks, bureaus and bunkers whereby, wherewith and wherein one is chained and bound if not enthused and abused. The alarm clock, on the other hand, is just a thin slice of the great toppled belfry, this index finger of history, and, waking by night from nasty dreams, one can hear this history loud and sweet, ticking inside the alarm clock, crumbling, on three crooked legs. (DR 1968)

c. Here DANIEL means the poet as *versographer* — not the poet as *topographer*. (DR 1968)

d. What in the west are called waitresses are called in the north *inner Kellners* (*Kellnerinnen* — the quite different if not completely opposite female form of *Kellner*), but higher up, in the mountains, in between the north and south — slightly closer to the north than the south — one finds the female children of SERVIN (opposites of the sons of that legendary hermaphrodite: his daughters), the serving girls. (DR 1968)

e. Probably SPOERRI'S birthday. (DR 1968)

f. On the subject of this picture and others he bought from me, ARTURO SCHWARZ [2, 52] recently wrote me very officially entreating me "to take note that on the collages to be repaired, all the organic matter (bread etc.) has been devoured by rats that infiltrated the storage room[g] during the month of August" and that it would be necessary "to bring replacements", enclosing with the letter a cheque for the trip to Milan.[h]

PIERRE RESTANY, on a trip to Milan, visited SCHWARZ, who showed him the fallen and damaged objects, carefully preserved like relics, which led RESTANY to ponder "the prolongation of object-fetishism through décollage."[jl] (DS 1962)

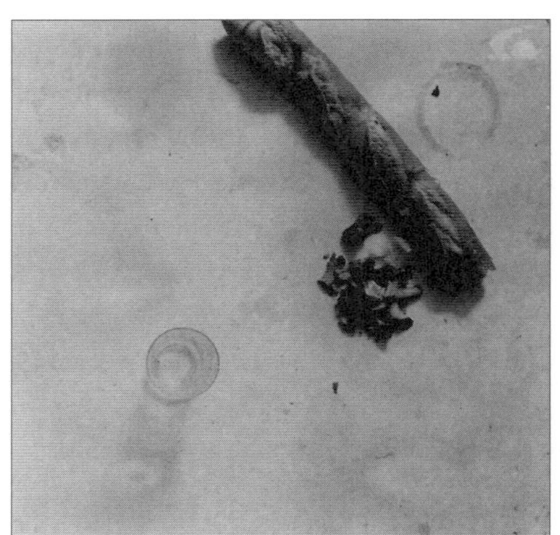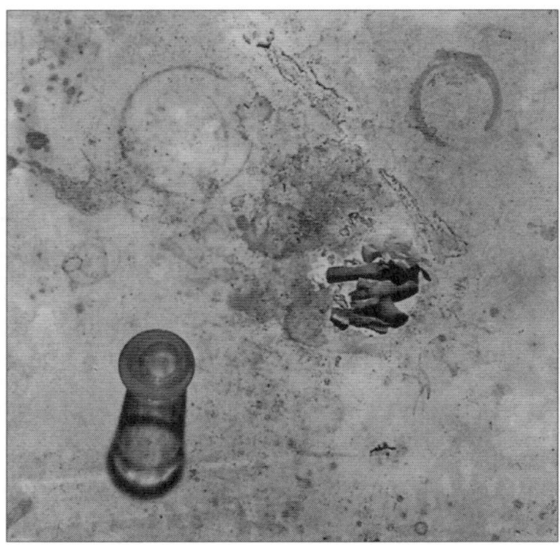

DANIEL SPOERRI, *Les os du szekely guljas*, 1960, private collection.
Before and after the collaboration of rats.

g. Probably brown rats. According to MAURICE BURTON, a big difference between brown rats and black ones is that black ones are more given to climbing. "That is why, in warehouses, brown rats are found on the ground floor and in basements and black rats upstairs." (EW 1966)

h. Fortunately I don't live in the 11th or 19th *arrondissement*, or, since last year, in the 16th, but in the 5th, for according to the newspaper *France Soir* of Thursday, March 22, 1962:

The city's rats by preference frequent the 11th and 19th *arrondissements*, and, since last year, the 16th. Since yesterday the thirteen RAT laboratory controllers (phone TAI 68-09), under the supervision of DR CORRE-HURT, chief of epidemic research for the prefecture of police, have intensified their activities, and the deratisation campaign will last until May 20.

Keep garbage cans[i] covered.

Keep cellars and courtyards clean.

Block up holes and large gaps under doors.

Cover vents with fine wire nets or grating.

Shield gutter spouts and drain-pipes.

These are some of the precautions recommended by the specialists. After these precautions, don't forget traps and poisons. (DS 1966)

i. I was eating paella with a friend in New York once, and when he saw me wrapping up chicken bones and mussel and shrimp shells to make a picture with he told me that his maid, who lives in Harlem, astounded him one day by doing the same thing after an elegant meal. She explained that she was going to take it home and put it in her own garbage can. It raised her status with the neighbours to have such high-falutin' garbage. (DS 1966)

j. The collaborating rats contributed, to some extent, to the utility value of the snare-pictures. At least these works of art were not simply gathering dust, the fate of so many paintings stacked in the storage annexes of museums and galleries. Fortunately, however, the collaborators were unable to pull out the screws and nails. Inspired by the Chinese proverb "*lou-shu-lai-kek-teng*" (a rat pulling out a nail),[k] CHARLES G. LELAND, better known under the pseudonym of HANS BREITMAN, a distinguished American philologist of the last century, composed the following poem in Pidgin English:

> One-tim one piecee lat
> Pull hard to catchee nail,
> And talkee when he come:
> "Look-see what largey tail!
>
> "But now my gettee out
> T'his ting no good — no how
> One piecee olo iron
> No blongey good chow-chow."

Supposey man lose tim
'Bout one long foolo tale,
He take you in — P'ho!
It all-same lat an' nail.

Pidgin-English Sing-Song, or Songs and Stories in the China-English Dialect, London: Kegan Paul, Trench, Trübner & Co. Ltd., 1904, p.73 (EW 1966)

k. There is a German version in KAN IN'CHEN, *Die Ratte im Haus erspart die Abbruchgesellschaft* (a rat in the house saves the demolition company). (DR 1968)

l. One feels inspired to ponder *the prolongation of décollage through décollage* when one reads WOLF VOSTELL.[m] (DR 1968)

m. Few will believe it, but this very afternoon, June 21, 1995, the editors confident that not another word would ever be added to their definitive edition of the *Topography*, the following fax beeped into my life. It is from RAFAEL VOSTELL, director of the Fine Art Gallery in Berlin. (RAFAEL is a son of WOLF, my old Fluxus colleague.)

"I am just preparing the return of your portraits to CARL SOLWAY in Cincinnati. When I went to my depot yesterday, I had to notice that the small bread of your *Portrait of DANIEL SPOERRI* fell off and broke. Terrible! I don't know how this could happen, as the works haven't been moved for months. My question and request is whether you could maybe restore the portrait."

So RAFAEL doesn't know how this could happen. Well, it could be the same breed of rats that devoured DANIEL'S picture at ARTURO SCHWARZ'S gallery in Milan [see **f** above]. But personally I think it's the fault of ROBERT FILLIOU, sitting up there cross-legged in his Buddhist Never-Never Land, jealous as hell that he can't be down here helping to re-anecdote the *Topography*. Aha, he's forcing me to do it for him! (EW 1995)

n. YES, JAPY'S LOVELY LARK[o] CHASED AS EVER EVERY JAPANESE LARK CHASER SWIFTLY OUT OF JAPY'S SPANISHY-PANICKY PYJAMAS! (DR 1968)

o. Lark = *Alouette* in French. (AB 1995)

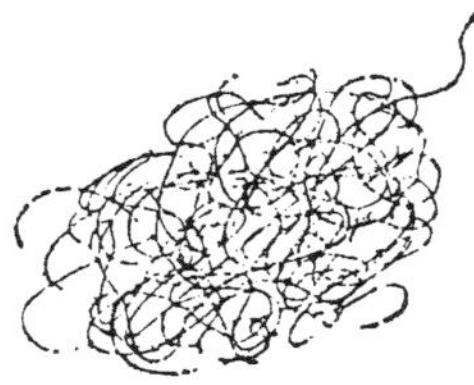

39. Strong black thread unwound from its spool [70].[a]

    a. One of the very few unannotated entries.[b] (DR 1968)

      b. It was, DIETER, until you discovered it. (EW 1995)

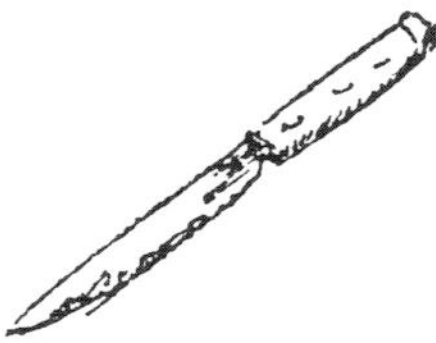

40. Ordinary knife with saw-tooth blade smeared with butter [1, 2, 27], white plastic handle.[a]

    a. I have had three such knives. Since all the handles got broken, the plastic is probably of inferior quality. (DS 1966)

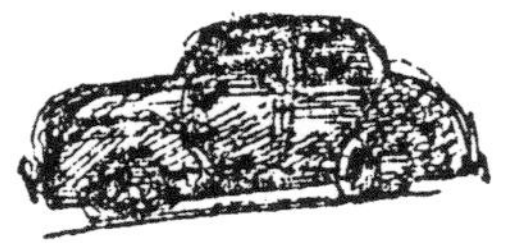

41. Microminiature[a] Norev model of a new RENAULT 4CV in its transparent wrapper, bought at the drugstore opposite the Hotel Beau Séjour [**26**] at the same time as a litre of alcohol for my stove [**7A**, **10**].

    a. Aha! The minimal! The fact is that where the table bears the miniature it is less table (and much less table there where it bears the microminiature) than where it doesn't bear the miniature. The table is more tableish at the edge, for instance, than under the car miniature, because under the miniature it is more of a road: MOTHER EARTH in the form of a road. That makes the table a road! (DR 1968)

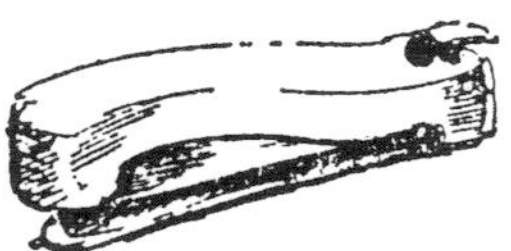

42. Green Swingline stapler [**34M**] bought for 24 francs the beginning of March to staple together the catalogues of the 1959 Édition MAT [**20, 34E**]. A year after this edition was terminated, I still had a pile of unbound sheets and the movement exhibition in Amsterdam gave me an opportunity to sell some of the catalogues (about thirty, at 1 florin each), and in that way I recovered at least the price of the stapler.

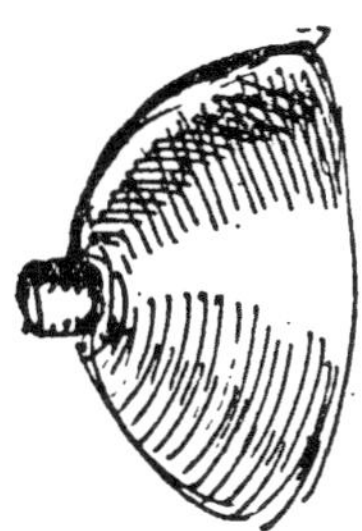

43. Push button for a bell in dark-brown Bakelite, the button of which, to be exact, is white, used in Nice during the Festival of Nouveaux Réalistes for the electric razor attached to "The Tripod" [**31**]; purchased close to ARMAN'S studio, along with an ashtray full of small electrical fixtures, bought as was for 70 francs, glued and given later to VERA. I used the gold-coloured wire attached to the button to make a lamp for KICHKA [**44**].

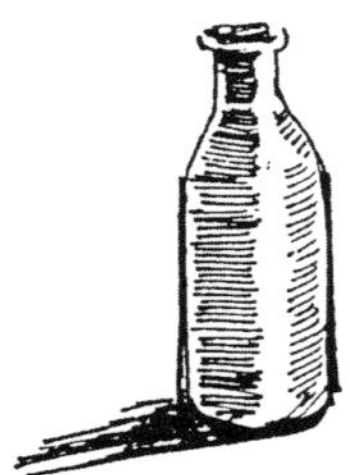

44. Very pretty dark-blue bottle with a large neck, bought in a shop opposite the Galerie RAYMOND CORDIER, Rue GUÉNÉGAUD, one day when for no apparent reason I visited the gallery; said bottle is topped by a socket and bulb, the whole forming a bedside lamp.[a]

    a. And not just *forming*[b] a bedside lamp. (DR 1968)

      b. We all know that form follows function. (EW 1995)

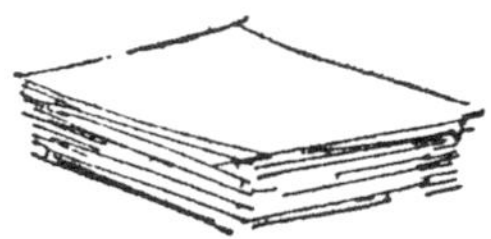

45. Pack of blue toilet paper with interfolded sheets, trademarked Soundproof,[a] which makes me think of Kangaroo men's shorts and EROS[b] deodorant cakes for toilets.[c] Some of these cakes, presented as "erotic objects", were in the surprise package given to KICHKA'S sister for her birthday [**2**, **17**, **22**, **29**, **63**].[d]

a. FRANÇOIS DUFRÊNE (who helped correct the French manuscript of the re-anecdoted *Topography*) called my attention to HANS ARP'S poem "Soundproof Blue" in the review *K*:

"With incongruous borborygmus the wind discharges… I hasten. At last I penetrate the soundproof blue of nostalgia."

(Meudon 1938) (DS 1966)

b. EROS is also the family name of MARIE-LOUISE, a young Hungarian of the quarter, who wrote a book of prayers and in whose room I made the snare-picture "Birthday Breakfast with EROS" the morning of my 32nd birthday. (DS 1966)

c. The, for foreigners, seemingly extraordinary language of the inordinately large piles of toilet paper — sitting in state above their antipodes, the provisions, in piles atop the topmost arenas of the supermarket shelves of the marvellous North Americas, filling the gaze of the devout with their soft mass — speaks to the unbeliever (the visitor from regions full of people who are corrupted by other forms of corruption than bowel eruptions or their opposite, obstructions) in the forceful but silent picture language *par excellence*, that of the pile or the piles. The piles of toilet paper speak there in markets where people suffer from inner corruption (being a symptom of outward prosperity), to those suffering from corruption in their innards (in this case in their digestive regions). Suffering, either from a decline in the ability to retain the digested, or a decline in the ability to egest the ingested. Suffering — from thick or thin. Constipative or eruptive. The pervasive and persuasive language, the slightly extraordinary figurative language of the pile of toilet paper up there now enters — or so it seems to the visitor from differently corrupt but similarly prospering foreign parts, who over-hastily shakes his head gently — softly yet persuasively, through thick and thin, the eyes of the provisions-buyers who are craning their necks and extending their arms in their relief, so that on top of everything else they also become toilet paper-buyers. For the enormous piles of paper have either paraded, stimulating or exciting, enormous heaps of business before their eyes, or if not, suggested a great act of soaking and wiping up, or of wiping down and out. (DR 1968)

d. The text of the *Topography* going through my head, I was intrigued to learn that while soundproof toilet paper is only optional in Paris, it is obligatory for garbage cans to be (see the decree of the prefecture of police of the Seine Department of March 1962). I also found and bought another brand of toilet paper that considers the whole thing a Bagatelle (registered trademark, B&B, Paris); but the Catholic Church does not consider it a bagatelle, and made the manufacturer of another brand of paper, Adios, back down. I learned this from reading *Der Spiegel* [e] (March 14, 1962) in an article titled "Blasphemy in Crepe". I asked *Der Spiegel* for permission to reprint excerpts from the article, which they very generously granted:

"The Catholic Church has compelled one of West Germany's richest firms to change its business tactics… Feldmühle, manufacturer of the old Servus paper, had decided to introduce 'a modern toilet paper, fully hygienic, perfectly detachable, of fine crepe in pastel colours' at the attractive consumer price of 60 pfennigs. In view of the broadened touristic horizon of West Germans, advertising psychologists added to the name Servus, borrowed from Austria, the Spanish word Adios. Feldmühle launched Adios with a half-million-mark advertising campaign. In train compartments, on advertising pillars and match covers the firm confided: 'Adios is better.'

"The new product had hardly been put on sale when, toward the beginning of

December, the Feldmühle telephone rang. On the other end of the line was DR JOHANNES NEUHÄUSLER, suffragan bishop of Munich, energetically demanding a bit of information: 'I've just learned that you are advertising a toilet paper called Adios. Didn't you realise what you were doing?'

"In a letter to the firm NEUHÄUSLER protested against the use of Adios for toilet paper, because according to the man of GOD the word offends religious sentiments: Adios means 'GOD be with you'.

"For fear that the Catholic clergy would call for a boycott from the pulpit, the directors called off the publicity campaign and an order went out to find another name acoustically similar to Adios that would not hurt religious feelings. Publicity writers came up with Arios, but almost immediately it was pointed out that this name, too, could insult the faithful. At the beginning of the 4th century A.D. the Arian controversy, which traced its origin to the presbyter ARIUS of Alexandria, threw the Christian world into an uproar. Because ARIUS had been anathematised by the Council of Nicaea for his teachings — he denied the consubstantiality of the Father and the Son — Feldmühle's directors recoiled from the name Arios.

"In their confusion the publicity men finally settled on Amios. But it was still not certain that the bishop would accept the new name. Amios recalls the Old Testament prophet AMOS who once warned against the inner corruption[f] of men in times of economic prosperity." (DS 1966)

e. Returning from the art talks in Vienna [see **66, a**], the author and I stopped off in Munich to visit SOPHIE VON BEHR-NEGENDANK of *Der Spiegel*. She gave us the key to a very comfortable apartment (equipped with TV, and across the street from where KANDINSKY'S atelier used to stand) owned by friends of hers then on vacation. One morning, planning an outing, the three of us were unable to agree on a destination. To decide the matter, SPOERRI placed a large map of the Munich area on the floor, shut his eyes, and dropped a coin: where it landed, we would go. It landed on Dachau. At Dachau I bought a book describing the German Catholic Church's opposition to HITLER and it was written by this very same suffragan bishop, who had been interned at Dachau during the Second World War. (EW 1966)

f. Do the cakes get rid of the odour? No, they simply drown the smell, and in fact they don't even drown it, but simply stink it out, so that an odour is stinked out by a stench! (DR 1968)

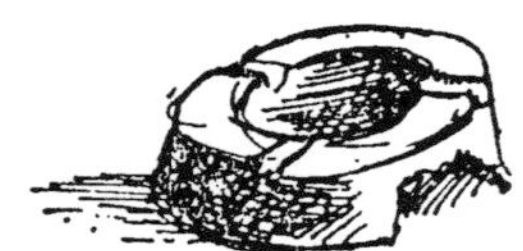

46. Greenish Bakelite ashtray broken on one side and burned in many places, fallen from a picture by GÉRARD DESCHAMPS exhibited at the Nouveaux Réalistes show in Stockholm (the beginning of June 1961) and returned to me by mistake. When he came to retrieve his picture, DESCHAMPS preferred it without the ashtray, which is easy to explain because it clashed with the other material — cloth, bras, slips etc. — with which he normally composes his pictures.[a]

a. DESCHAMPS, when this paragraph was read to him, explained that he really left me the ashtray because he didn't want to nail it up again, and that he hoped to see it some day in a good spot on one of my snare-pictures. (DS 1962)

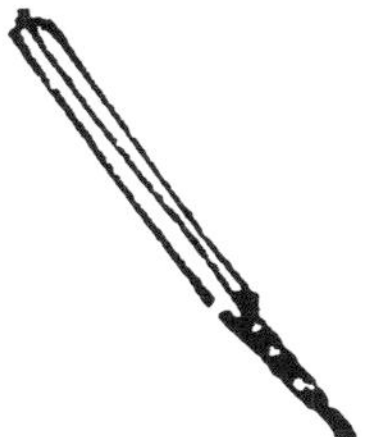

46A. Burnt match in ashtray **46ᵃ** [**7, 7A, 10**].

a. One can call symbols discarded commodities, because commodities — so long as you need them — lead an unconscious or unseen life, because they exist down in the unconscious of the people who use them (the hammer lives in the hand, the shoe lives beneath the foot, the match lives up front, before the cigar, and so on and so forth), and the commodities only first rise up into the so-called consciousness when — on being thrown away, say — they fly past your eyes and their image flies into them and slips into your brain where it calls out its name (e.g. "Here's match!"). And when the discarded commodity summons its image and calls out its name up there in the brain, the person listens intently inside, or outside, and the person sees all manner of different things in the process — not just the falling match, for instance, but also sticks and stakes and staves and pillar-like objects and much more. And when he sees inside himself pillars he hears pillars simultaneously, and he hears pillars and killers and then he thinks for instance of thrillers and so on and so forth. These images, the images of discarded objects — with their trains of kindred images and sounds behind them — sometimes have, or can have, a train that contains the whole world. That's to say: obviously just the whole world that you can name, see, think of, in short: the world you perceive inside in yourself or outside outside yourself. And these things, which are thrown away and have a train (as has just been described) trailing behind them, these are symbols. Symbols are all old, discarded stuff. [To be continued in **47**] (DR 1968)

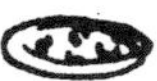

47. White shirt button[a] [58, 59, 73].

a. [Continued from **46A**] And with that something crazy happens: the objects lie around, consumed, after being used, or the objects lie there unconsumed, before being used. And images, the names and the whathaveyou rise up from them as a cloud of a definite-indefinite nature, but one that stimulates certain people. And now they come, the people whom it stimulates, who see it — picture-makers, writers and madmen — the people, human beings in general, and they take what is rising up and use it. They need it as the object of their picture-, sound- or gesture-language — as characters, and then these become commodities once again, and no one can tell any longer what they are because they have become commodities which no one can tell what they are because they have not yet flown away and have neither produced a train nor allowed a cloud to rise up. But then once again these things grow old, stupid or the like, are used and thrown away, and the old familiar train trails behind them — and so they are once more really lovely symbols. And then they fall to the ground and remain there — in museums, libraries and warehouses, and the charged, plump cloud rises up from them, and so on. And that's the way it keeps going on. (Real finesse here dictates that naturally one cannot say: that's the way it goes on! because everything keeps happening simultaneously, so all that one can really say is: yes, that's the way it keeps on going!) (DR 1968)

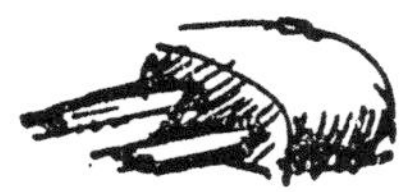

48. Electric plug connected to the snare-picture "I'm Not Allowed to Dance". The star-shaped pin bearing this inscription (in German) I found about the time I gave up dancing;[a] along with a lot of other stuff I had collected over the years, it finished up on this picture and gave it the title. The plug is connected to a small lamp on the work, which can be turned on.

a. I had just taken up dancing when I met MAX TERPIS, ballet master of the Berlin Opera during the 1920s. (The Nazi rise to power ended his career.) By the time I met him he had become a psychologist (before becoming ballet master he had been an architect). I mention this meeting here because it is to him that I owe most in life. Over the years we saw one another every day, and thanks to him I realised my potentialities. Once I acquired my own individuality, however, it inevitably conflicted with his, and I saw him only rarely the last years of his life, which he spent alone. After his death in 1958, his brother, in announcing the decease and informing me that TERPIS had remembered me generously in his will, justifiably reproached me for my ingratitude. (DS 1966)

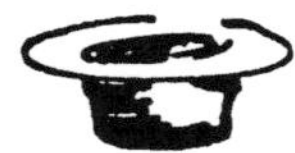

49. Tricoloured plastic stopper, black-green-red, from a bottle of Vin des Rochers [3, 25, 34L, 57, 67].

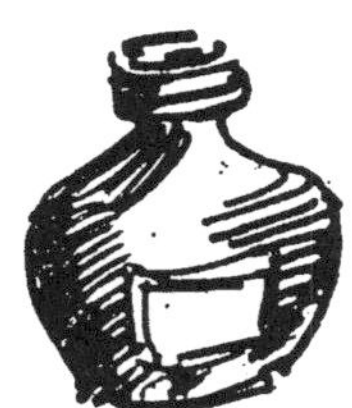

50. Sample of Olfran aftershave lotion (77%) found inside the electric-razor bag [**31**], which I used only once;[a] half empty due to evaporation.

a. Once I went for a walk in a forest and I came upon a clearing where a couple of pine trees had been felled. And I think of a walk like that today, and I see the pines, which is a beard in pine green that grows on my face when I think of the pine forest. When I think of the clearing I feel how my green beard is being shaved away, and when after all that I read about aftershave it rains on the clearing in the pine forest, but suddenly the sun shines once more, the ground dries and becomes parched — and I need a drink. (DR 1968)

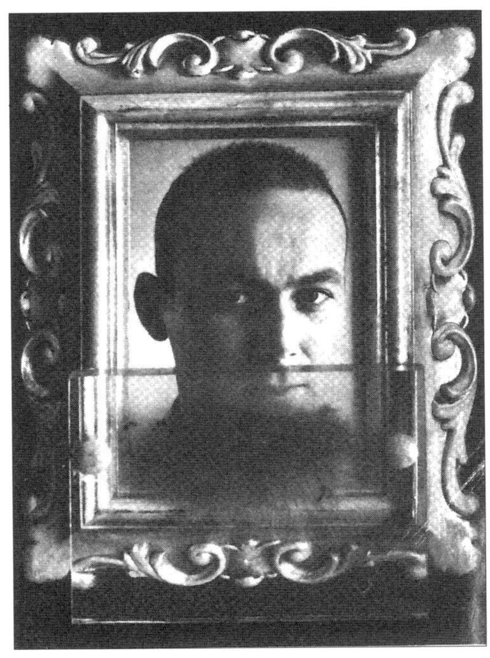

DANIEL SPOERRI,
Portrait of Diter Rotbarsch, assemblage, 1971.

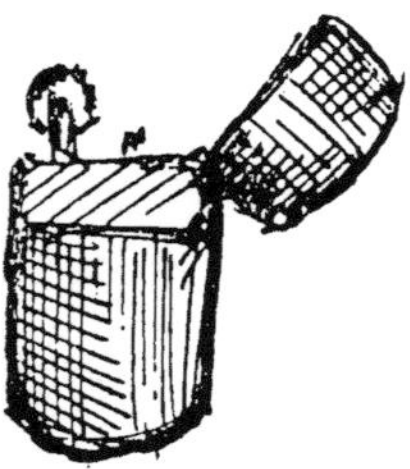

51. Small dispenser of cigarette-lighter flints bought, although I didn't have a lighter, because the system of ejection seemed ingenious to me. **a**

a. A note unencumbered by annotations. (DR 1968)

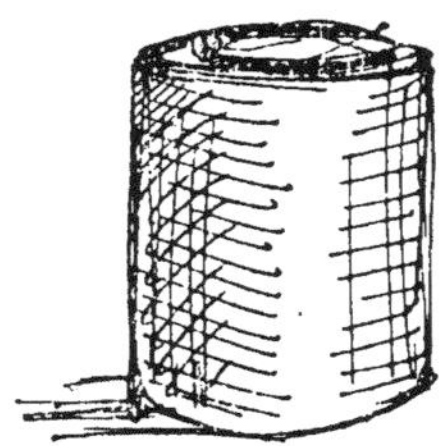

52. Two-pound container of Vinavil glue bought, with four others, in Milan during my exhibition, on the advice of ARTURO SCHWARZ; the best glue I have found so far. Forgetting that I wasn't returning directly to Paris but via Amsterdam, I had to pay a surcharge for them on the plane. In Amsterdam I was visited by a friend who was hitchhiking back to Paris and who bravely undertook to carry the ten pounds of glue to my room. This is the glue I subsequently poured into the flexible apparatus described in **16.**[a]

a. I am now in the happy position of being able to announce that my worries about glue are about to disappear. It was at the Bazar de l'Hôtel de Ville that I fell upon Araldite (sold in America as Epoxy) which FELIX LEU[b] had already described, but not by name, as miraculous, which I can confirm as true now that I have used it.

During a trip to Basle, where FELIX LEU was born and lived for 16½ years, I visited the laboratories of CIBA, manufacturers of Araldite. A chemist there agreed that the problem with Araldite is not making it stick, but unsticking it when necessary. Which made me think that FRANÇOIS DUFRÊNE could find himself without an art if they ever start using Araldite for pasting posters. (DS 1966)

b. When I see, outside on the ferry, down in Basle, up on the Rhine, the sign sitting there that says LEU, and painted on it a lion with its twice-two limbs: two legs and two arms, I start to see two LEUS before me for all those twos. And when, later, in winter, I glue a piece of transparent paper over two cherries that are printed in two colours on yellow card, I can think up all manner of things in the evening, before going to sleep, such as: when I glue a piece of transparent paper over two cherries and when I think to myself that I have two cherries in my mouth, and when in addition I myself am two LEUS and two cherries — here inside of my head — and then when I let myself swim across the Rhine in the form of two LEUS, each with two cherries in its mouth… is the Rhine there really yellow and is it summer, or does it just seem that way? And is a lion really a vegetarian and does it love children, or does it just pretend to? (DR 1968)

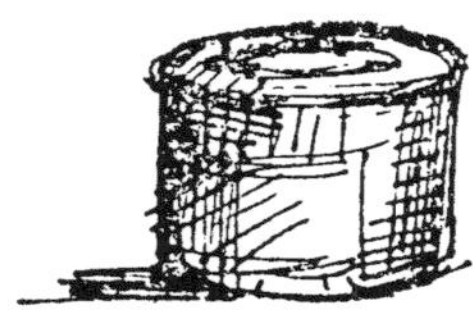

53. Jar of powdered coffee the brand name I forget; after the first tracing of this *Topography* the jar got lost. But one thing is certain, it wasn't Nescafé, most likely a Danish imitation bought at IRMA'S [**15**, **19**, **21**].

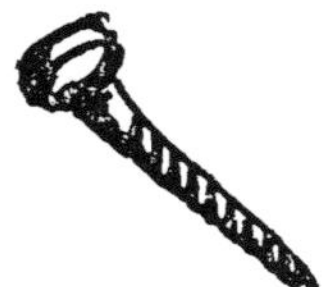

54. Screw, 2.5 cm. long, from the assortment I generally use to fasten objects, bought from a hardware store on the Rue Mouffetard. The dealer is certainly surprised by my diligence, but he doesn't know that most of the screws are scattered about and glued to the pictures themselves.

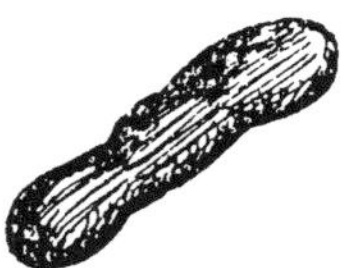

55. Peanut presented to me by MR PEANUT, the peanut vendor in the quarter, my brother ("yessir, you're my brother"), an old one-armed Algerian with a wrinkled face, who likes to recount the story of his missing left arm: "When I was little I fell out of a tree, yessir, really. Then my arm turned completely black, yessir, it really turned completely black. Afterwards I was able to remove the hand and throw it away, yessir, and later the whole arm turned black, and one day *it* fell off, yessir, that's the truth, because we didn't have any doctors, nobody went to see a doctor in those days, and that's really true, yessir."

56. Screw.[a]

a. This simple entry should appeal to purists. (EW 1966)

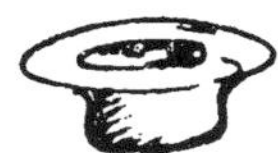

57. Stopper[a] **from Vin des Rochers**, tricoloured, this time red–white–yellow. [3, 25, 34L, 49, 67]

a. Crossing the Pont Neuf accompanied by ROBERT and probably MARIANNE and KICHKA, we all noticed at the same time a truck whose tyre bolts were decorated with multicoloured stoppers, which excited us and incited us to take down the licence number and name of the firm, to be able to include it here:

RUFÈRE & Co.
Pigs[b]
8356 GL 75[d]   (DS 1966)

b. Sometimes one person says to the other: "Stupid pig!" And if it so happens that the other person believes the first, the other often says to himself: "Hmph, that's clipped my wings that has!" because he had said to himself that pigs have short legs.[c] And then before long he feels he's a despondent old boar and asks himself: "What if someone were now to slaughter me?" Finally he says: "What a silly sausage I am!" Yes, that's the way it goes when people believe the nasty things that are said to them — regardless of whether it's someone else or themselves that say it. (DR 1968)

   c. A paraphrase of the German proverb "lies have short legs". (MG 1995)

   d. Eight minus five is three is five less two is eight minus six plus two is a G plus an L equals eight minus one the first equals seven with five behind or back to front five with seven behind like the numbers of the paragraph one more than the sum of the last two digits of the first group as well as one less than the first two of the first ones and one less than the last ones as many as the spaces half as many as the digits of the first ones. (DR 1968)

58. White shirt button[a] [47, 59, 73].

a. This simple entry is probably too dirty for EMMETT the puritan. (DR 1968)

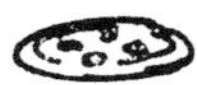

59. White shirt button[a] [47, 58, 73].

a. Puritans may well delight at this simple shirt button, however. (DR 1968)

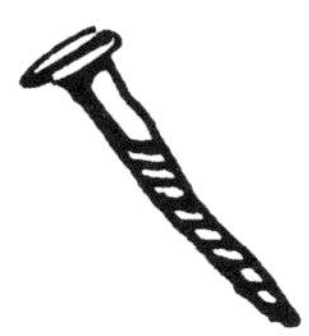

60. Screw, 1.5 cm. long[a] [**54, 56**].

a. This should appeal to EMMETT. (DR 1968)

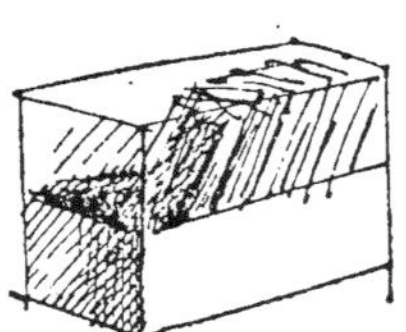

61. Plastic box containing 20 transparency frames, used during direct projections with polarised light (a method invented by BRUNO MUNARI)[a] on an evening at the I.C.A. (Institute of Contemporary Arts [see **34B**, **34O**, **77**]) in London in February 1960. The audience consisted of about 150 people and I was afraid the evening would be boring, but everyone was delighted and took part, with as much application as at a nursery school, gluing and arranging the slides. A jury selected by the audience chose the winning compositions, so everybody signed their frames. Among the names on the frames in said plastic box are MAPUJAHA, TABAKOBUF, IRMA BODLEY, A.B., SPEARPOINT, LEE PENROSE, ROSALIE DE MEVI (?), EARL KOHN, I.H., LEONIE KOHN, S. RANKIN, BANKS, FRANÇOISE GILOT, TONY and TOM GARLAND.[b]

a. *"Direct Projections with Polarised Light*

"This method uses projected light and breaks its course like the prismatic phenomenon by using a polarised slide which changes the colour composition. The audience is invited to make compositions with different materials such as cellophane and cellotape, which become coloured by the polarisation. The different colours are produced by the number of superimpositions of the same material. Materials which are already coloured do not give as many possibilities for changing colour.

"Start experimenting by folding a piece of cellophane or two pieces of different colours, a small square of black paper, a drop of mastic squeezed between two pieces of colourless rodhoid. Black or opaque papers in opposition to the coloured parts give more depth.

"Cleanness is important, for any trace of dirt or any speck of dust, no matter how small, will be magnified by the projection."

— English text distributed to the I.C.A. audience (DS 1962)

b. Rummaging through the author's room, I found these other names on slides used during the same evening at the I.C.A.:[c] UG, A, CROSBY, EILEEN, G. WISE, M. MORRIS, J. (?) BAKKER, VISCOTI, DAVID, VANE BIER (?),[d] LAMI, D.G. and DAVENPORT. (EW 1966)

c. This morning (21 September 68) I looked through 20 slides (showing pictures of an exhibition) in my room in Reykjavik. Here are some of the names on them: KODAK, KODAK, KODAK, KODAK, KODAK. (DR 1968)

d. In my note **h** to **Introduction I,** I call attention to a review of the original French version, in the *Times Literary Supplement* of September 3, 1964, that praised the book for its "scholarly style that any bibliographer, museum director or art historian might be proud of…" In a recent letter to me dated May 21, 1995, 07:17:17 p.m., ALASTAIR BROTCHIE, an editor of the present edition, upholds this tradition of painstaking research and accuracy. "By the way," he writes, "the 'amateurs of contemporary art' includes one VANE BIER (with a ?). I think this must be the Yugoslavian Surrealist artist VANE BORE, who lived in the UK from the war years onwards; he died recently I believe. When he found out what his name meant in English, he changed it to STEVEN ZIVADIN." (EW 1995)

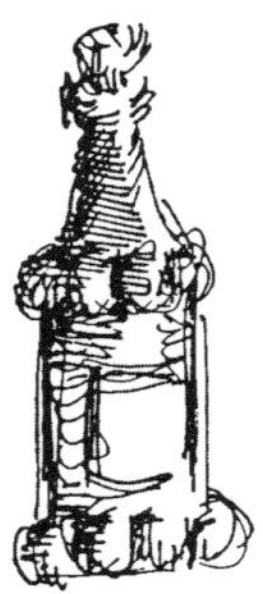

62. Bottle of SAUZÉ, *eau de cologne* for men, verbena scent, three-fourths full, around the neck a black bow KICHKA gave me the day I received an invitation[a] to the preview of the "Art of Assemblage" exhibition in New York which stated that guests had to wear black ties.[b] I had remarked to KICHKA that since I didn't have one I wouldn't be able to go to New York.[c]

a. Text of the invitation (DS 1962):

The President and Trustees of The Museum of Modern Art
request the pleasure of your company
at the Contributing Members' Preview of the exhibition
the art of assemblage
on Monday evening, October 2 from 9–11:30 o'clock

Tickets are required for admission
R.S.V.P.   11 West 53 Street New York 19   Black tie

b. After reading the manuscript, PIERRE RESTANY, theoretician of the Nouveaux Réalistes, explained to me that "black tie" is the fashionable phrase for evening dress, that the tie can be black or white, which makes the immediate purchase of a black tie unnecessary. (DS 1962)

c. I should point out that this exhibition was organised by WILLIAM C. SEITZ, who spoke to me about it in Amsterdam [**34D**] during an agitated evening when we had had a lot to drink and I insulted him, for which I offer my apologies here. After the opening of my exhibition at Galerie LAWRENCE (Feb. 9 to March 7, 1962), SEITZ, passing through Paris, visited the gallery and, seeing one of my snare-pictures that caught his fancy, went against his principle of not collecting to the point of taking it off the wall himself and carrying it with him to the airport. He was unaware that this snare-picture — the top of a suitcase — had quite a story behind it. I told him all about it in my reply to his letter announcing the hanging of the picture:

The Museum of Modern Art
New York 19

February 27, 1962

Dear DANIEL,
Just a word to tell you that the frying pans, etc., are now hanging on my wall and look great.

With best regards,

BILL

(WILLIAM C. SEITZ)

Associate Curator

WCS:sjk

Paris, March 17, 1962

Dear BILL,
Just a word to tell you that the letter, etc., is now in my pocket and feels great.

With best regards,

DANIEL

(DANIEL I. SPOERRI)

P.S. It might interest you to know the story of the suitcase top. I was invited by an awful modernistic architect to participate in an exhibition he had arranged at his house in Cologne… A few years ago, when I was going around Europe exhibiting the Édition MAT (multiplied art objects) I always wanted to be able to carry all the works of the artists in one suitcase. Once I even asked some of them to make their work small enough to fit into a suitcase. So on this new occasion… I took up the idea again and I asked ARMAN, CÉSAR, DESCHAMPS, DUFRÊNE, HAINS, RAYSSE, NIKI DE ST. PHALLE, TINGUELY and DE LA VILLEGLÉ to participate with me in a suitcase exhibition. I made use of an old suitcase of mine that I was then using as a kind of table; the snare-picture that you bought is the top of this suitcase. By chance, a young gallery owner from Cologne — HARO LAUHUS — came to see me the same week I was working on the suitcase, and proposed an exhibition at his gallery, to follow the first performance at the architect's house.

So I went. BOB RAUSCHENBERG, who was at that time also in Paris, offered to participate in the exhibit, then said the only thing he'd like to do was furnish a padlock to lock the suitcase with, and to throw the key away. And I did it. It was rather difficult to cross the Franco-German border with my locked suitcase, but I succeeded in explaining to the customs officials that I was an illusionist, and that I couldn't open the suitcase without ruining my whole act — and from the way the top of the suitcase looked, they were ready to believe me… I arrived, with my suitcase, at the house of the architect as scheduled (June 10, 1961). About 200 people were there, including DAVID TUDOR. The architect asked me not to take more than ten minutes, but I think the whole performance lasted about an hour and a half. First I had to saw the padlock, then I hung all the things on the wall, explaining irrelevant things about each artist and his work. NIKI had given me sugar candy to distribute to the public, TINGUELY asked me to blow soap bubbles, GHÉRASIM LUCA made a poem that I handed out, DUFRÊNE screamed a few lettrist poems on a tape, we shot at one of NIKI'S pictures, two sculptures of TINGUELY had to be mounted together (they were attached to the suitcase), and so on. Anyway, I succeeded in what I wanted to do… Next evening was the *vernissage* at the gallery… And that's the story about the Blue GILLETTE Blade.

P.P.S. For the sake of exactness, I inform you that ROBERT FILLIOU has since made an even smaller exhibit. He carries small "works of art" in his cap, over his head, through the streets. He calls cap and contents "The Legitimate Gallery".**d** (DS 1966)

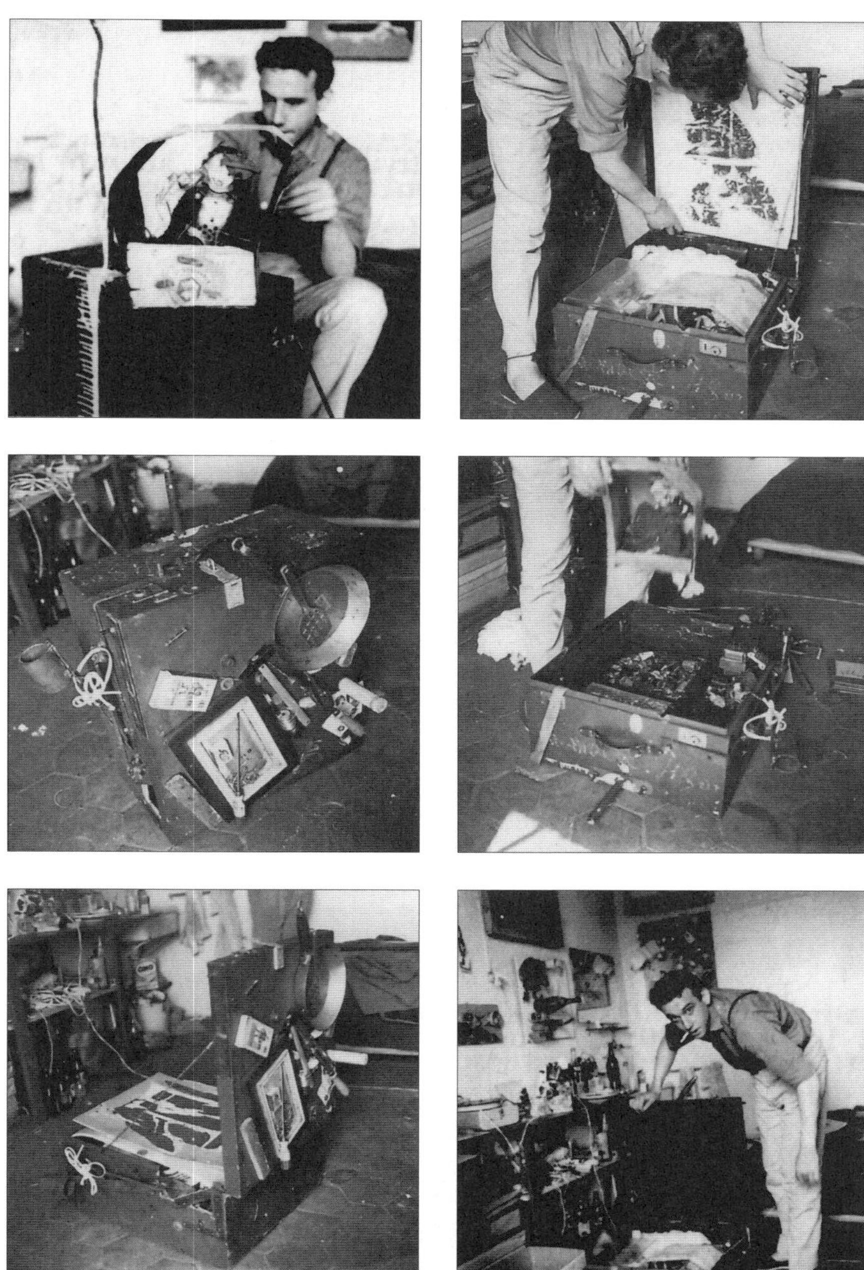

DANIEL SPOERRI assembling the "suitcase", 11 June 1961.

d. This Legitimate Gallery also has a history. The idea was born during a tumultuous evening at the sumptuous seaside villa of AAGARD ANDERSEN near Helsingør where we drank a great deal, and where FILLIOU insulted MESDAMES ANDERSEN and HALLING KOCH, for which I don't know if he has been pardoned. In any case, he got the idea of starting a wheelbarrow gallery in Paris, where he was returning soon because of his expulsion from Denmark. Everybody present — TINGUELY, NIKI DE ST. PHALLE, ADDI and TUT KOEPCKE, the ANDERSENS and his wife,[e] the HALLING KOCHS, the USSINGS and I — was bowled over by the idea and, convulsed with laughter, made preposterous suggestions, which FILLIOU took seriously. And to prove to us that he was serious, the following day he sent TINGUELY this letter:

Dear TINGUELY,

Pursuant to our conversation of last evening, I confirm that the *vernissage* of the Legitimate Gallery will take place during the month of October (or as soon as possible) with an exhibition of your work. The Legitimate Gallery is itinerant. It consists of a wheelbarrow or pushcart, according to need. It travels (legitimately) through the streets, in the highest creative tradition. Upon receipt of your works, I promise to maintain them in good condition, respect your prices, and to follow an itinerary to be worked out with you. My commission will consist of the usual 33 per cent.

On your part, you will contribute to the launching of the gallery by sending out invitations to your exhibition, and taking care of publicity (press, television, collectors).

The Legitimate Gallery will open as soon as legal formalities are arranged. If the price of the licence surpasses my means, you will be expected to advance me the money, to be deducted from my commission.

In exchange for your assistance in launching the gallery, I promise to exhibit your "legitimate works" whenever you express the desire, in Paris as well as in the provinces and abroad (I intend to take the gallery to such cities as Brasilia, Tokyo, New York, Moscow, Peking etc.), respecting, of course, contracts with other artists (NIKI DE ST. PHALLE and DANIEL SPOERRI have already given their consent). Your confirmation of receipt of this letter will serve as our bond of agreement.

So long,

R. FILLIOU

Incidentally, I would like to quote the song FILLIOU sang, completely soused, to the tune of the COLONEL BOGEY March the rest of the evening, almost bursting our eardrums:

GOERING has only got one ball
HITLER has got them very small
HIMMLER
Is very similar
And poor old GOEBBELS has no balls at all.[f]

explaining each time that only the English could call their worst enemy "poor old GOEBBELS" and that's why they won the war.

To conclude the history of the gallery: FILLIOU was not able to get a licence from the city of Paris, so he decided to reduce the dimensions of the Legitimate Gallery and carry it around on his head without a licence. Thus the Legitimate Gallery turned out to be an illegitimate gallery.

I myself was so drunk that evening that I'm certain it was there I infected my finger, and not in the door of a taxi, as I once supposed; after two days the infection had spread almost up to my shoulder, and I was sent to a doctor: if I had come two days later, he said, I probably would have died of blood-poisoning. I don't know how the art critics of Copenhagen got wind of the infection, but EJNER JOHANSSON, the best known of them according to MARIANNE (anyway, he writes in the best paper, *Information*), said of me in an article dated Tuesday, Oct. 10, 1961: "He recently exhibited in Copenhagen, where he walked around with a serious blood infection that frightened his acquaintances."[i] (DS 1966)

e. GRETE. (DR 1968)

f. *GÖRING hat nur eine*
  HITLER ganz kleine,
  HIMMLER
    hat ähnliche Bimmler,
    und der arme alte GOEBBELS keine.[g] (DR 1968)

g. I hope the editors keep the German translation of the song.[h] Although I can't fit DIETER'S words to the rousing strains of the COLONEL BOGEY March, as a Berliner-by-choicer I find them topical, as well as topographical, especially the Himmler-Bimmler bit. I'd like to point out, in this connection, that in the telephone directory (in German *das Telefon bimmelt*) of the former capital of the Third Reich I can find only seven Bimmlers, as opposed to 91 Balls and 131 Sacks. As you might expect, there are pages and pages of Peters and Wieners. There are also 82 Bonks, 66 Wangs, 60 GOERINGS, 40

Dicks, 23 Butts, 19 HIMMLERS and 19 Wanks, 16 Dings but only seven Dongs, nine Bubs and nine Fucks, seven Pricks, six Fuckers, five GOEBBELSES, four Fluxes, three Cocks, a pair of Titts, a solitary Pecker and one lonely Frigger, but not a single HITLER. While we're exploring this subject, there are three DIETER ROTHS (not related, so far as I know), one EMMETT WILLIAMS (the one and only), but no ROBERT FILLIOU, no DANIEL SPOERRI, no TOPOR. The closest thing to a *Topography of Chance* is a *Topographie des Terrors*. (Not to be re-anecdoted, I pray.) (EW 1995)

h. We have. (MG/AB 1995)

i. Curiously enough, I was afflicted with the same malady in June 1966, and was likewise close to death's door. Towards the end of May, I accompanied BROOKLYN JOE JONES to an exhibition called "New Art for New Jersey" in Hoboken, where JOE was exhibiting three of his electrified violins which play inside brightly coloured plastic Japanese bird cages. Bored with the proceedings at the gallery, JOE and I left to find the nearest bar, which turned out to be rather far away. After several beers we set out to find a more interesting place, and on the way passed the Hoboken Pig Store. Inside the window, next to an effigy of a pink pig, were three boxes each containing three bottles of Underberg bitters, in my opinion one of the highmarks of German civilisation. I went inside and purchased all three boxes, and between glugs on the way back to the gallery I told JOE that Underberg was also one of DANIEL SPOERRI'S favourite beverages, that SPOERRI, GEORGE BRECHT and I once drank ourselves into insensibility by consuming five or six dozen bottles of the stuff in a Cologne hotel room, and that SPOERRI once wired me (while I was finishing the English translation of the *Topography* in Germany) to send him 50 bottles to be incorporated into a snare-picture called "Hommage à EMMETT WILLIAMS". After finishing the Underberg JOE and I returned to the Gallery — it was formerly a fire station — where we more than helped ourselves to champagne for four or five hours, during which time I made at least one profound comment on electronic art. A gushing dowager sporting a fur collar, despite the time of year, remarked that JOE'S composition "Winter Bird" was not functioning. I butted into the conversation and informed her that of course "Winter Bird" wasn't functioning because it was May. Soon after our friend TOM WASMUTH [see **36, n; Appendix V**] arrived, the gallery owner cut off the drinks, and JOE, TOM and I indignantly left. My memory fails after this, except that we were thrown out of one bar, and that we were run out of town by the police after I was caught shitting behind the bushes in a chic residential area. TOM and JOE were forced to clean up the pile and take it with them. They did not have it with them when we returned to New York, so the three of us assume that we got rid of it somewhere in Hoboken. DIETER ROTH was waiting for me when I got back home. He made a considerable fuss over my right hand, which was covered with a bloody rag. I washed the hand, applied a Band-Aid and went out — somewhere, somehow — with DIETER, allegedly to discuss the forthcoming publication of his selected writings. A week later the "scratch" turned out to be an ugly sore, and BARBARA MOORE, who prepared the manuscript for the publication of the American edition of the *Topography*, sent me to her doctor, who gave me a tetanus shot and applied a larger bandage. A week later, only minutes after I had told CHRISTO over the telephone that I was on my way to meet him at the CASTELLI Gallery, I felt a shooting pain in my arm, and noticed a red streak running all the way from wrist to elbow. I rushed out to ST. VINCENT'S hospital, where I was informed gently that it was a pretty bad case of blood-poisoning, and that if I had waited any longer it might have meant the loss of the arm. For two weeks I was on penicillin and pain killers, it was scraped and soaked daily, and my arm was immobilised in a sling for three weeks. The most embarrassing part of the episode is that I could not tell the doctors how the accident occurred. JOE remembered nothing, and TOM had only a faint recollection of my falling off a church wall. To one and all I said simply: "I slipped and fell in Hoboken." (EW 1995, written 1968)

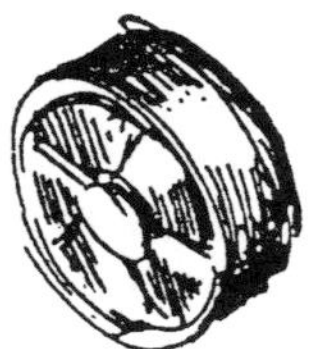

63. Roll of Scotch tape, used up, with which I sealed the surprise packages for KICHKA'S sister on her birthday [**2, 17, 22, 29, 45**].

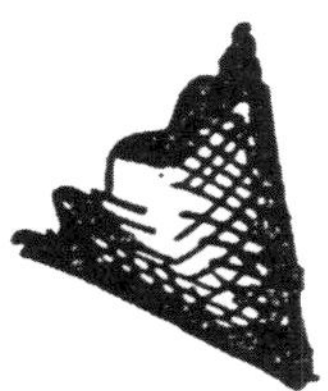

64. Corner of a half-litre container of milk, Blue Circle brand. This container is one that has taken my fancy, and contains, in effect, a lesson in applied geometry. Cylindrical at the start, it ends up a pyramid.[a]

a. From the *Petit Écho Diététique* No. 46, June 1960: Blue Circle sells milk in this special container at the same price as bottled milk. It is the ideal container for milk. This simple and hygienic modern method for distributing pasteurised milk [see **9**, **a**] comes to us from Sweden, a country with a very high dairy reputation [see **34D**] and in which hygiene has advanced as nowhere else.

Why the strange shape? We are often asked the reason for the curious shape. Those who have seen our packaging machine in operation have been left spellbound and fascinated by its technical and mechanical perfection. The qualifying adjective "ingenious" has often been pronounced: this is in no way an exaggeration. How simple,[b] how clean, how hygienic. It is not a prefabricated container, which is later filled; in a single operation, without handling or human intervention, the machine shapes the container around the milk, and seals it… vacuum-packed.

The container is not just a fancy carton: it is made from very special paper. The side that comes in direct contact with the milk is not coated with paraffin, but with pure polyethylene, used pre-eminently for packaging food products. It is absolutely harmless.

Why not a transparent container? Because light — natural or artificial — spoils milk, as well as many other products. The more exposure to light through a window, the sooner the exposed products deteriorate. Light "eats" colours, causes oxidation, corrosion and burning.

What does light do specifically to milk? In a matter of minutes it destroys vitamins A, C and B2, accelerates oxidation of fatty matter, and causes the distinctly unpleasant sensations known as "oxide taste" or "fishy taste" or "metallic flavour". (DS 1962)

b. What complications, what filth, what extremes! What a mingling and mushing! What excrements! (DR 1968)

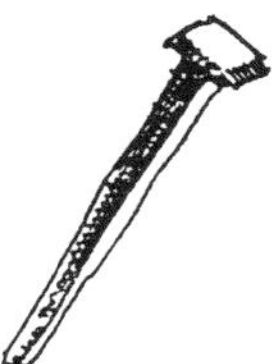

65. Nail, 3.5 cm. long, brought from Sweden, square. In France, as far as I have been able to find out, nails are round and make wood fart.[a] Square nails are the only ones that don't have this defect, as ULTVEDT pointed out to me.

a. *Péter* means "to fart" in French, and that is what the author says ULTVEDT told him square nails prevent wood from doing. But it seemed a harsh word for such an activity, and I queried another sculptor, LAURENCE WHITFIELD, in London, who obliged with the following data:

Nope, I ain't never heard of any wood that farts. I've known wood that splits, warps, dries in, swells out, twists, cracks, shakes and runs, but no sir I ain't never heard of any wood that farts. I thought I knew every kind of wood in GOD'S creation but this is a new one on me… Happy to say that I do know something about your other query, though. I think the term "square nail" is a misnomer though there is an actual square nail made, which is used largely in packing-case manufacture, but I don't think that it has any advantages over the ordinary round nail, though perhaps it can be clenched over easier when it comes through the other side of the wood as it does in packing cases. But I think the ones you mean are called "cut nails" or "brads". Nails were at one time made individually by blacksmiths, each one beaten out on an anvil, and so they had square corners. The first machine-made nails were stamped out from sheets of steel and so these too had square corners, and because of their rough edges gripped the fibres of the timber well. They don't have a sharp point like wire nails have, but have a flat tip.

A thickish nail with a sharp point, when driven through a piece of timber, parts the fibres to allow the shaft of the nail through, but is really acting like a wedge and has a tendency to split the wood. With the cut nail, however, the square flat tip severs the fibres as it is driven in, in effect making a hole for itself, and so this lessens the chances of splitting, anyoldhow, that's enough about nails. Tap-Tap-Tap... Q: What is a grub screw? A: A poke in the lunch hour. (EW 1966)

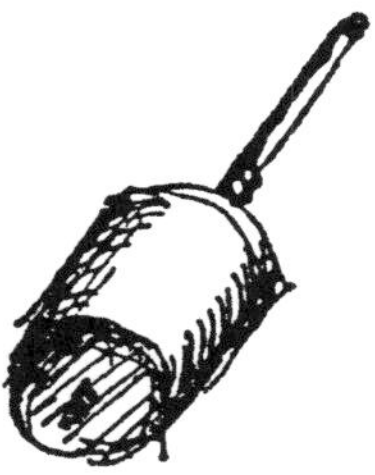

66. Ordinary cork,[a] on a corkscrew, the missing handle of which was broken off a long time ago. I have continued using it with the aid of pliers because I keep forgetting to get a new one.

a. The French word for cork is *liège*, but the Flemish city has no more to do with the bark of the cork-oak than has County Cork (which means swamp). Yet the ordinary cork (*bouchon ordinaire en liège*)[b] gave SPOERRI an opportunity to digress on the contents of the right pocket of his black suit coat in an essay printed in a special number of the *Daily Bul* (published at La Louvière, Belgium) devoted to "A Stethoscopic Examination of the Belgian Continent". During this embryonic strip tease the author commented that the "*bouchon ordinaire en liège*" in his pocket "is not Belgian because it is stamped with the words 'fine wine'."

The same black coat and the suit pants as well were submitted to a more thoroughgoing strip tease in Vienna. The summer of 1963 I accompanied SPOERRI to the IX. Internationale Kunstgespräch in the Austrian capital. We were installed in the apartments of prince-bishops at the Stift Klosterneuburg, where we plotted our strategy in baroque splendour. The title of the lecture-event was "Vortrag Über Das, Was im Augenblick zu Sagen Wäre, Mir Aber Vielleicht Nicht Einfällt". SPOERRI removed the contents of his pockets and discussed each item in the fashion of the *Topography*. While he lectured away (this was 9 a.m. Sunday morning, and we had been swimming nude in the Danube only a few hours before) I played a taped concert of music ranging from rock and roll to Romanian love ballads, served beer to everyone in the audience, took photos, passed out hard-boiled eggs, refilled the beer cups from time to time, gave away cigarettes, bonbons, lollipops and bubble-gum, interrupted him when he omitted what I considered relevant data (much in the fashion of my notes to this volume), handed out copies of the *Topography* to the spectators page by page, conducted a lottery (won by ARNULF RAINER) and presented everyone an autographed photo of SPOERRI and myself. SPOERRI was brilliant. Then why did I interrupt him, and drown out his words? Well, what can be more boring than an art lecture? Anyway, it was a perfect collaboration. And even the Jesuit MONSIGNOR PROFESSOR DR OTTO MAURER, who every Sunday spellbinds the faithful from the pulpit of ST. STEPHAN'S Cathedral, found it "amusing nonsense" (*charmante blödelei*).

I might add that in May 1965, after his return from New York, SPOERRI discarded his famous black suit, which I salvaged from the trash pile and wore during the translation of the greater part of this *Topography*. (EW 1966)

b. Excerpt from an inventory of my right jacket pocket. I did not buy the jacket in Belgium, and I would never have written this text if ROBERT FILLIOU had been in Belgium.

a) GREETINGS CARD from someone I don't know, although he took the trouble to gum a photo-portrait on it in place of his signature. He cannot be a Belgian even if, as KICHKA opines, he looks like a Belgian.

b) CORK (*bouchon de liège*) which cannot come from Belgium because it is inscribed with the words "*Vin fin*".

c) NOTE bearing the telephone number (GOB 4128) of the restaurant Les Cinq Billards which cannot be found in Belgium, but only in the Contrescarpe, Paris 5. The note is to remind me to phone KICHKA. She was neither in the Contrescarpe, though, nor in Belgium, but rather "very sick" — a piece of news that later proved to be false.

d) SWISS 1,000-FRANC NOTE, roughly 12,000 Belgian francs, half of the costs for my journey to New York that I have been about to embark on for the last three months.[c] The journey is neither to Niort — as DUFRÊNE keeps telling everybody — nor to Belgium.

e) KEY to KICHKA'S front door. She does not live in Belgium, has no wish to live in Belgium, and wouldn't even consider ever living in Belgium. But under no circumstances will she give me the key to her room. She says that that would make her "embarrassed".

f) LIPSTICK made of coconut butter, not Belgian, trademark Lip Aide, from ROGER & GALLET (protects your lips and keeps them soft and fresh).

g) SMALL FATHER CHRISTMAS made of wood, 30 cm. tall and 18.5 cm. wide, with a solid German — and certainly not Belgian — look to it. KNUT left it here today for me to repair. CLAUDE RIVIÈRE, the Belgian art critic, would have used the word *fixer*.**d**

h) SMALL SCREW coated in white plastic, definitely not Belgian. How did it come to be in my pocket — the right pocket of my black jacket which I did not buy in Belgium?

DANIEL SPOERRI, 20.1.1964, 11:30 p.m.

P.S. I dictated this text to DUFRÊNE and then read it out to KICHKA ("It's good, so long as the cork hasn't been inserted intentionally"), then GINETTE DUFRÊNE ("The Belgians will never accept that"), and then I put it in my right jacket pocket which… etc.… but not in Belgium. (DS 1968)

c. Aha, quite colossal! The idea that the earth there where it is coated in shadows — from the things which stand around and live on it — is more earth than there where it has no shadows — where it is coated in light and not shadows. Or the earth as a volcano which, as something medium-sized does not have any stature — for comparisons with things large or small — and which, being less than medium-sized, is — when compared with largeness as such — just a tiny little phut. That defies all description! (DR 1968)

d. Why? (DR 1968)

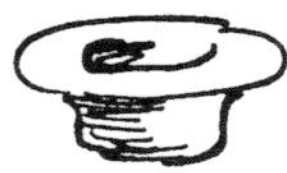

67. Plastic bottle-stopper, tricoloured, red–white–yellow [**3**, **25**, **34L**, **49**, **57**].

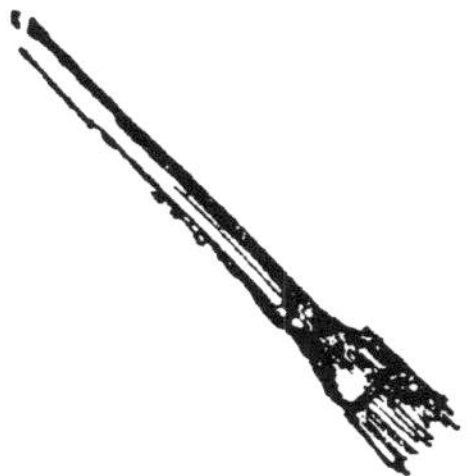

68. Paint brush, 28 cm. long, bought at the paint shop opposite the Greek restaurant on the Rue DESCARTES, the owner of which has called me Mr Constanza ever since he learned that I am Romanian by birth. The Romanian port of the same name caused his ears to be boxed when he was a schoolboy in Athens and wasn't able to solve a textbook problem about seamen making purchases in Constanza; ever since, Romania for him has equalled Constanza. This brush replaced another of the same size on a snare-picture called "Édition MAT" [**20**, **34E**], now in TINGUELY'S possession, so named because all the tools and other material used to make the objects in the MAT collection are on it. The first brush was lost during the Nouveaux Réalistes exhibition at the Galerie J. in June 1961.[a]

a. Two brushes wanted to demonstrate here by two means how one avoids living in a trap — either by evading it (the first) or by avoiding it (the second). And one might be forgiven for thinking that if they have not been found again (the first) or glued tight (the second) they will live happily ever after in liberty. But then you see straight away that the two of them are once again caught in a trap, cosily next to each other, on the same page of the book. (DR 1968)

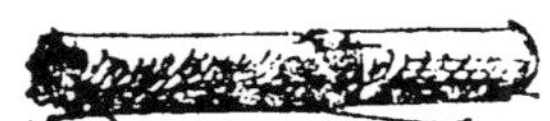

69. Aluminium tube full of pistachio-green Dolorostan[a] pills[b] bought while I was vacationing[d] in Nice after a sudden attack of rheumatism that seemed all the more violent because it was my first. After three days I went to see a doctor who told me the pills were "not worth shit" and that there was nothing more effective against rheumatism than plain old aspirins.

a. Inscription on the tube:

"Pain-chasing Dolorostan / Directions for use: 2 to 6 pills daily before meals. For gout, rheumatism, sciatica, arthritis and affections of the liver and kidneys. Dosage: Extr. graminis 0.008g — extr. fraxini 0.024g — extr. sarothamhi 0.0064g — extr. juniperi 0.019g — extr. hyascyami 3 millig. 2 — extr. sarsaparilloe 0.0011g — extr. sassafras 0.012g — extr. scilloe 0.012g — extr. convallariae 0.002g — extr. guaiaci 0.0064g — natr. salicylicum 0.05g ½ — natr. bromatum 0.02g (per tablet). DUMONTIER Laboratories, Rouen, France."

(In addition, there is a pretty little picture of a chapel on a mountain slope.) (DS 1962)

b. In all likelihood tablets.[c] (DR 1968)

c. It gives me a big headache to think that I made a mistake, but since I have no Dolorostan *pilules* (*sic!*) on hand I'll cure myself by thinking that DIETER'S brash note is really the answer to the question "Upon what did GOD inscribe the Ten Commandments?" and belongs in another book. (EW 1995)

d. *sic!* (DR 1968)

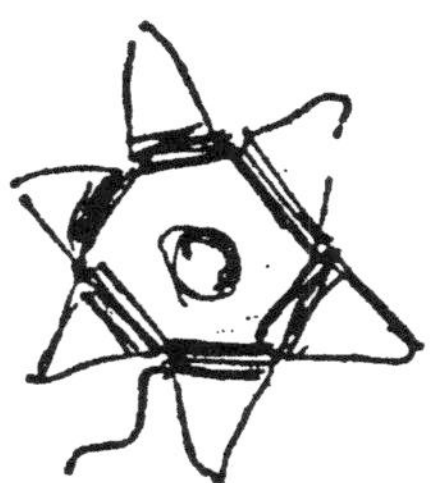

70. A spool that isn't one but a cardboard star of black thread [**39**] bought several days ago at my newsdealer's, as well as a needle. At Les Cinq Billards café [see **3, b**], where I went after making the purchase, I met ANNIE, a young woman of the quarter: seeing me with these two objects, she offered to sew on the button missing from my fly[a] [see **66, a**]. She started at once, on the spot, which reminded MADELEINE the waitress that one day back in the Auvergne she sewed two buttons on a customer's fly, that it was difficult to do without touching it, and that everybody had laughed.

a. I recall the teacher in grade school, HERR MOLL, who never remembered to button his fly after going to the lavatory. Our big pleasure consisted in pointing out to him: "You left something open, HERR MOLL" — which never failed to embarrass him very much.

At the house of my brother, a future minister who teaches school in the mean time,[b] I copied down this composition of one of his students, KÄTHI HELD, a young girl of 14, considered the brightest student in the class:

I want to be a seemstress. That is a nice job. You can sit in the room and still earn something in sumer and winter. Only it is expensive to learn about 3 years that is a long time. To learn it right. It is hard but even so it is still nice. That would be my wish when I am out of school and could learn to sew. It takes pashents and you have to try hard.[c] (DS 1966)

b. Today, 29 September 1968, he is a minister! (DR 1968)

c. KÄTHI'S composition was translated from the German by my daughter PENELOPE, age 12. Instructed *not* to better what she called "very bad German", she attempted to render it in "very bad English". I find the result very satisfactory, although my daughter LAURA is puzzled that such sloppy writing is going to be published.

To return to the subject of HERR MOLL'S fly:[d] my son EUGENE one Thanksgiving Day convulsed a dinner guest by pointing his finger and shouting "One two three four five six seven eight nine ten — the hot dog stand is open." (EW 1966)

d. Much ado about strip tease, EMMETT! (DR 1968, in English in the original)

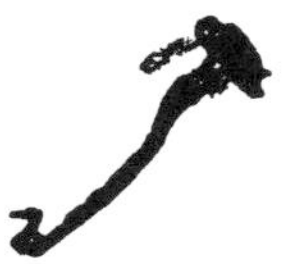

71. Rusty nail[a] [65].

a. *La même nuit où RAYMOND HAINS me parla [3, **e**] pendant qu'il me disait au sujet de ce clou, en réponse à ma question sur son idée du clou de la Palissade: "Quand ma Palissade est au clou, ma tante est au Mont de Piété," ANNETTE, la propriétaire du café de la rue THOUIN où nous nous trouvions alors par coïncidence, racontait à un client: "… et moi je traversais les clous en dehors des clous, alors le flic me rappelle et me dit: 'Vous allez faire le passage des clous dix fois' — alors à la dixième fois je suis partie en biais sortant des clous — j'étais terrible quand j'étais petite."* [b] (DS 1962)

b. This note has been kept in the original French for three reasons: it abounds in untranslatable puns, shows how the author handles his adopted language, and affords students of French an opportunity to show off. But mostly for the first reason. (EW 1966)

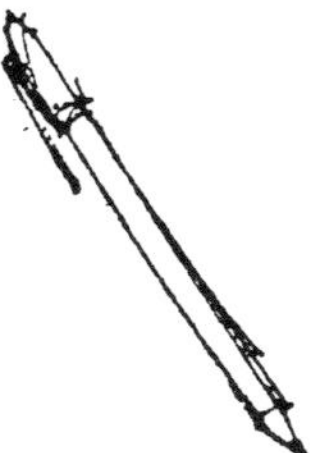

72. Ball-point pen, Bic brand, black ink, with grooved no-slip grip, which says nothing to me except something I prefer to keep absolutely to myself, for the sake of propriety. I am in the process of using it while writing these very lines.[a]

  a. I am writing these lines on ARNAR'S ERIKA. (DR 1968)

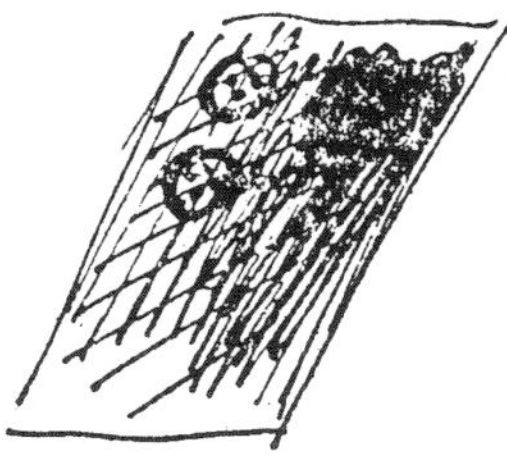

73. Small white card to which nine white shirt buttons were originally sewed; only two of them remain[a] [**47**, **58**, **59**]. The card is torn at one corner and partly covered with crumpled silver paper.

    a. Unencumbered note (alleviated card). (DR 1968)

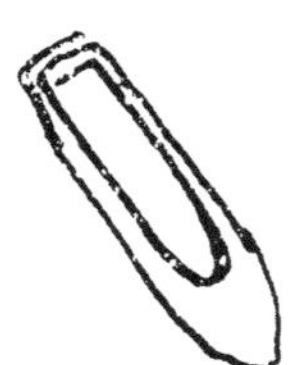

74. Paper clip.[a]

a. "trom•bone\ (ˈ) träm¦bõn, (ˌ) trem'bõn\ *n* -s [It, aug. of *tromba* trumpet, of Gmc origin; akin to OHG *trumpa, trumba,* trumpet — more at TRUMP (trumpet)] 1 a (1): a brass wind instrument that has a cupped mouthpiece, that consists of a long cylindrical metal tube bent twice upon itself ending in a bell and that has its first crook as a movable slide thereby permitting the player to control the length of the vibrating column and produce any pitch within its compass of E to b_b' — compare VALVE TROMBONE (2): a player on this instrument b: a large-scale pipe-organ stop of a quality similar to that of the trombone 2: an early blunderbuss having a large trumpet-shaped muzzle 3: a U-shaped section that resembles the slide of a trombone and that adjusts tuning in a wave-guide or coaxial-line circuit."

— WEBSTER'S *Third New International Dictionary*, G. & C. Merriam Co., Publishers of the Merriam-WEBSTER Dictionaries, 1961

(None of these trombones, but a paper clip.)[b] (DS 1966)

b. Unfortunately for the English and American reader, a paper clip in the shape shown at **74** on the topographic map [see endpapers] is called a *trombone* in French; I say unfortunately, because it deprives him of the lusty exchange between PIERRE RESTANY[c] and SPOERRI that appeared in the original French edition of the *Topography*. To supplement the definitions of *trombone* in the *Petit LAROUSSE* and the *Petit LITTRÉ*, both of which standard French dictionaries ignore the contemporary commercial and administrative use of the word, RESTANY suggested the following:

A clasp or holder for letters, bills, clippings etc., made of metal or plastic, bent twice upon itself (the large crook embracing the smaller one), the shape of which resembles the musical instrument from which the name is derived. Use: place the edges of the papers to be clasped or held together between the two crooks until the upper extremity of the trombone is level with the edges of the papers; to remove, turn rather than pull the trombone to avoid puncturing the papers. Historical: this type of fastener (certainly posterior to the war of 1914-18: GUILLAUME APOLLINAIRE did not know of it) has forced out of use[i] such anterior methods of ligature as paste, wire, pins. Its predominancy is nevertheless placed in question at the present time…[j] above all by the automatic stapler, although this method has the distinct disadvantage of marking the paper in the form of two holes approx. 10 mm. apart and the size of a pinhead…[k]

I should like to point out that the LAROUSSE *Dictionnaire Moderne Français-Anglais* does list the administrative and commercial use of *trombone*, an insight I attribute to the genius of ROGER SHATTUCK whose hand I detect (rightly or wrongly) in the more interesting entries of this useful work. (EW 1966)

c. The following letter from PIERRE RESTANY, in which he criticises my vocabulary, was printed on the wraparound of the first edition of the *Topography*:

Can Day, AMÉLIE-les-Bains, 30-12-61

Salut!

The *Topography* holds up briskly under a second reading in the calm of the Pyrénées. I have not succeeded, however, in digesting the term "*anecdotée*" (*Topographie Anecdotée du Hasard*). After an extensive examination of the *Grand LAROUSSE Encyclopédique* in seven volumes I point out for your benefit:

1 — that the orthography *anecdoté, ée*, which presupposes the verb *anecdoter* (non-existent), is not listed, and that it is thus necessary to consider it a neologism of your invention, a rather inharmonious one.

2 — that the word *anecdote* in its original sense (from the Greek *anekdotos*) signifies "things unpublished": I forward this observation for your cogitation.[d]

3 — that there exists, on the other hand, the word *anecdotomanie*, from which one can very properly build *anecdotomaniaque*, and which means mania for research, for telling anecdotes. It offers, moreover, the advantage of being recognised by the Academy (in the spirit of a "*nouveau réaliste*").

PIERRE RESTANY (DS 1966)

d. During the course of a conversation on Feb. 15, 1962, KICHKA'S sister, told of EMMETT WILLIAMS'S declaration that "people will kiss your arse[e] for the next fifty years because of your book," suggested rephrasing the sentiment to read "people will kiss your book for the next fifty years because of your arse," adding that that is what happened to the MARQUIS DE SADE.[f] (DS 1966)

e. Figuratively speaking. (EW 1966)

f. BAZON JÜRGEN HERMANN JOHANNES VLADIMIR HANS JOACHIM PHOENIX PHLEBAS BROCK, who once started to translate the *Topography* into German, told me with enthusiasm several years ago, in an intellectual fashion I have never been able to understand (his thesis, "Die Kategorien der Selbstbestimmung und Fremdbestimmung des Geistes", helps confirm my incomprehension), that the *Topography* represents the materialisation of a method of writing propagated by JAMES JOYCE. I replied that I had never read JOYCE, but that I knew from an anecdote about him that I read in *Der Spiegel* that JOYCE had never read his colleague MARCEL PROUST. Some weeks later I found in *l'Express* of Feb. 15, 1962 the same anecdote: according to JOYCE, the conversation at the meeting of the two geniuses was restricted to the word "No." PROUST asked JOYCE if he knew the Duke of ————. JOYCE answered no. Their hostess asked PROUST if he had read such and such a passage in *Ulysses*, to which PROUST answered no.

According to another version of the meeting, PROUST regretted that he did not know JOYCE'S work, and JOYCE said he had never read PROUST, and the conversation stopped there. (DS 1966)

The *Topography* also reminded certain people of the *nouveau roman*, which I knew no better. So in order to find out what it was about, I bought a book by ROBBE-GRILLET (I think it was called *Jealousy*), but I didn't continue after reading three pages. All that I read from cover to cover is *Der Spiegel*[g] — which is where I read the JOYCE-PROUST anecdote the first time — or thrillers, like *The Woman Trap* I am reading at the moment, and last week *Stick to the Compass*. (DS 1968)

g. I must ask SPOERRI whether he still (in 1968) reads *Der Spiegel* from cover to cover.[h] (DR 1968)

h. At present I'm reading *The Savage Mind* (*La Pensée sauvage*) by CLAUDE LÉVI-STRAUSS, along with *On Aggression* by KONRAD LORENZ. (DS 1968)

i. Is it possible that "use" is something hollow (perhaps even with a bottom) in which something can be put? It must definitely be hollow, for otherwise nothing could be forced out of it (and it must in fact have a bottom, for otherwise what was inside it would fall through and out of it before it was forced out) — or has the "use" perhaps no bottom after all, i.e. has the stuff inside not been placed but stuffed inside it so that it sits there tight — without falling out on its own — until it is forced out? (DR 1968)

j. This question also seems to be something hollow, for it seems that the predominancy can be placed inside it. Without now placing the question — is a question something hollow? — itself in question (and perhaps additionally the question: what is a predominancy, in contrast, say, to a postdominancy?), one can say here words to the effect that it's impossible to say whether the question has a bottom. Hence one cannot tell whether the predominancy stands in the question like a flower in a vase. Nor can one say whether or not the question has no bottom, so that the predominancy (of the existence that is placed in question) stands on something other than the bottom of the question: a table or whatever? And whether it leans on the walls of the question from inside, or perhaps stands bolt upright (on the table, in the hollow question, with the question also on the table) and does not even touch the question? (DR 1968)

k. Yet another something that is hollow, and one asks oneself: perhaps all this stuff here (use, question, vase and so on) is not merely hollow, but actual holes? That would be the hollowness of the hollowness, that which had been holed out of the hollowed objects. Is it not the case that one can always still put something into everything? So that everything is at least something hollow? And if one then goes so far as to say: the whole caboodle, all this stuff, is not just hollow but holes! Then one asks oneself: if things are holes, then holes in what? (DR 1968)

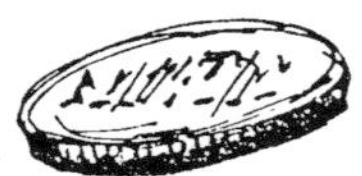

75. Bronze token[a] inscribed on one side "Métamatic — TINGUELY — July 1959 — Paris" and on the other side "Métamatic" across the middle, and in a circle around the rim "VIVA EVA —YVES — HENRI — IRIS — XAVIER — PONTUS." They could be purchased for 3 francs during the exhibition of Métamatic[b] machines at IRIS CLERT'S gallery in June 1959, an exhibition that had wide repercussions, particularly in the press, which wrongly interpreted the machines as only a joke at the expense of abstract painting.

a. Aha, the pecuniary! The fact that it glitters and rolls — and yet lies there and grows mouldy — and that it lives and breeds — and yet is unborn and hasn't even an ass — that's its secret! The fact that they who have the eyes to see it, that even the glittering light of the stars which roll about in the heavens above tells of shit and mould, that's what's so astonishing! (DR 1968)

b. "Letters patent / P.V. 798.710 / No. 1.237.934 / International classification: B 43 h–B 44 d / French Republic / Industrial Ministry / Bureau of Patent Rights / Drawing and painting machine / JEAN TINGUELY, Swiss resident / Applied for June 26, 1959, at 1700 hours, Paris. Issued June 27, 1960 / (Letters patent of which the issuance has been postponed in pursuance of article 11, section 7, of the law of July 5, 1884, modified by the law of April 7, 1902) / The present invention has as its objective a machine of simple construction, for drawing or painting in a manner which, in practice, is wholly automatic, human intervention being limited to the selection of one or several

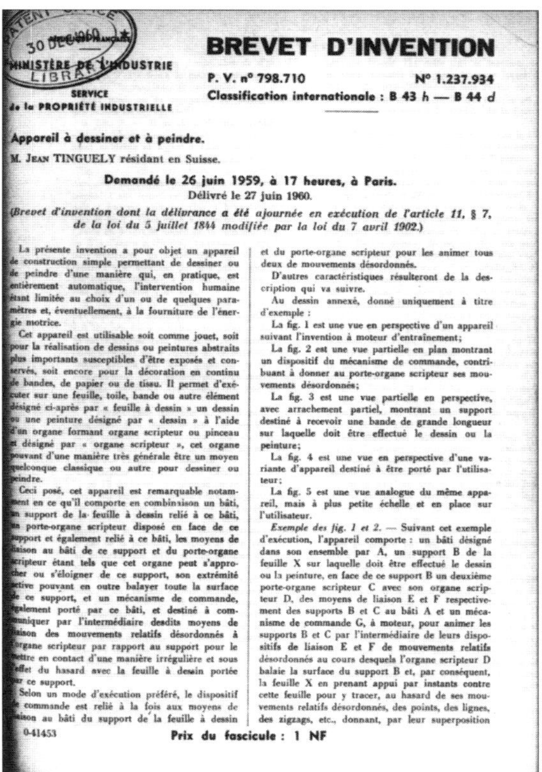

parameters and, on occasion, furnishing motor energy.

"This machine can be used as a toy, for the realisation of abstract drawings and paintings capable of being exhibited and preserved, for the continuous decoration of rolls of paper or cloth. It permits the execution on a sheet of paper, canvas, roll or other element referred to hereinafter as 'drawing sheet' a drawing or painting referred to as 'drawing' by means of a writing instrument or brush and referred to as 'writing instrument', this instrument being able in a very general way, accepted or other, to draw and paint. This granted, the apparatus is noteworthy in that it comprises in combination a frame, a support[c] for the drawing sheet attached to this frame, a writing-instrument holder placed in front of the drawing-sheet support and also connected to the frame, the means of liaison between the frame of the drawing-board support and the writing-instrument holder being such that the writing instrument can approach or withdraw from the support, its active extremity being able to sweep across the surface of the support, and a control mechanism, also attached to the frame, and destined to

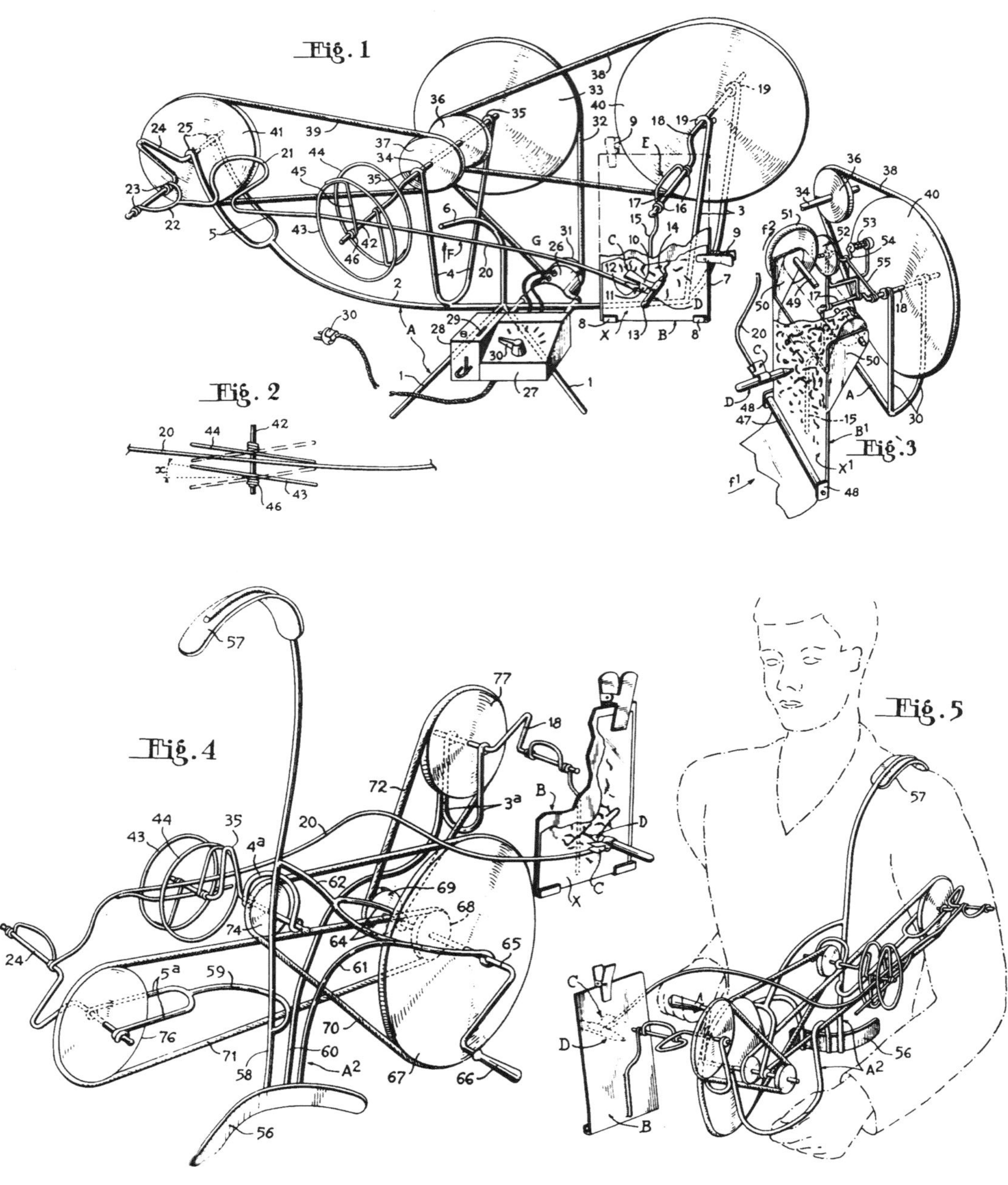
Fig. 1
Fig. 2
Fig. 3
Fig. 4
Fig. 5

communicate, through the intermediation of said means of liaison, connected unsystematic movements to the writing instrument in relation to the frame to place it in contact in an irregular manner and under the influence of chance with the drawing sheet held by the support.

"According to a preferred method of execution, the control mechanism is attached to the means of liaison, to the frame of the drawing-sheet support and the writing-instrument holder, to impel both with unsystematic movements.

…

"In another variant, the machine is portable, its frame adapted to fit easily the body of the person carrying it.

…

"JEAN TINGUELY (by proxy): LAVOIX, attorney-at-law" [Excerpt] (DS 1962)

c. And once again we are very concerned. Sometimes about the frame, sometimes about the support, sometimes about the drawing, sometimes about the sheet. Sometimes about the support in its frame, sometimes about the drawing sheet in its support stockings, sometimes about what is suspended in the holder, sometimes about what is held in the suspender. Sometimes about the stocking suspender with its stocking wearer inside, sometimes about the stocking suspender with its stocking wearer outside, sometimes about the stocking on its suspender on its wearer, sometimes about the foot on its bearer inside of the stockings with the suspenders outside of their wearer with his brain up above from which a cloud ascends on which is written, *Das Wandern ist des Müllers Lust*: "rambling is the miller's great delight".**d** (DR 1968)

d. In the German original of this note, a pun is being made once again on the word *Sockel*, used here to mean "frame". (MG 1995)

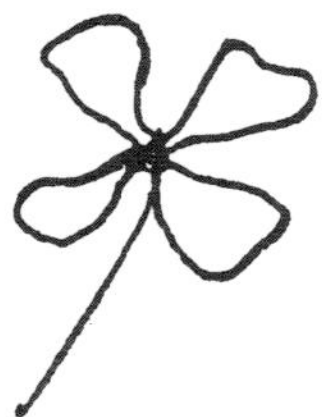

76. Four-leaf clovers, gilt, pinned to a small card that tells my fortune and describes the good-luck charm.[a] I got the small white rectangular card by taking a chance at a bakery at the Flea Market in the company of KICHKA and KICHKA'S sister, then instructor of English at a school in Dijon and now assistant professor at the University of Nantes, who provided the 10 centimes.

    a. Text of the card:

    "Don't let reversals upset you. React against the weaknesses you show from time to time. Avoid a person among your acquaintances who tries to learn your secrets in order to divulge them to others and harm you." (DS 1962)

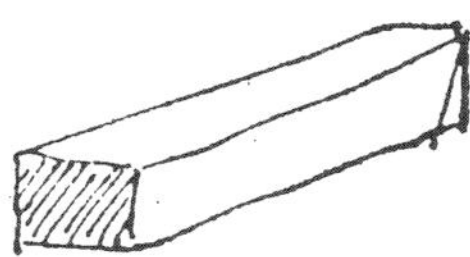

77. Cover[a] **for the plastic box** [61] containing the projection frames. On it, a Magic Marker [78].

a. When it turns dark it's because the plastic box has a non-transparent plastic cover (apart from the fact that it is itself opaque), and you are there inside and someone has put a cover on top. If the cover were transparent it would have remained light (even if the box itself was opaque). But it has turned dark, and you start to ask: Whether the darkness is a stone, whether you are also one, or whether perhaps the light is a stone? And how far the light (if it wasn't dark right now) would penetrate your body? If you were then to say, for example: The light brings the images! and also to think to yourself: It comes from the things, from this stuff here, and brings the stuff in the form of images! Then you put two and two together and ask yourself: What becomes of all the stuff that the light brings with it and stuffs in to me (especially when the light stuffs it in deep), am I then full of stuff? (DR 1968)

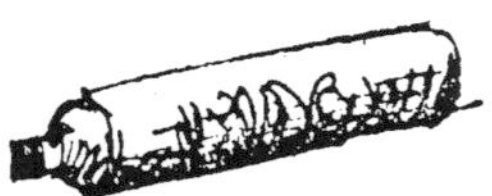

78. Magic Marker, black ink. The pictures exhibited at Galerie KOEPCKE [6] in Copenhagen were signed with it. I found it there, in the apartment of FILLIOU, who helped me write this text in French because I was born March 27, 1930, in Galati, Romania, and he was born Jan. 17, 1926, at Sauve (Gard).[a]

a. Thinking it might be diverting to review the facts of my life up to the present, I asked ROBERT FILLIOU to write my biography from details MICHÈLE RICARD [**25, a**] received from my mouth:

DANIEL was born DANIEL ISAAC FEINSTEIN March 27, 1930, at Galati, a Romanian port on the Danube. He lived there until he was 12. His father, a Jew converted to Protestantism, had founded a mission there to convert other Jews. After his death at the hands of the Germans in 1941, the family fled to Switzerland, where DANIEL was adopted by his maternal uncle, PROF. DR DR H.C. DR H.C. DR H.C. THEO-

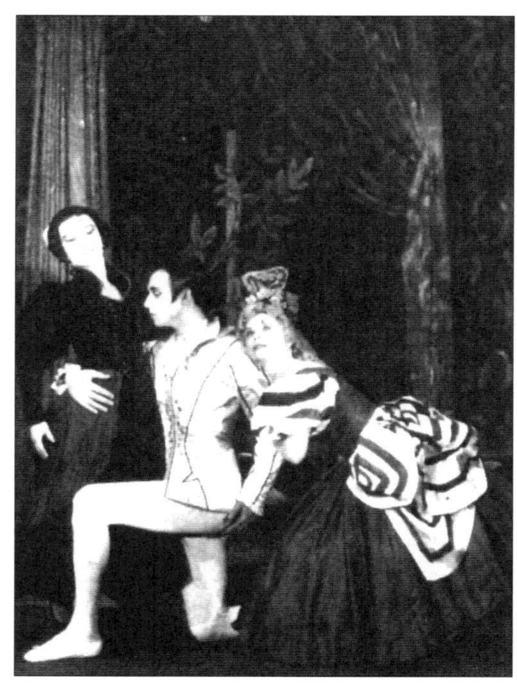

PHIL SPOERRI, rector of the University of Zurich. He was a bad student, and was apprenticed to an import house. He stole large quantities of postage stamps and was dismissed. He became an apprentice bookseller in a bookstore that also sold stuffed animals. He stole a mounted frog and was dismissed again, which pleased him because, recently converted, he had decided to become a missionary in Tibet. But he lost his faith after reading COUÉ'S "Autosuggestion" at a model farm where he had been apprenticed while waiting to enter missionary school. He left the farm and headed for Basle where his family enrolled him in a commercial school. He was thrown out because he spent his time reading poetry (especially RILKE, HOFMANNSTHAL and STEFAN GEORGE). After that he lived alone, without a regular job, under the surveillance of the minors' control board, from whom he escaped many times during trips to Amsterdam, Paris and Marseilles. He stole fruit on the street, hired out as an unskilled labourer, waited tables at a café, and wrote poetry until all his manuscripts were stolen while he was sleeping under a bridge of the Seine, then stopped writing poetry altogether. He studied photography, but not for long. Then he started dancing nights in a Zurich jazz cellar, and shortly afterwards entered a school of classical dance, which he attended more or less regularly for two years. In 1952 he was in Paris studying classical dance, with PREOBRAJENSKA and mime with DECROUX. He guided tourists around Paris and escorted pilgrims to Lourdes. In Paris he renewed his acquaintance with TINGUELY, whom he had known in Basle. Together they conceived a colour ballet with mobile décor, which collapsed the day of the final rehearsal. In 1954 he was first dancer at the Bern Opera.[b] He staged several avant-garde plays ("The Bald Soprano" and "The Lesson" of IONESCO, PICASSO'S "Desire Trapped by the Tail" and works of TARDIEU, BECKETT and TZARA). He taught mime and jazz choreography, and directed several studies for the experimental theatre. In 1957 he became an assistant to GUSTAV RUDOLF SELLNER at the Landestheater in Darmstadt, Germany. He took part in the movement exhibition at the Hessenhuis in Antwerp, where he exhibited a wood sculpture transformable by the chance participation of spectators, and, with the help of TINGUELY, the Autotheatre, which turned the spectators into actors. This was in 1958, after he had published a series of articles with CLAUS BREMER on experimental theatre. In 1959 he left Darmstadt and went to Paris with VERA. The rest is in the *Topography*.[c] (DS 1966)

b. *Opposite*: DANIEL SPOERRI as first dancer at the Bern Opera in 1955 (*left*: SYBILLE SPALINGER, opera ballet master). (AB/MG 1995)

c. Not in *my* copy. (EW 1995)

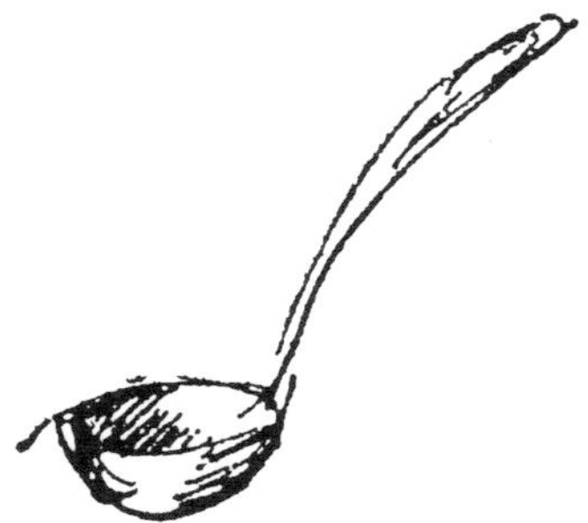

79. Tin sauce ladle rejected by KICHKA from a pile of shoemaker's tools with which she herself wanted to make a picture, all bought at the Flea Market for 25 francs.[a]

a. MONSIEUR RIES, whose sole trip outside of France was to Metz (part of Germany before 1914), and who now runs the café-grocery-telephone at Grégy-sur-Yerre where TINGUELY has a barn, and a former second-hand dealer who still knows a bargain when he sees one, says to me every time he sees me: "You have a small truck and you know the Flea Market so well, you ought to get into the second-hand business. You can't make anything out of art. But you'd make a good second-hand dealer. During the week you could drive around the countryside and visit farms — I can give you plenty of addresses — and on Sunday set up shop at the Flea Market and show off your things all cleaned up. You'll see, sometimes nothing happens, then all of a sudden, when you least expect it, zap! you'll have a wad in your pocket."[b] (DS 1966)

b. MONSIEUR RIES has been otherwise immortalised in another of SPOERRI'S works, the trilingual *L'Optique moderne* [see **Introduction I, d**], in which the author models something misnamed and mis-spelled "Assymetrical eye-blower".[c] This turns out to be a pair of eyeglasses with one powerful lens and one of plain glass ("Mister Ries model"), the type worn by the former second-hand dealer of Grégy-sur-Yerre, short-sighted in his right eye.

But perhaps the most spectacular of the spectacles demonstrated in this unusual book are "ROBERT FILLIOU'S glasses, reduced to powder, promised to the collection". Their

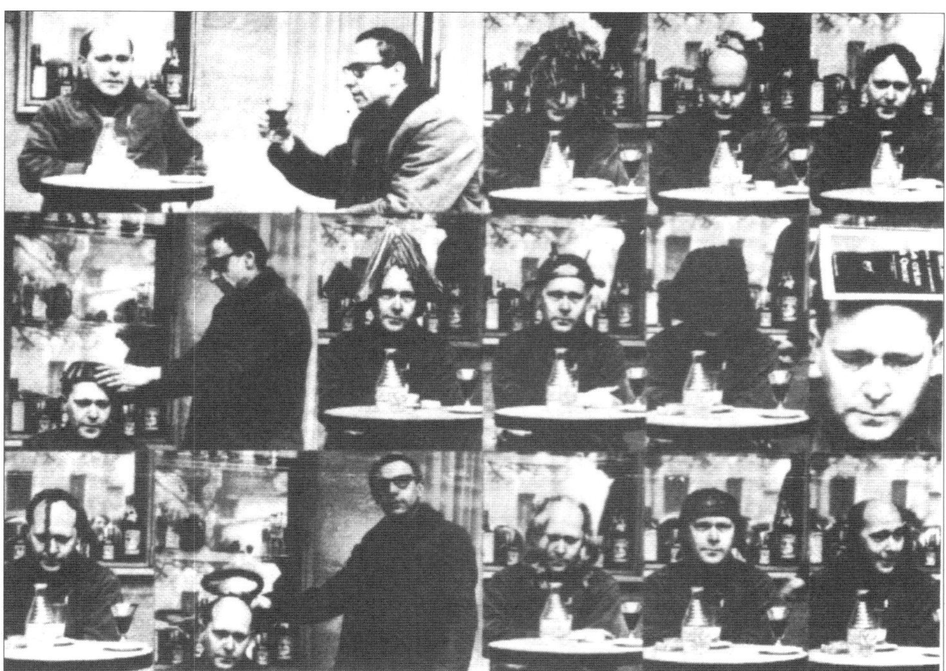

reduction to powder is shown in twenty-five photographs of "Thirteen Ways to Use EMMETT WILLIAMS' Skull", a composition by ROBERT FILLIOU. Here is the script:

On stage: EMMETT WILLIAMS, bald since the age of 17, designated by the initial E, and ROBERT FILLIOU, who has worn glasses since the age of 4, designated by the initial R.

E is seated on a chair. R stands behind him. From a bag, R takes a wig and places it on E's skull. R removes the wig, and replaces it with a second. He repeats this operation until he has placed the thirteenth wig on E's skull.

As R leans over to see how the thirteenth wig looks on E, E suddenly snatches the glasses off R's face and snaps them in two. Then he throws them on the ground. He stands up and stomps on them. He produces a grinder,**d** scoops up the remains of R's glasses, stuffs them into the grinder, and reduces them to powder. Next he takes an envelope from his pocket, pours the powdered glasses from the grinder into the envelope, extracts a piece of paper and a pen from his pocket and writes: "Dear DANIEL, here, to augment your collection, are FILLIOU'S glasses, reduced to powder."

R casts his eyes heavenward and intones: "Powder! Oh heavens!" E puts the letter in the envelope, seals it, stamps it, addresses it, then reads in a loud voice: "DANIEL SPOERRI, 24 Rue Mouffetard, Paris 5." E leaves, saying to R in parting: "I have to mail a letter."

And this really took place outside of the Chope, a café only a stone's throw from the Hotel Carcassonne, to the utter bewilderment of passers-by who thronged to watch (unknowingly) the perpetrators of this *Topography* at work. (EW 1966)

c. Although it is tempting to translate "Assymetrical eye-blower" as "Assymetrischer Augenbläser" (that would be the correct — i.e. not completely correct — mis-spelt translation), one feels compelled here to reproduce most exactly the German expression that was given for MONSIEUR RIES'S eyeglasses in *L'Optique moderne* that EMMETT mentioned earlier: *Assymetrisches Augenvergrößerungsglas (Modell des Herrn RIES)*. Once again, one can say in unison with EMMETT: misnamed and mis-spelt. (DR 1968)

d. The last sheep landed up in humanity's hands. They slit it open and put it to the knife. They carve it up, and share out the parts among themselves. Then one man says: "Let's make minced mutton!" "But we no longer have any cleavers or choppers," the others reply. The man answers back: "But we have the wolves!" **e** "Wolves?" the others reply, "but there are no more wolves either!" "'Sright, exterminated by mankind," says the man, "but the meat grinders, what about them?" "Ah, meat grinders, we've plenty of them." And everyone went home with their bits of lamb, and the lamb was put through the gorge of the grinder with vim and vigour.

There you are, in the end people are the sheep's wolf! (DR 1968)

e. The German word *Fleischwolf*, literally 'meat-wolf', means meat-grinder. It is often abbreviated simply to *Wolf*. (MG 1995)

80. Cigarette burn[a] on the first tracing of this *Topography*.

    a. *Publisher's note (1966)*: Illustration is manufactured by carefully burning the book[b] with a cigarette.

      b. Which book?[c] (DR 1968)

        c. Good question, DIETER. We've got to fight this book-burning syndrome. (EW 1995)

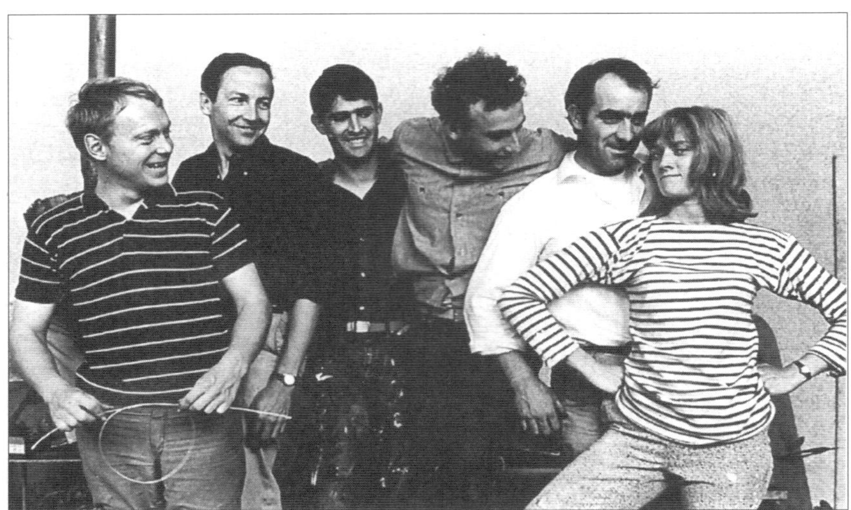

Group photographs, with names of artists in the *Topography* capitalised. *Above*: Dylaby Group, 1962: PER OLOF ULTVEDT, ROBERT RAUSCHENBERG, MARTIAL RAYSSE, DANIEL SPOERRI, JEAN TINGUELY, NIKI DE ST. PHALLE. *Below*: Antwerp, 1959: Frau Mack, Heinz Mack, Otto Piene, JEAN TINGUELY, DANIEL SPOERRI, POL BURY, YVES KLEIN, EMMETT WILLIAMS.

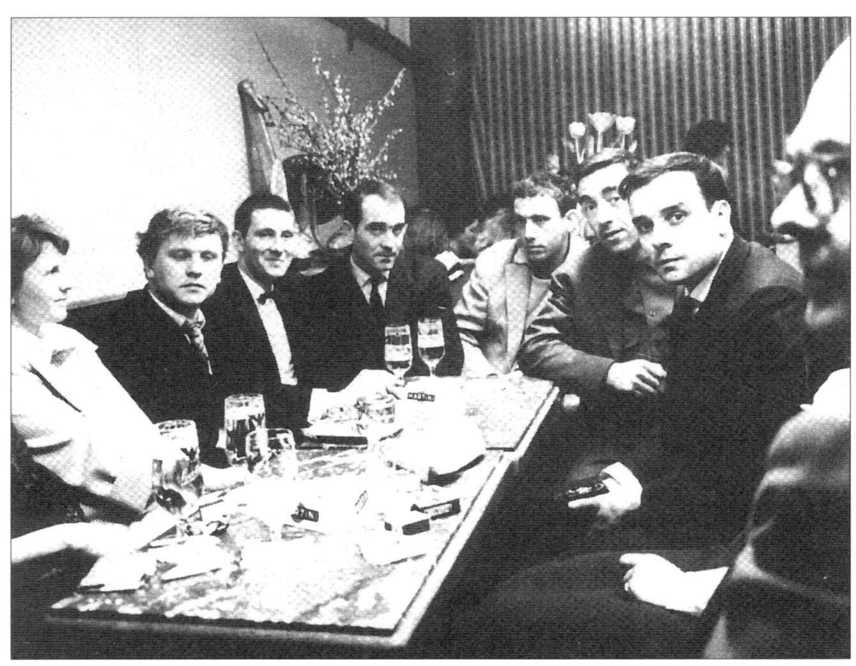

APPENDICES

APPENDIX I. TOPOGRAPHIC RELIEF INDEX

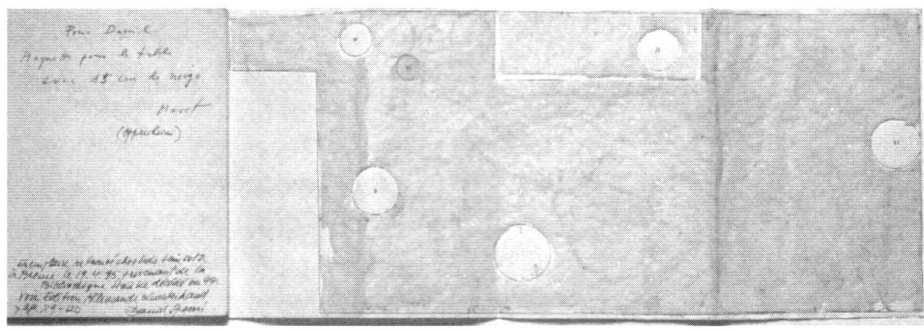

For the benefit of readers who have not seen MERET OPPENHEIM'S composition based on the relief features of this *Topography* (see **Introduction III, m,** and the maquette from March 1962, above), which consists of the topographic map covered with cotton representing 15 centimetres of snow, the contours of only those objects exceeding 15 centimetres in height cut out (underlined in the list below), here are the heights of all the objects,[a] measured at her request Feb. 28, 1962:

1. *ca.* 1.5 cm.	**21.** 7.3 cm.	<u>41 cm.</u> (with socket and bulb)	**62.** 12.3 cm.
1a. *ca.* 1–3 mm.	**22.** 1.5 mm.		**63.** 1.5 cm.
2. 2.8 cm. (egg cup)	**23.** 8.5 cm.	**45.** *ca.* 3 cm.	**64.** 1.2 cm.
ca. 5–6 cm. (egg cup with shell)	**24.** *ca.* 7.5 cm.	**46.** 1.5 cm.	**65.** 3 mm.
	25. 1 cm.	**46a.** 1.5 mm.	**66.** 2 cm.
3. <u>32 cm.</u>	**26.** 1.7 cm.	**47.** 2 mm.	**67.** 1 cm.
4, 4a. *ca.* 1 mm.	**27.** 2 cm.	**48.** 1.5 cm.	**68.** 1 cm. (on **45**; together *ca.* 4 cm.)
5. 0.5 mm.	**28.** 7.5 cm.	**49.** 1 cm.	
6. 6.9 cm.	**28a.** 0.0 mm.	**50.** 1.3 cm.	**69.** 2.4 cm.
7. 1.5 cm. ⎫ 1.65 cm.	**29.** 1 mm.	**51.** 3 mm.	**70.** 0.5 cm.
7a. 1.5 mm. ⎭	**30.** 7.3 cm.	**52.** 13 cm.	**71.** *ca.* 2 mm.
8. 6.1 mm.	**31.** *ca.* 10 cm.	**53.** *ca.* 7 cm.	**72.** 0.9 cm.
9. <u>21.5 cm.</u>	**32.** 1.3 cm.	**54.** *ca.* 4 mm.	**73.** *ca.* 3 mm.
10. 1.5 mm.	**33.** *ca.* 3.3 cm.	**55.** *ca.* 1 cm.	**74.** *ca.* 1 mm.
11. 13 cm.	**34.** 9.5 cm. ⎫ <u>32.8 cm.</u>	**56.** *ca.* 4 mm.	**75.** 2 mm.
12. 12.5 cm.	**35.** <u>23.3 cm.</u> ⎭	**57.** 1 cm.	**76.** *ca.* 0.5 cm.
13, 13a. 2.5 mm.	**36.** *ca.* 5 mm.	**58.** *ca.* 2 mm.	**77.** 2 cm.
14. 4.5 cm.	**37.** 1.7 cm.	**59.** *ca.* 2 mm.	**78.** 1.7 cm.
15. 7.3 cm.	**38.** 11.7 cm.	**60.** *ca.* 3–4 mm.	**79.** 3.5 cm.
16. <u>14.5 cm.</u> (cut out only partly)	**39.** 0.5 mm.	**61.** 4 cm.	**80.** 0.0 mm.
	40. 1 cm.		
17. *ca.* 2–3 mm.	**41.** 2.8 cm.		
18. <u>15 cm.</u>	**42.** 5.6 cm.		
19. 7.9 cm.	**43.** 3 cm.		
20. 11.2 cm.	**44.** <u>26 cm.</u> (bottle)		

a. Total height: 3812.62 mm. Average height: 44.33 mm.[b] (DR 1968)

b. Corrected total height: 167.7″. Corrected average height: 1.94″. (MG 1995)

APPENDIX II. DEVELOPMENT OF THE SNARE-PICTURE

1. *material*: Between 1957 and 1959 I published a journal for concrete and ideogrammatic poetry. Concrete inasmuch as the authors avoided any kind of subjective interpretation[a] — ideogrammatic because they primarily represented their ideas visually. Contributions were made by ROTH, WILLIAMS, LUCA, BREMER and myself, among others, and there were five issues.

In the game that was suggested in *material*, the reader was to assume the personal position that the author had vacated. As such, he was invited to participate as his own author. And why should the author force his personal views on the reader?

2. *Édition MAT*: Multiplication of artworks which move or can be changed. An attempt to multiply art outside of the customary methods of reproduction (printing, casting, copying etc.).[b] The inherent possibility of change in all of the works I produced made each number of a series an original. At the first exhibition of the *Édition MAT*, November 1959, I showed works by AGAM, BURY, DUCHAMP, GERSTNER, MAN RAY, ROTH, SOTO, TINGUELY and VASARELY.

Here the visitors became performers: either involuntarily (when their movements before the picture produced an apparent movement in the latter) or deliberately (when they were able to set the objects in motion themselves).

Were these multiples really originals? What is an artwork worth? Why not admit that an artwork has scarcely any value,[c] apart from one that you might give it? (The works of the *Édition MAT* were sold at a standard price, regardless of the artists' market value.)

Three ways of questioning marketable value:

a) At the MAT exhibition in London, March 1960, I built a machine from which the buyers had to draw lots to see whether a work would cost nothing or twice the price.

b) SINCLAIR BEILES exhibited a scribble in his hotel room in 1960 which was supposed to cost one pound. Beside it hung a framed pound note which could be bought for a penny. The purchaser had, however, to buy both. (Somewhat later I made a snare-picture out of a waitress's tray on which her tips for that day had been stacked; I sold it for twelve times the amount of the glued-on money.)

c) In Copenhagen, June 1961, ROBERT FILLIOU offered his works in exchange for things he needed at the time: a sack of potatoes, a bed, a residence permit, a crate of beer and so on. For one of the works he requested money.

3. *Exhibition Bewogen Beweging* (1961, Amsterdam, Stockholm and Louisiana): as an almost logical consequence — and conclusion — to the *Édition MAT*, an exhibition was organised with the aim of providing an overview of the fifty years' development of those artworks that move or can be altered.**d**

Again, the visitors were incorporated so directly into the exhibition that they became performers. Does the viewer in an exhibition *have* to act passively? Are quiet and meditation**e** indispensable requirements for understanding art?

4. *Snare-picture*: objects found in chance positions, in order or disorder (on tables, in boxes, drawers etc.) are fixed ("snared") as they are. Only the plane is changed: since the result is called a picture, what was horizontal becomes vertical. Example: remains of a meal are fixed to the table at which the meal was consumed, and the table hung on the wall. I first exhibited pictures of this kind at the *Festival d'Art d'Avant-garde*, Paris 1960.

5. *Snare-picture squared* (snare-picture of a snare-picture): the tools used to fix the objects in a snare-picture are themselves snared along with the objects, in the position they occupied at a certain "snared" moment.

6. In the "Grocery Store" at the Galerie KOEPCKE in Copenhagen in October 1961, groceries were recognised as individual works of art without being incorporated into an assemblage. They were stamped "Caution, Work of Art" and bore my certifying signature [see **6**]. Nothing else about them was changed, and the price was the current market price of each article.

7. Dark glasses equipped with needles to poke out the eyes made necessary and possible the recreation of objects through memory and the imagination. The objects found on a table, instead of being fixed and exhibited, are simply indicated on a numbered topographic map, with anecdoted descriptions of the objects in an accompanying text. Example: the present volume.

8. Once the creation of objects through the imagination is accepted (at first the imagination was totally rejected), the false snare-picture enters. It consists of imagining and composing a situation in which the details appear to be a chance situation, so that the result cannot be distinguished optically from a real snare-picture. Example: a play-pen with scattered objects

and toys that a baby might have left in disorder, except that the pen was never used by a baby.

9. Working with chance situations implies the acceptance of chance as a collaborator after the initial result has been achieved, of transformations due to time, weather, corrosion, dirt etc. Example: the rats who devoured the organic matter on two of my snare-pictures at Galleria SCHWARZ in Milan [see **38, f**] have been accepted as collaborators. Taboos have as their objective the preservation of traditions and forms, an objective that I reject: at the Galerie KOEPCKE "Grocery Store", sandwich rolls, in which garbage and junk were mixed during the kneading, were baked and sold as "taboo catalogues".

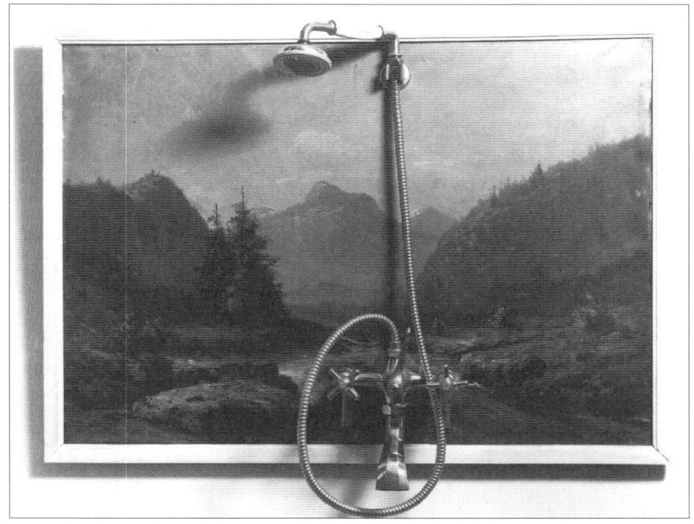

DANIEL SPOERRI, *The Shower, détrompe-l'œil*, 1961,
Musée Nationale d'Art Moderne, Paris (Centre POMPIDOU).

10. When the supporting element of a snare-picture represents something (if it is a realist painting, for instance) a relationship is automatically established between the snared objects and the supporting element. This relationship destroys the false perspective of the representation: a deliberate choice of added objects interprets, profanes and changes the *détrompe-l'œil*: a romantic view of the Alps — a valley with a stream flowing towards the spectator — is augmented by bath-taps and a shower.

11. Chance and creation merge, the difference[f] between the snare-picture and the false snare-picture gradually disappears when the real snare-picture is multiplied by false ones. In the "art multiplier", a chance situation is fixed to a mirror, and the same situation is reflected into another mirror joined to the first by hinges. In addition, the objects are reflected and multiplied in proportion to the angle at which the mirrors are set.

12. Everything is a snare-picture, anybody[g] can choose a chance situation and make a picture out of it. To demonstrate this, I accepted an invitation to exhibit at the Danish "Salon de Mai" in 1962 on the condition that ADDI KOEPCKE be allowed to choose and fix situations in my name. The following certificate of guarantee was printed for the occasion:

BREVET DE GARANTIE
TABLEAU - PIÈGE

Fabriqué sous licence par : ....

....

Titre : ....

Date : .... Lieu : .... Dim. : ....

en foi de quoi - pour que ceux qui ont des yeux voient -

j'autentifie :

....

(DANIEL SPOERRI)

13. The foregoing principles can be applied to the other arts. A conversation between four persons, snared on tape and reproduced as was, became the play *Yes, Mamma, We'll Do It*, first performed at the Municipal Theatre in Ulm, Germany, in October 1962. This true snare-play became a false snare-play when it was acted out on the stage; but it became a true snare-play in the second part of the play when the actors listened to themselves speaking their roles in the first part and commented spontaneously.

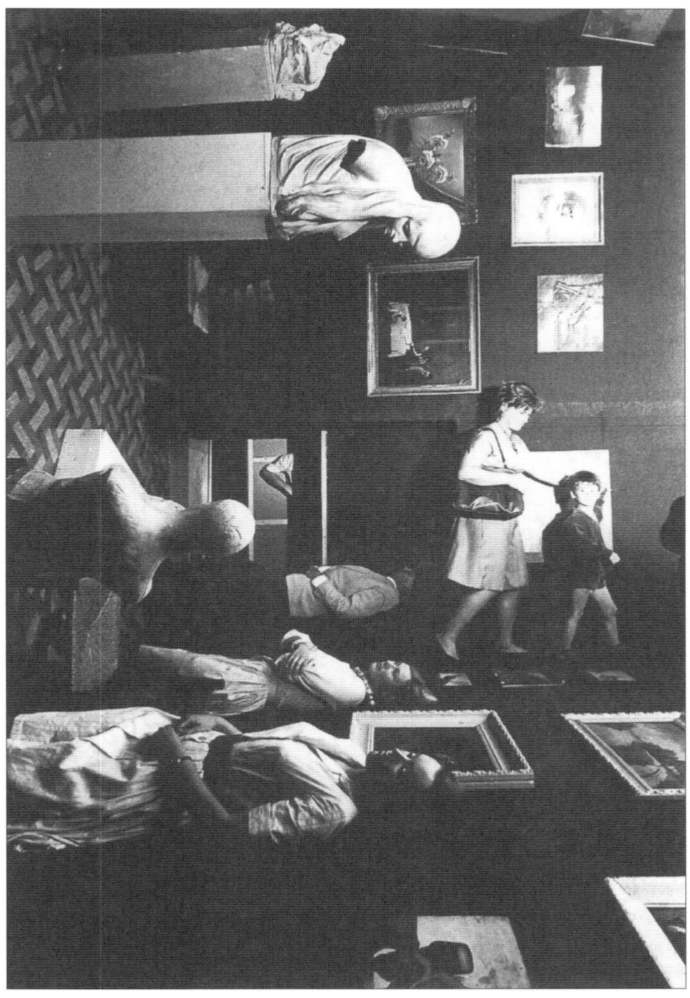

14. During the group manifestation "Dylaby" (dynamic labyrinth, see p.228) at the Stedelijk Museum in Amsterdam in September 1962, I transformed two rooms of the museum. In one, converted into a dark labyrinth, the spectators were exposed to sensory experiences (warm and humid surfaces, varied textures, sounds and odours) as if, blinded by the dark spectacles equipped with needles (see above), they had to develop their senses to appreciate the environment. In the other room, a principle of the snare-picture (changing of plane) was applied to a whole room containing an exhibition of *fin-de-siècle* painting and sculpture. The real floor was "hung" with paintings, so that it was transformed

into a wall; sculpture "stood" on one of the real walls, transforming a real wall into the floor; and the other walls shifted their position in relation to the new "floor".

15. In my "collections", a definite object, preferably commonplace (cooking utensils and gadgets, eyeglasses, shoe stretchers), is shown in as many variations as possible, as found at different times and places. Here the goal is not to show the chance relationship of the object to the other objects around it, but its evolution and transformation. For this reason the objects are not fixed to a supporting element, but placed or hung ready for use.

16. In the "Restaurant" [see **Appendix IV**] several of the foregoing independent ideas were integrated:

a) The restaurant tables became snare-pictures.

b) As in the "Grocery Store", the foodstuffs were exhibited as works of art without being incorporated into assemblages.

c) The prepared dishes were transformed (eaten etc.) during the meals, almost like the remains the rats gnawed from my pictures at SCHWARZ'S.

d) EVERYBODY could produce, under licence, his own snare-picture from the remains of his meal.

e) The sense of taste was added to the visual, descriptive, tactile aspects of the exhibition, recalling the mastercooks ESCOFFIER, PLON, Mère FILLIOUX.[h]

f) The "collection", in this case cooking utensils, found its ideal use.

17. In March 1963, a composite photograph of my room, composed of 55 individual shots, was exhibited as a snare-picture at the "Comparaisons" exhibition in Paris.

18. In the Dorotheanum (Non-Profit Suicide Institute), at DOROTHEA LOEHR'S gallery in Frankfurt-am-Main[i] in October 1963, different facilities for suicide were offered in eleven rooms. (No one took advantage of the opportunities offered.)

19. In March 1964 at the ALLAN STONE Gallery in New York I exhibited 31 "Variations on a Meal",[j] extending the variations-on-a-theme principle of hard-edge art to include the collaboration of chance. Thirty-one identically set tables were transformed through the agency of the invited guests. The results were exhibited.

20. The "word traps" made together with ROBERT FILLIOU[k] were an attempt to visualise

proverbs and sayings. Example: "Raining cats and dogs", in which toy cats and dogs were fixed to the top of an open umbrella.

21. The exhibition of my hotel room. [See **34D, b**]

These principles developed in an unmethodical fashion, and are much less precise categories than they might seem as outlined above. It is not my intention to disparage other people's accounts, but simply to give my own. Perhaps it was not in fact necessary to hold this history of the developments under other people's noses when in actuality it only concerned myself (and, at the most, my friend ROBERT FILLIOU, without whose help I would never have written it, and who also translated it into French)?

— DANIEL SPOERRI, Dec. 1961 to Jan. 1963. (During my last visit to Ulm, 6 February 1963, I forced my friend CLAUS BREMER to translate it into German.)[1]

a. Is the so-called subjective really itself? Is it not I who possesses and constitutes the subjective? So isn't it a part of me, and thus not something that one can quite calmly give a name to as if it were a being?

And is the objective really itself? Is it not I… and so on, as above.

So are the subjective and the objective actually different? Shouldn't one rather avoid calling them by some name or other — first, because both are not themselves, and second, because both *are not* in the same way? (DR 1968)

b. SPOERRI'S train of thought can be illustrated so: The edition of a non-changeable picture (the additive artwork) would be *the picture + the same picture + the same picture etc.* And the edition of a changeable picture (the multiplied artwork) would be *the picture + a similar picture + a similar picture etc.* But what is here termed a multiplied artwork does not yet seem to reach SPOERRI'S ideal — which would be perhaps an edition of the always different, i.e. *the picture + something else + something else etc.* (DR 1968)

c. Nothing and no one has a value other than man, that's for sure, because when man invented himself, he invented himself as his own value. And so it has remained, something he will chew on for a long time until he has chewed the whole value business out of his body. But the question is: what will then be left of him? (DR 1968)

d. At first people made — here and there — these things because they flickered or twitched or rattled so nicely. And SPOERRI the anecdotalist and story-writer came along and collected these people together with all their junk. And it seemed that people had done these things so as to demonstrate what is called an idea — multiplication or the *bewogene bewegung*⋆ (⋆MG: roughly "impelled movement") or the like. But already the businessmen jumped on it and called it Op Art, and already it looked different again — as if the things had been made to feast people's eyes. And suddenly it was called kinetic art, and it looked very much as though people had wanted to say from the outset: "Hey, everything's moving and turning!" And the fattest, grandest mechanical-production-business-entertainment-industry was in full swing, and it looks quite truthfully as though everything had (although — as it is so nicely put — unconsciously), right at the onset, right from the outset — at the beginning of this story, and on top of everything behind closed doors — as if everything had been felt through in advance and was intended to be introduced to the world around in a carefree manner. (DR 1968)

e. When man invented himself, he did so in the form of an artwork. But then he invented himself once again, in the form of time. And he looked at this constellation: man-artwork-time, which was sometimes so arranged that time ended up between him and the artwork, so that when on top of all that man began to say: time is space, he saw space sitting there between himself and his artwork. And as he further insisted that time is money, a heap of money lay between him and his artwork, and with that he began to meditate, i.e. he placed himself between himself and the artwork (at the same time edging time, space and money out of their intermediary position, as it were) and felt how he became one not only with himself, but also with the artwork. And he saw that man and the artwork and he himself are the same, and thereupon he recalled that he had in fact invented all three — as himself. And with this he feels at ease again. And because he feels at ease when he meditates, he meditates (especially before artworks. Because at first he always feels uneasy before artworks on account of the time, the space and the money), silently before the artworks. (DR 1968)

f. It would be possible to develop SPOERRI'S idea and illustrate it so (DR 1968):

Snare picture = (support)(junk)

(Snare picture)$^{(2)}$ = (support)(tools)(junk)

(Snare picture)$^{(2)(2)}$ = (wall)(support)(tools)(junk)

(Snare picture)$^{(2)(2)(2)}$ = (collector)(wall)(support)(tools)(junk)

(Snare-picture)$^{(2)(2)(2)(2)}$ = (SPOERRI)(collector)(wall)(support)(tools)(junk)

g. Who is this ANYBODY? Probably someone like SPOERRI, because why else should SPOERRI say: ANYBODY can do what I do? But why does SPOERRI sign what this ANYBODY has done with: SPOERRI — and not with: ANYBODY? (DR 1968)

h. That's Mère FILLIOUX with an "x", mind you, no relation to our very dear friend ROBERT. The famous gastronome "Prince" CURNONSKY classed this 19th-century *cordon bleu* with Maréchal FOCH, ANATOLE FRANCE, MISTINGUETTE and other stars in the French hall of fame. The most famous speciality served at her bistro was *Volaille demideuil* or "chicken in half-mourning", loaded with truffles, and the knife she used to decapitate an estimated half a million young chickens to make it with is enshrined in the ESCOFFIER Museum in Villeneuve-Loubet. Still, ROBERT'S mother, without an "x", has her own claim to culinary fame: the recipe for rusty-nail soup preserved for posterity in BARBARA MOORE'S ReFlux Editions *Cookpot*. (EW 1995)

i. Which is lovely, although the sun never shines there. (DR 1968)

j. At this point JOSEF ALBERS would say: I have nothing to do with *variations*. I make *variations*! (DR 1968)

k. When ROBERT FILLIOU worked together with DANIEL SPOERRI, they were involved in getting ensnared in the snare, and sticking and nailing and tying things tight (and if they've not escaped, they'll sit there happily ever after).

When ROBERT FILLIOU worked together with GEORGE BRECHT, they were involved in a book — *The Cedilla Takes Off* — about letting loose and flying off (and if they've not fallen down, they'll fly happily ever after). (DR 1968)

l. And translated even deeper into German by DR on 6 October 1968. (DR 1968)[m]

    m. This appendix to the Something Else Press edition had been revised for the German edition of 1968 and was translated for the Atlas Press edition of 1995 by MALCOLM GREEN. (AB 2015)

APPENDIX III. TOPOGRAPHICAL RECONSTRUCTION OF A CRIMINAL ACT

1. S.E.I.T.A. matchbox, half full, with drawing of an Alsatian man in traditional costume, lying face down. (EMMETT tells me that in this position one doesn't snore.)

2. Freshly opened pack of Gauloises,[a] bought at Les Cinq Billards (where I was waiting for EMMETT, living in the room next to mine, to get dressed[b] and come with me to lunch at LOU'S apartment), after I discovered I had left my cigarettes upstairs in my room.

3. Wine glass, one finger full of smoked wine. [See 11]

4. Matchbox, same design as 1, face up and empty. [See 11]

5. LOU'S scissors, used to cut silver foil. [See 10, 11]

6. Milky-porcelain ashtray with red CARLSBERG trademark, containing seven cigarette butts (one of which, only a quarter smoked, probably belonged to LOU), 14 burned matches,[c] some of them only a quarter of an inch long [see 11], and ashes.

7. Two small bars of Suchard chocolate, offered to EMMETT and me by LOU, who wondered what the word *croquer* in "*chocolat à croquer*" on the wrapper meant. I explained it by telling her what *croqueuse de diamants* meant.

8. Small sewing kit, in a clear plastic case, called Multifil (patent not protected by the French government), containing interwoven strands of multicoloured thread and four needles. The fifth needle, double-threaded with black, was used to punch holes in the silver foil. [See 11]

9. Cork [from 10] inscribed "*Plan de Dieu*".

10. Part of the base of a bottle of Côtes du Rhône, "*Plan de Dieu*", bought near the Place de la Contrescarpe with EMMETT on the way to lunch with LOU, to help convince her that the delay in our travel plans was a Plan de Dieu. (My Milan show was postponed four days after ARTURO SCHWARZ, the gallery owner, broke two ribs in an automobile accident.)

11. Medicine bottle with plastic top, originally containing a very expensive antibiotic available only with a prescription, partly refilled with *canabis indica*.[d] A rubber band around the bottle top secured the folded silver foil [see 12] after completion of the criminal act. Following lunch, which consisted of eggs scrambled with onions, beans with corn, sliced ham, croissants, pumpernickel, butter and Gala cheese, LOU brought the medicine bottle to the table and

offered to show us how to play hooka-ooka, poppety-boo, or something similar, I forget the expression she used. Then she closed the curtains to darken the room. EMMETT seemed to know what was about to happen, but as usual he hid his knowledge behind a mischievous smile. Then LOU outlined the rim of a glass on the silver foil, and cut around it so that it would fit over the top of the glass with enough space below the rim to allow for a rubber band to hold the foil in place — like one does with opened cans and jars. She took the needle and punched 20 or 30 tiny holes in an area about the size of a 1-franc piece near the rim of the glass, and opposite the tiny holes she cut a narrow slit (she called it a mouth) with the needle. I was mystified by these activities, not knowing why one should drink wine out of a glass prepared in such a fashion. LOU told me to wait and see. Then she put a small amount of *canabis indica* over the holes, and after lighting it told me to suck through the slit. Then I understood. To make LOU and EMMETT happy I participated in this strange cult. But it gave me little pleasure or inspiration. LOU said that she did it just for fun, but EMMETT seemed to enjoy it. I must admit that I found the resultant aromatic wine [see 3] superb.

12. Silver foil cut too small, in haste, to cover 3 properly. [See 11]

13. Original position of EMMETT'S Gitanes, moved by him to position indicated in 15 during reconstruction of the criminal act.

14. EMMETT'S wine glass, one-third full of "Plan de Dieu".

15. EMMETT'S Gitanes, after removal from position indicated in 13.

16. Pink saucer used as an ashtray, containing five cigarette butts, five matches (length indicated that they were not used in the criminal act), ashes, one Kleenex with wine stains, one pit and a wrapper from Chun Pi Mui (orange peel plum) furnished by LOU. LOU and EMMETT enjoyed this Hongkong delicacy, but I spat it out as soon as I tasted it.

17. Wrapper of chocolate bar eaten by EMMETT. [See 7]

18. LOU'S empty wine glass.

(This crime took place at LOU'S apartment April 1, 1963, and was reconstructed immediately afterwards. The text was dictated by me, DANIEL SPOERRI, in very poor English [constantly corrected aloud by LOU], and hastily put into the present form by EMMETT WILLIAMS. First printed in the YVES KLEIN memorial number of *KWY*, Paris 1963.)[e]

    a. The word *Gauloises* makes you think of something blue. And then sometimes you think about blind people and what they think when they hear the word *Gauloises*? And then you also reflect that perhaps from the outset language has only had words for what is seen with the eyes (and that language is still that way, even though it — and the people who use it — act as though it would be as easy as pie for it to talk about the invisible). And so you are prompted to bemoan the injustice of speaking, describing and painting towards the blind and the invisible. (DR 1968)

b. What about reversed strip tease, EMMETT? (DR 1968, English in original)

c. The destruction of the matches reminds one of one's own. For I believe there is someone inside me who seeks my destruction (I am talking about destruction in this life and this world, and about me in this life and this world). And when I talk like that I hear myself saying: Since it is I who finds living this life in this world difficult, it cannot be someone else who (apart from me) sits here inside myself and wishes to witness my destruction. Rather it must be I myself, so it seems, who wishes to see my destruction, for it is I who have difficulty with life. (Irrespective of the fact that I, when I say I, am unable to talk of something inner or outer because I am both my inside and outside.) But if one was to allow thought — and above all speech — to remain with such opposites (for one has the suspicion that it is not thought that is talking here but speech that has succumbed to the mania of erecting opposites), how could one then think and speak? (DR 1968)

d. A compounded error. For one thing, *cannabis* is mis-spelled (in the German edition too!). More important, it wasn't *cannabis indica* in LOU'S medicine bottle, it was *cannabis sativa*. My old friend BRION GYSIN (God rest his soul) pointed this out to me in Venice once, while we were thumbing through the Something Else Press version of the *Topo* and reminiscing about our old Paris days and ways. "*Cannabis indica* is hemp, all right," he explained, "but hemp without the *bhang*. You might as well smoke old rope. But you guys weren't smoking rope." He knew about all these things, and yes, BRION himself committed a criminal act when he slyly slipped the recipe for hashish fudge into the *ALICE B. TOKLAS Cookbook*, a crime that helped push the book on to the best-seller lists. ALICE, according to BRION, was shocked and embarrassed when she found out about it in the book review section of *Time*. No, ALICE B. TOKLAS and GERTRUDE STEIN never touched the stuff.

Nor did GEORGE MACIUNAS, I might add, and he often warned ROBERT and myself and other Fluxus artists with criminal tendencies that smoking anything but especially hash would make us impotent as well. But the parsimonious father of Fluxus knew at least one rope trick. GEORGE once invited LARRY MILLER to a tea party. He made tea with rope, just plain old rope, which he claimed contained lots of nutrients, yet still remained perfectly good rope after having been brewed. LARRY tried the tea, and, believe it or not, it tasted just like — plain old rope. (EW 1995)

e. DR translated it post-haste into German on 7 July 1968, then copied it quite calmly into a fair hand on 7 October in the same year, followed by the last ten accompanying words on the 25th of the same month. (DR 1968)

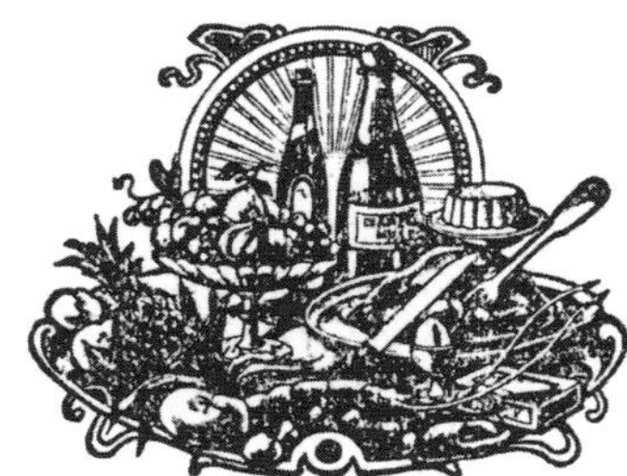
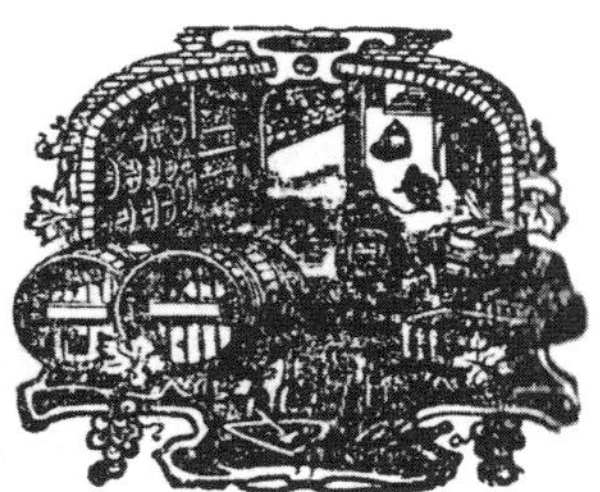

RESTAURANT
DE LA
GALERIE J.
8, Rue de Montfaucon
PARIS (6ᵉ)   DAN. 30-65

A l'occasion de l'Exposition de Daniel SPOERRI
" 723 USTENSILES DE CUISINE "

la Galerie J. annonce l'ouverture d'un Service de Restaurant

du 2 au 13 Mars 1963

8. RUE DE MONTFAUCON — PARIS (6')

La Galerie fermant ses portes sur l'Exposition chaque jour à 19 heures,
le Restaurant ouvrira à 20 heures (fermeture hebdomadaire le Dimanche).

Aux Fourneaux le Chef SPOERRI " DANIEL "
Les Critiques d'Art assurent le Service

Attention : Le nombre des couverts étant limité à 10 par
soirée (sauf le buffet exotique qui sera de 20 couverts) les
amateurs éventuels sont priés d'indiquer le menu de leur
choix, soit en téléphonant à DANton 30-65, soit en faisant
parvenir le bon ci-joint sans délai au Service Restaurant de
la Galerie J., le cachet de la poste faisant foi pour les
priorités. (Les places retenues et non occupées demeure-
ront à la charge de la personne ayant fait la réservation)

L'activité gastronomique du Chef SPOERRI " DANIEL " entraînant
d'immédiates conséquences esthétiques (dans la plus pure orthodoxie du
Nouveau Réalisme), le public est prié de venir juger sur pièces, le lendemain
du jour de clôture du Restaurant : **le 14 Mars à partir de 17 h.**

VERNISSAGE DES MENUS-PIÈGES

COCKTAIL

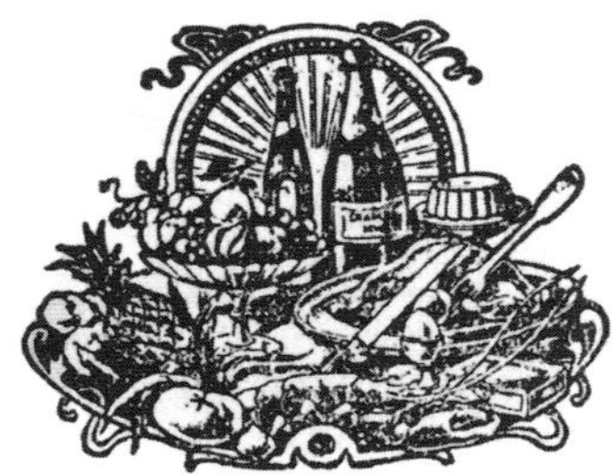

RESTAURANT
DE LA
GALERIE J.

D I N E R S

Cuisine soignée

PRIX MODÉRÉS

Réservation obligatoire
(ouvert du 2 au 13 Mars, à partir de 20 heures)

Apéritifs, Hors-d'œuvre, Fromages, Fruits, Café, Pousse-café,
1 Bouteille de vin, Couvert, Pain compris dans les prix indiqués
——————— Service : 15 % en sus ———————

Samedi 2 Mars

MENU FRANCO-NIÇOIS (servi par Michel Ragon)

Pastis
Salade Niçoise
Testicules à la crème fraîche et aux champignons
Boursault à l'ail
Noix
Café Marc

15 francs

Dimanche 3 Mars

Fermeture

Lundi 4 Mars

MENU DES INDES OCCIDENTALES & ORIENTALES (servi par Pierre Restany)

Punch froid
Salade fraîche
Poulet aux pommes, ananas, curry et chutney
Gingembre confit et en sirop
Café Alcools

15 francs

Mardi 5 Mars

REPAS INTERNATIONAL (servi par Jean-Clarence Lambert, opposant)
MENU DE PRISON

Soupe maigre aux choux, 125 gr. de pain

1 franc 50

Mercredi 6 Mars **MENU ROUMAIN** (servi par Tony Spiteris)

Apéritif Roumain (Tuicâ)
Hors-d'œuvre : Salata de vinete, Mititei, etc.
Tocanâ cu givets cu mâmâliga
Fromage : Brînza
Confitures de Roses, Rahat
Café-Turc Alcools   15 francs

Jeudi 7 Mars **MENU FRANÇAIS** (servi par John Ashberry)

Dubonnet, Picon ou Suze
Langoustines au vin blanc flambées à l'Armagnac
Le plateau de fromages
Mendiants
Café Alcools   15 francs

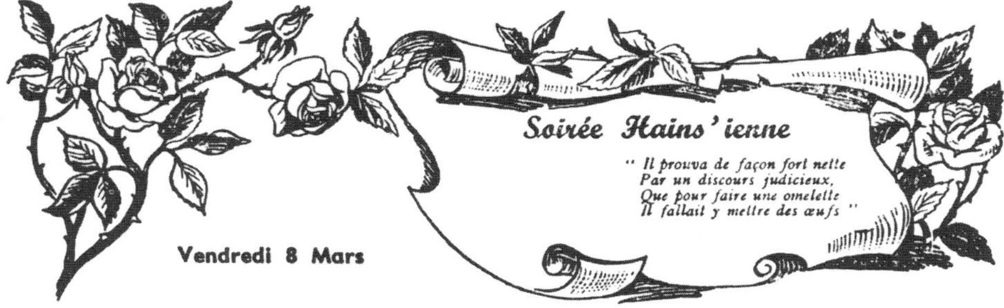

Vendredi 8 Mars

MENU-HOMMAGE A RAYMOND HAINS

L'Abstrait, Sigisbée de la Critique, par Pierre Restany et Daniel Spoerri

Potage lettriste
Coquilles St-Jacques au gratin, Mahé de la Villeglé
Araignée de mer, sauce Heinz
Ramereaux aux olives, à la Toulouse-Lautrec
Bœuf écorché nouvelle mode
Pommes de terre à la Dubourg ou en robe des champs
Fromages : Gala Claudel, petit Briennois
" Les Entremets de la Palissade "
Far Breton, éclairs *
Négresse blonde en chemise
Himalaya, Mont Blanc
Charlemagne, Napoléon
Les Vérités de La Palisse
Vin : Clairette de Bellegarde
Champagne Heidsieck — Cognac Hennessy
Cigares Néos   25 francs
SUPPLÉMENT : Hommes-Sandwich
Vin des Rochers   2 fr. 50

* Fournisseur : André Breton, Boulevard du Montparnasse, Paris

Samedi 9 Mars

MENU HONGROIS (servi par Jean-Jacques Lévêque)

Apéritif Barak
Hors-d'œuvre : Paprikas szalonna
Szegedi gulyas
Rétes
Café — Tokaji   **15 francs**

Dimanche 10 Mars

Fermeture

Lundi 11 Mars

MENU SUISSE (servi par Alain Jouffroy)

Apéritif Suisse
Pommes de terre en robe de chambre
Bündnerfleisch
Fromages, beurre et petit suisse
Salade
Birchermuesli
Café — Trasch   **15 francs**

Mardi 12 Mars

BUFFET EXOTIQUE (self-service)

Itinéraire gastronomique international rassemblant
les spécialités les plus rares des cuisines les plus
exotiques du Mexique à la Chine, du Danemark
à la Bulgarie, du Tessin à l'Auvergne...   **25 francs**

Mercredi 13 Mars

MENU SERBE (service surprise)

Apéritifs Sliboviza
Lentilles au lard dans leur vin
Langue de veau au citron et aux amandes
Salade de poivrons
Le plateau de Fromages
Café — Pousse-café   **15 francs**

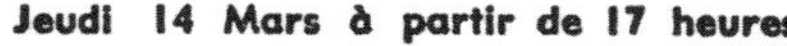

Jeudi 14 Mars à partir de 17 heures

VERNISSAGE DES MENUS-PIÈGES

COCKTAIL

Menus LABEILLE - PYR. 95-06

APPENDIX V. A LISTING OF THE OBJECTS

on the blue table at 9 p.m. on the first day of December 1964 when EMMETT WILLIAMS began the translation of the *Topography* in DANIEL SPOERRI'S room, SPOERRI having left Paris for his New York exhibition. Objects marked with an asterisk were not on the table when SPOERRI departed.

Serving tray
*Christmas gift shopping bag from Amsterdam in which LYDIA LUYTEN had wrapped:
    *One loaf of home-baked bread and
    *One jar of homemade hip jam
Can of Bel Canto olive oil
*Quarter of a pound of butter
Can of Primis olive oil
Pfeifer & Langen Kölner sugarloaf
*Carving knife given me by RENATE KIRCHHOFF
*Blue Circle dairy store bag
*One egg, on top of the Blue Circle bag
Honey
Candied sugar
*Chunk of Parmesan cheese
Bulgarplodexport Jam of Roses
One almond, in the shell
Garlic salt (German)
*Eggshell
*Top to teapot
Roses Petal Jam (*sic*)
Jar of Amora mustard
Green Label curry paste
One whole nutmeg

*Royco bouillon cube
*Knorr bouillon cube
Viandox bouillon cube
*Liebig bouillon cube
TWINING'S Ceylon breakfast tea
Sauermann's Paprika Speck
Colorant Rosière
Cane sugar from the Antilles
*Note from JENNIFER CUSHING:
"Dearest Twerp, I came by but nobody was at home (turn s.v.p.) Hey ho nobody home Drink nor sleep nor money have I none (turn over) So… bye love YUK"
*Chopstick glass
*Ten pairs of chopsticks
Vinegar
Van Houten's powdered chocolate
Dessaux mustard
*Salt, spilled
Vinavil, the Universal Adhesive
Sambal Kemerie
Sweet mustard
*Package of Kinortine BEA salt and pepper shakers
Caraway seeds
*TOM WASMUTH'S passport

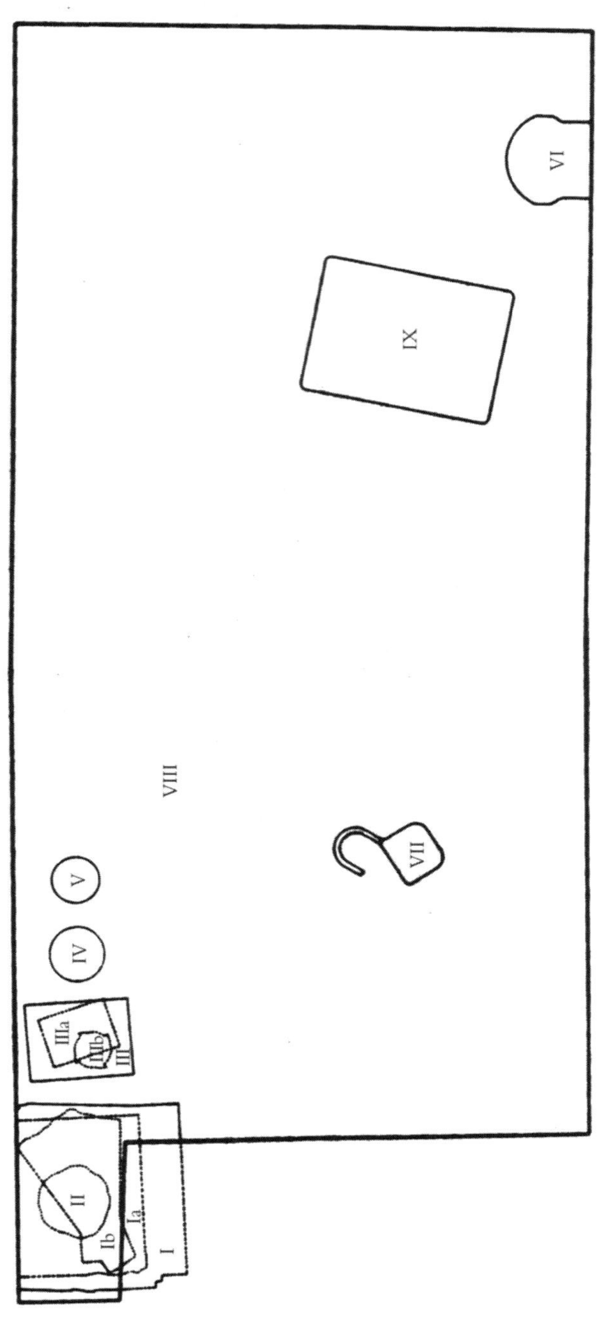

VI
IX
VIII
VII
V
IV
IIIa
IIIb
III
II
Ia
Ib
I

APPENDIX VI. ANECDOTED TOPOGRAPHY OF ORDER
[See *Postscriptum* to **Introduction I**]

I. Typing paper, thin, for carbon copies,[a] cut in four for personal needs. From a package of 500 sheets bought for 4 francs from my newsdealer.

    Ia. Flat pack of interfolded toilet paper, trademark Bagatelle [see **45**].[b]

    Ib. Sheet of toilet paper from the pack described above, crumpled but brought back unused from the public convenience in the stairwell.

II. Yellow rennet apple, beginning to rot, but not enough to throw it away, placed on I, Ia and Ib as a hygienic paperweight.[c]

III. Box of Gitanes kitchen matches [S.E.I.T.A., see **7, b**], bearing an advertisement for Champigneulles, "the queen of beers, leading brewery in the Common Market. Ask for it at your café or grocer." Bought at the tobacconist at 26 Rue Mouffetard, for 70 centimes.

    IIIa. Small box of matches, undoubtedly S.E.I.T.A. (I have lost the box), on top of the large box and spotted with paint.[d]

    IIIb. Small flint dispenser [see **51**].

IV. Cupping-glass, one of a dozen bought at the Kremlin-Bicêtre Flea Market the end of January 1962 for 5 francs. In the glass, filled with water, an onion is sprouting.

V. Cream-coloured plastic salt cellar, a present to me from VERA, brought from Frankfurt-am-Main by BAZON BROCK.

VI. Small vice, for the amateur or part-time mechanic, cast iron, blue varnish, weight 1 kilo 250 grammes. Bought for 10 francs from SINCLAIR BEILES who, in need of money, sold it to me the beginning of February 1962.

VII. Combination lock with secret [see **37**] combination: one clockwise turn to 1, counter clockwise to 9, then clockwise to 11. Bought in the cutlery shop at the foot of Rue Mouffetard for about 4 francs 30 centimes.

VIII. Red or yellow petal fallen from a bouquet of flowers.[e]

IX. Diary for 1960, bound in red imitation leather, probably given away as publicity by the

Reederei Rhine shipping company in Switzerland. I found it the summer of 1960 in the back seat of TINGUELY'S Peugeot 203, during the era I was constantly with him. It must have been lost by a Swiss the night of a party in the woods of the Chevreuse Valley organised by a South American. Each guest had to pay 10 francs, to cover the cost of wine, bread and mutton roasted on a spit. TINGUELY and I took part only because the others didn't have transportation. I suppose the person who lost the diary went with us, because I found it the day after the party while accompanying TINGUELY to a junkyard. Even on first reading it I found it so significant and important that I thought right away about publishing it. But it kicked around my room and got lost, and I found it again only a few weeks ago while I was looking for a catalogue to show BAZON BROCK. After re-reading it I decided to integrate the text in the next edition of the *Topography*. I could certainly have stuck it in somewhere as a note to one object or another, but the contents seemed so strange and outside of my world that I decided to place it deliberately on the blue table when I made the *Topography of Order*. Thus this opuscule is the only object in the two topographies that found its way on to the table by design.

The entries begin on New Year's Eve of 1959 and finish Wednesday, Jan. 27, 1960. The name and address of the owner are written in the diary, as well as the names and addresses and telephone numbers of his friends and acquaintances, but for obvious reasons all of these have been changed. I find the day-by-day entries so impressive, and the life of the author so well presented, that I take upon myself the risk of publishing the text, leaving the reader free to interpret as he sees fit.

Thursday, St. Sylvester, 31 December
New Year's Eve with Monika. Late Christmas present for her. A nice coat that we both like. Met Margie: martial type. Even without ski a happy new year's eve. Ate caviar again at Margie's. Monika is very lovely in her coat.

Friday, Jan. 1
Bad weather. Warm, rainy.

Saturday, Jan. 2
Miserable weather. Friends at Andermatt.

Sunday, Jan. 3
At the swimming pool with Monika. Things going well between us now. Getting myself ready for new job. Ever in an unholy rage against Cliché Hoch.

Monday, Jan. 4
Started new job at Lift and Spranger as copyist! Crumby place, same atmosphere. Real contrast with Hoch. Little work, therefore boring. Ulf sick. In the evening plodded through French.

Tuesday, Jan. 5
I was second in French. Later at the Mosque. (EW's note: the Mosque is a pseudo-Arab café in Basle, real name Atlantic, but known to teenage jazz fans as the Mosque.)

Wednesday, Jan. 6
Tried in vain to telephone Zurich. Was pretty furious. After work drove to Zurich. Ate a Twelfth-night cake.

Thursday, Jan. 7
At the Turkish bath. Freddy brought Rust to the Mueslin. He has a beautiful complex.

Friday, Jan. 8
Gym. Good workout.

Saturday, Jan. 9
Left Basle with Hermann at 6:30. Light snow. 3½ hours of driving. Many more slalom spectators than before. Clouds and snow gusts hampered the descent. Burgers completely suburbanised — eat in restaurant and go to bed. With Hermann in the village. Car, music, French people.

Sunday, Jan. 10
Began with a fight between Bernie and his wife. She's terribly complicated. Slalom fascinating although Swiss very bad. The Burgers going to carouse again in this good weather — just fill up their bellies. Irritating remarks from Annemarie. Weather and descent fantastic. Marvellous landscape. Biting cold, about -20°. Fiat wouldn't start. Snow in Basle!

Monday, Jan. 11
2CV wouldn't start, had to crank it. Got skis fixed. Mosque.

Tuesday, Jan. 12
Like the job better already. Time passes relatively fast copying. Tried French pronunciation on tape. Makes me too nervous. Good pronunciation but rhythm German. Practice! Mosque. It's snowing! Long telephone talk with Monika. She's getting tired.

Wednesday, Jan. 13
Swimming pool. It's boring and I'm tired. Very cold in Basle, -14°. Read *Du*.

Thursday, Jan. 14
2CV wouldn't start. Very cold. Meeting of the ski committee. Headache.

Friday, Jan. 15
Hans brought his Porsche. Very fine car. Telephoned Monika. I was upset.

Saturday, Jan. 16
Going to Zurich instead of ski meet. Monika getting along relatively well. I'm terribly sad, lost something. Feel like after a funeral. Also very tired.

Sunday, Jan. 17
Good rest. Better spirits. Such fine weather outside makes me think of the slopes. One gets older. Plugged battery in in room, otherwise motor won't start. Monika very sad, worries a lot. Intense pains.

Monday, Jan. 18
For apartment, Wanda's. We ate spaghetti. She's very nice. Peter started! She's going to marry money. Happy with the apartment. 160 francs. Late to bed.

Tuesday, Jan. 19
French dictation. Not good, because I don't know the forms. Went with Wanda to an excellent film, *The 400 Blows*. Mosque.

Wednesday, Jan. 20
Wanted to make some enlargements. But I'm too tired. Talked too long on the phone with Monika. She's better. Mosque.

Thursday, Jan. 21
Turkish bath. Mandi on vacation. Freddy sick. Mosque.

Friday, Jan. 22
My birthday. I am 33 years old. Very nice to me at home, and always a little awkward. — At Monika's. Nicely arranged table, pleasant atmosphere. She's very beautiful, and I love her very much.

Saturday, Jan. 23
Weather heavy: slept a lot. Monika has a headache.

Sunday, Jan. 24
Still heavy weather. Toured the lake. Very beautiful. Discussion, and I threw a fit. Terribly sad. Returned home late. 2CV has a flat.

Monday, Jan. 25
Much too warm, I'm tired. (Illegible passage.) Didn't follow the plan.

Tuesday, Jan. 26
French. Trouble with the *passé composé*. Went downtown with Tony and Wanda. They hatch incomprehensible politics. Saw Marcel.

Wednesday, Jan. 27
At Monika's. She always has a headache and must be X-rayed. We're both incorrigible. Returned home late.

Here the daily entries stop. On the pages that follow there are only such sketchy notes as these:

Feb. 4: 10 o'clock, Dr Hubert, teeth.

Feb. 21: Sick, walk in the park.

and dates of ski meets:

March 6: Stoss.

March 13: Jochpass.

and after that, nothing until:

Saturday, June 18: PARIS.

I think it was close to this date that I found the diary, because it is blank after that. At the very end, however, on the unlined pages, one finds:

Work — not very interesting. Possibilities not sufficiently explored. Result — inaction and fatigue. Antidote — get interested in photo production. How, and in what manner, can one make slides? Prepare for a new job through French, German and language courses.

Pleasures — not satisfactory, makes me nervous and leads to lack of sleep and dissatisfaction. Antidote — stay away from cafés, find rewarding amusements, create (absolutely) a larger circle of friends, moral stiffening, and more personal initiative.

Health — state of health continually bad, like insomnia, instability, chronic fatigue, resulting in the disproportion described above. Antidote — satisfying way of life (see above), gymnastics more times a week, walks, swimming pool twice a month, ski outings in the spring, summer excursions, kayak with Hermann.

In the near future — enlarge vacation photos, and portraits. Work at French and answer letters. Visit Hans for fixing up interior. Guitar, reading. Keep in contact with lots of people.

Addresses and telephone numbers follow. In a pocket at the end of the book are the following cards and papers:

1. Receipt for 40 francs for furnishing and dishes, dated Basle, ——— the 25th, 1960, signed by Frau ———.

2. Membership card in the Basle Jazz Club, No. ———.

3. Piece of yellow paper with the following pencilled note: "Apartment. On the entrance door, fix photo emblem on Pavatex (the eyes of a skier). In the kitchen, paint cabinets and other things. Redo tables and chairs. Repaint the smallest room myself. Go see about the plugs. This afternoon change the wheels, remove the seat. 13 h. 25 change the plates. See classified ads for furniture. Telephone?"

4. Floral postcard:

Jan. 22, 1960

My dear Walter,

Today, the day that you perhaps think with a certain amount of regret that you have grown a year older, I wish you with all my heart the happy fulfilment of all your wishes. My love will accompany you through all your trials, and will always be your joy.

Your Monika

I wanted to refrain from anecdoting the objects found in order on the blue table, Wednesday, Feb. 21, 1962, at 8:07 p.m. The order in effect condemns the objects to a specific use, while disorder and chance free them, thanks to the unusual rapprochements that stimulate the memory. But I can't refrain from saying:

— that SINCLAIR BEILES was the first man in space, put there during TAKIS'S exhibition of "The Impossible" at IRIS CLERT'S gallery.

— that the paint stains on the matchbox are due to ERIK DIETMANN who was in my room to restore paintings used for my *détrompe-l'œil* exhibition.

— that EMMETT WILLIAMS has written a novel, which I have never read, that takes place in toilets and lavatories.

— that the yellow or red petal has to be yellow or red since it came from a *détrompe-l'œil* consisting of a bouquet on which I fixed an empty bottle of TUBORG beer containing a dried bouquet of yellow and red flowers, and that now belongs to MERET OPPENHEIM.

— that SINCLAIR BEILES was shut up for the second time in ST. ANNE'S psychiatric hospital, as false rumours said TITOV had been after his conquest of space.

— that the bolt of my new lock was forced twice, once by the hotel proprietor during one of my nocturnal absences because there was a fire in the adjacent room and she thought it was in mine; another time while I was on a trip to Germany, accompanied by ROBERT FILLIOU, during which my phonograph was stolen.

— that in Germany there exists a serious problem for the city water supply during TV programme intermissions because everybody rushes to the toilet at the same time, and this necessitates stepped–up water pressure.

— that if Champigneulles beer calls itself the leading brewery in the Common Market it is not the only one, since all French beer pretends to be the best, while everyone knows that all Common Market countries except France produce good beer, but so what, I prefer wine and I prefer France to all other countries and not only for that reason.

— that VERA sent me the salt cellar to remind me of the many pounds of salt we used during our marriage in Darmstadt because she must have remembered the old Romanian proverb that you don't really know a person until you've eaten a sack of salt together.

— that I placed the other cupping-glasses on a painting of a nude woman that became the *détrompe-l'œil* "LEDA and the Swan", thanks to the little porcelain swan between her thighs.

— that SINCLAIR BEILES believed he would receive the NOBEL Prize for his conquest of space.

— that until a few years ago there was a tax on cigarette lighters in France, that they were engraved that the tax had been paid, and that the police could fine the owner of an illegal lighter.

— that I like to see not only onions growing, but all vegetables and herbs.

— that there is no longer a padlock on the door, but a security lock, and since I don't live there any more there is no reason to force the lock to room No. 13 on the fifth floor of the Hotel Carcassonne at 24 Rue Mouffetard where, to the right of the entrance door, between the stove and the sink, there used to stand a table that VERA painted blue one day to surprise me. (DS 1966)

> **a.** You have already written a comment to the lovely words carbon copy and it lies before you, but the weather is so so cold today and the wind whistles down the streets because winter has arrived and Christmas is just around the corner; things are piling up in the shop windows, the world wants to bathe in presents. That makes you (me) really sick, so you say: "Shit, I can't be bothered to make the comment!" (DR 1968)

> **b.** Thinking of apartments makes
>   you feel flat
>   thinking of lavatories makes you feel
>   crap
>   thinking of lav paper makes you

> shiny or matt
> thinking of trifles makes you flabby
> and fat. (DR 1968)

c. "An apple doesn't fall far from the lavatree." (DR 1968)

d. The sheet on which this text is being written in fair hand has a sheep liver sausage stain on the front side which has oozed through to the back side. (DR 1968)

e. When the leaves fall from the trees and the flowers fall from the bouquets, when the rabbits run home and the seals still swim although they have been shot dead (because they have spent all summer guzzling themselves), then it is time to think of art and to say: "Even writing is an art." And when the writing falls on to the leaves and the leaves on the heap, when one lets the heap fall on the table and sits down at the table, then it is time to remember that the table is also a heap, and to say: "The table is a heap." Those who say such things act as if the one (the table) could be the other (the heap). And this sentence acts as if the one was beside the other. And this makes it seem as if something was there. And this sentence is a description like — for instance —: "The rabbit runs home." And that *shows* a rabbit, and *is* a rabbit, and *shows* me and *is* me and says in addition that I am a rabbit. *It acts as if I were a rabbit.* And this sentence is actually a question, but also an objection, and even more. (DR 1968)

Object 3. After making this drawing, I realised that the bottle is absolutely not the kind that Vin des Rochers comes in.

6. I have never seen Danish Nescafé, but to make up for it I met a Dane one night at the Restaurant Échaudé, with whom I talked theology at great length.[a]

16. Bizarre object evoking anything but a container of glue. In fact, it evokes nothing.

28A. Ink stain wishing to resemble a wine stain.[b]

34. My drawing of the box resembles a shoe box more than anything else. Maybe because I bought a pair of shoes today, and since it was raining, the box broke open on the way home and the old shoes tumbled out on to the wet pavement.

34E. The object referred to in the text doesn't have, more than likely, saw-tooth edges, made less and less, and I personally regret it.

34H. A door (*porte*), because I don't know how to make a case for drills (*porte-mèches*). For me, a case for drills calls nothing to mind. Done the night of July 15-16, 1965. I stopped drawing because the birds are singing.[c]

> **a.** Did TOPOR make a connection between *échaudé* (light pastry), the theologically inclined Dane, and Danish pastry? (EW 1966)

> **b.** This could, of course, be taken as a portrait of SPOERRI [see **28A, a**]. The situation of one inanimate object wishing to be another reminds me of ROBERT FILLIOU'S poetic construction, "A Bottle of Milk Dreaming It is a Bottle of Beer", exhibited at the Danish Salon de Mai several years ago. Just before the exhibition opened, the bottles fell off the construction and broke on the floor. The custodian came with a broom to sweep away the mess, but I managed to talk him out of this drastic step, roped off the area strewn with broken glass, and posted a notice to the public that the metaphors of ROBERT FILLIOU are extremely fragile. (EW 1966)

c. A moment ago he said: "When the bird calls!", but what he said there he had said in town and the town is large, so there, in the town, is a dog, and the dog is weeping. "Okay," he said to himself, just now, "the dog's weeping. So what if the dog is weeping?"

Because the stomach — which is a brain — it thinks: "The brain is thinking up a bird (the lonely waterbird) on the large solitary lakeful of water set in the large, empty countryside. Singing there where he who hears it (he thinks up a listener for the water-song-bird), is or was or could be lonely, and where he who hears or heard or could hear the singing may also be lonely and able to sing — and also really sings. There he sings, out there together with the bird. But he sings thoughtfully, with his stomach, the brain, and this is now (as is often, in fact always, the case) the dog which is weeping there in the town: the dog is weeping there where it is impossible to be lonely (which is just why it is weeping). The dog, this dog, weeps in the town. And the man, this man, weeps, too." "And the man, would he like to be a dog?" you ask yourself. And you receive a reply, for instance: "Oh no, the man would simply like to be alone. That doesn't mean you have to burst straight into tears, you can sing, out there on the water, just the way you weep in town, right?" But then perhaps another says: "But what if the dog is not a dog but a bitch?" "In that case replace man and dog in the story with the words woman and bitch (the bird remains the same)," someone answers, perhaps. (DR 1968)

PHOTO CREDITS (WHERE KNOWN)

Front cover: (Daniel Spoerri) D. Abadie; (Robert Filliou) Vera Spoerri; (Dieter Roth) Bernd
    Jansen; (Topor) Ad Peterson

Front endpaper: Spoerri's original drawing of the *Topographical Map of Chance* is reproduced
    with the permission of Collection Gerstner, Weserburg / Museum of Modern Art,
    Bremen

83 André Morain

111 (The Boxes) Fabrizio Carghetti; (Monsieur Bitos) Bacci

156 (After) Bacci

222 Erismann

230 Joachim Fliegner

233 Bacci

272 Alastair Brotchie

Rear endpaper: Vera Spoerri

INDEX

Numbers indicate page numbers. Entries marked with one asterisk were new to the 1966 edition; two asterisks: the 1968 edition; three: the 1990 edition; four: the 1995 edition. Authorship of these notices corresponds to the author of the texts in which they first appear.

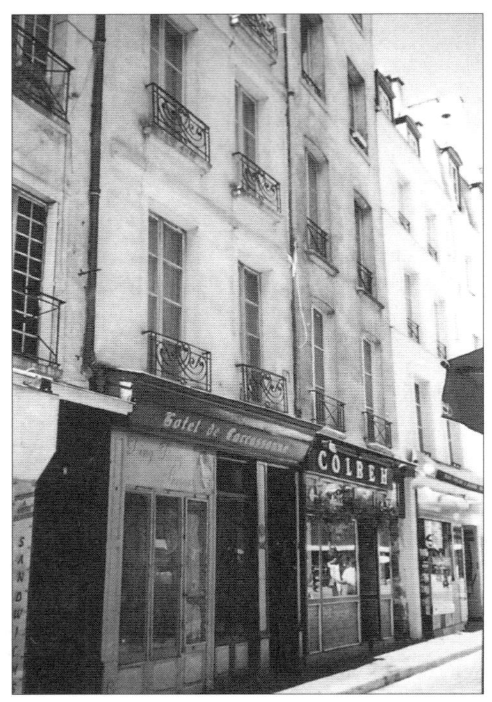

The Hotel de Carcassonne

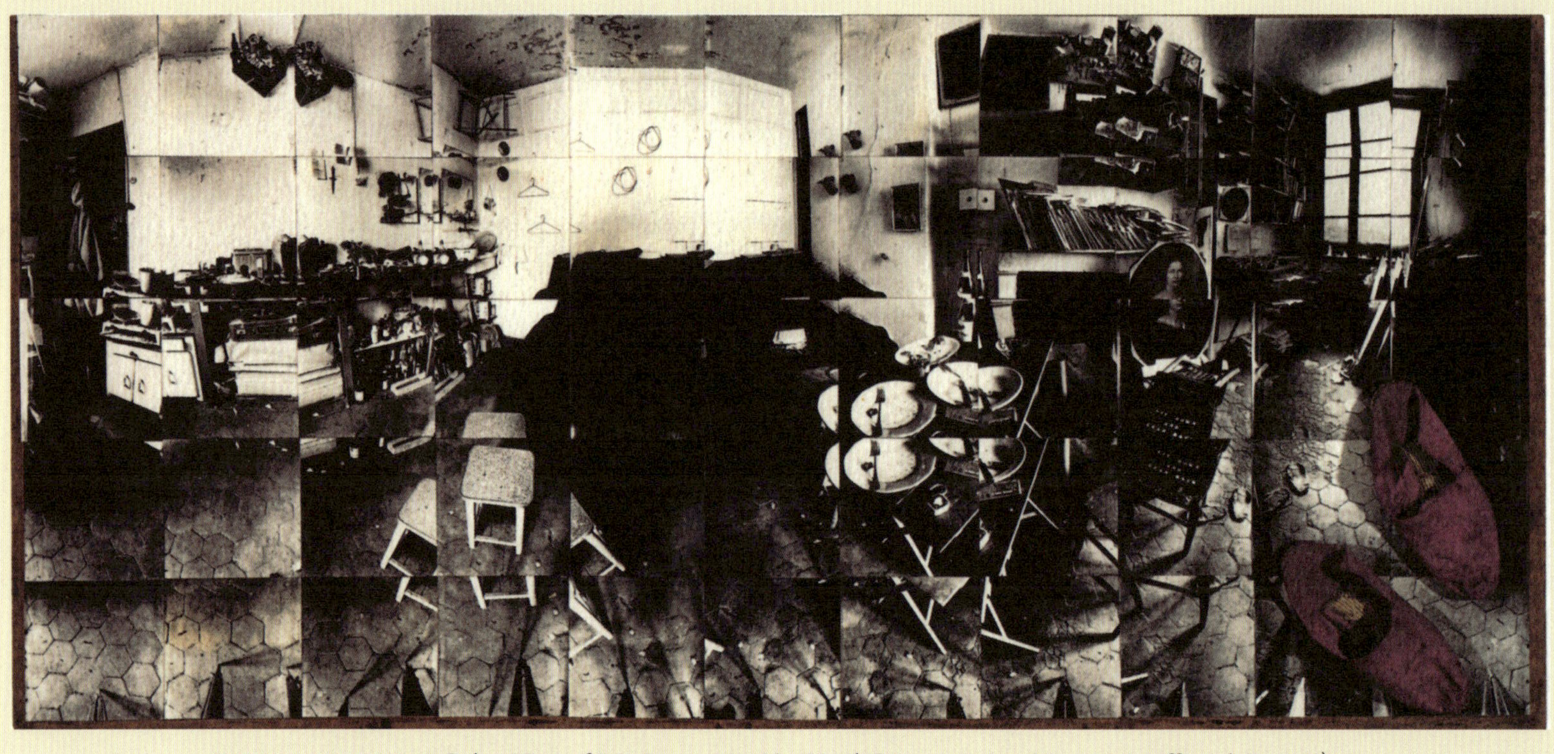

DANIEL SPOERRI, *Cubist View of My Room, No. 13, Hotel Carcassonne*, at 24 rue Mouffetard, Paris 5ème, taken according to my directions by Vera Spoerri in 55 individual photographs and mounted on plywood (with the espadrilles that appear in the photographs attached). Collection Kunstmuseum, Solothurn.